W9-AHF-513

"Gripping."
—*USA Today*

A MISSING MAN

Even the dogs had taken up the chorus, and were howling, caught up in the troubled excitement. . . . I did not have a good feeling; I was convinced Keizo was beyond the limits of our farthest perimeter.

The wind was still so strong that you could barely hear the man twenty feet from you shouting into the bleakness. Running into the wind a horrific image filled my mind: carrying Keizo's frozen body to the finish at Mirnyy tomorrow, on his sled in a sleeping bag, draped with the flag of Japan. I shouted more desperately—"Keizoooo . . . Keizoooo." . . . If we did not find him soon, and alive, the expedition would be a total loss.

"The real thing. A bold journey, a dramatic story told with candor and affection."

—*Joe Kane, author of* Running the Amazon

"A wonderful, gripping book. . . . A great adventure."
—*George T. Frampton, Jr.,*
President, The Wilderness Society

CROSSING ANTARCTICA

WILL STEGER and
JON BOWERMASTER

A LAUREL BOOK

Published by
Dell Publishing
a division of
Bantam Doubleday Dell Publishing Group, Inc.
666 Fifth Avenue
New York, New York 10103

A portion of this work was originally published in *National Geographic*.

ISBN: 0-440-21460-2

Reprinted by arrangement with Alfred A. Knopf, Inc., New York, New York

Printed in the United States of America

Published simultaneously in Canada

February 1993

10 9 8 7 6 5 4 3 2 1

OPM

Dedicated to the preservation and protection of Earth's most paradoxical continent.

"What castles one builds, now hopefully that the Pole is ours!"
Robert Falcon Scott, January 5, 1912

"The Pole. Great God! This is an awful place."
RFS, January 17, 1912

CONTENTS

EPILOGUE

ACKNOWLEDGMENTS

APPENDICES

All temperatures are in Fahrenheit.

All mileage is in accordance with the calculation of the Argus Processing Center, Toulouse, France.

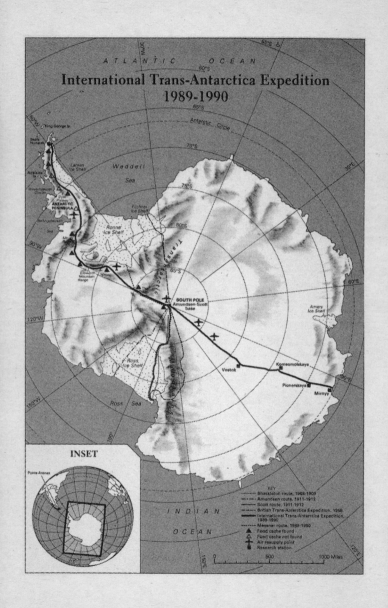

International Trans-Antarctica Expedition
1989-1990

ATLANTIC OCEAN

Weddell Sea

ANTARCTIC PENINSULA

Ronne Ice Shelf

Filchner Ice Shelf

Ross Ice Shelf

SOUTH POLE
Amundsen-Scott base

Vostok
Komsomolskaya
Pionerskaya
Mirnyy

Amery Ice Shelf

Ross Sea

INDIAN OCEAN

INSET

Punta Arenas

KEY
Shackleton route, 1908-1909
Amundsen route, 1911-1912
Scott route, 1911-1912
British Trans-Antarctica Expedition, 1958
International Trans-Antarctica Expedition, 1989-1990
Messner route, 1989-1990
Food cache found
Food cache not found
Air resupply point
Research station

500   1000 Miles

CROSSING
ANTARCTICA

PROLOGUE

ST. PETER,
HERE WE COME

JULY 25, 1989

The stench of wet dogs, kerosene, cigarette smoke, molding cheese and sweat-stained clothing saturated the air of the Soviet "flying coffin" as we closed in on Antarctica. Fifty-odd passengers readied themselves for what we fully expected to be a crash landing. My partner in this expedition-to-be, a diminutive Frenchman named Jean-Louis Etienne, was standing beside my seat. He leaned over and insisted the smell that permeated the tense cabin and increased the tension was one he recognized; it was, he said, the smell of adventure.

The Ilyushin-76, used back home in the Soviet Union for carting tanks and missiles, rumbled and whined as it neared touchdown on King George Island, the Antarctic atoll seventy-five miles off the tip of the mainland. We had taken off just two hours before, from Punta Arenas, Chile, the second-to-last stop of a tragicomic week-long juggernaut that would take us from Minneapolis to the seventh continent, via Cuba (where we'd lost two sled dogs to heat exhaustion), Buenos Aires and Perú. The passenger list included myself and five other explorers, reporters from the U.S., France and Japan,

Soviet and American support staff, French, U.S. and Soviet film crews, photographers, mechanics, copilots, a nurse, a translator, and forty heavy-breathing ninety-pound sled dogs. Each of us said our prayers as the pilots, neither of whom had ever landed on a comparable sheet of ice before—in fact, no one had ever landed a wheeled plane this big anywhere in Antarctica—descended toward the tiny runway at Chile's Teniente Rodolfo Marsh base.

As we dropped through the high clouds tomorrow's head-lines formed in my mind: INTERNATIONAL TRANS-ANTARCTICA TEAM KILLED BEFORE SETTING FOOT ON CONTINENT. I envisioned what it would be like to die in this windowless shell of steel. Our twenty thousand pounds of gear—including 150 gallons of heating fuel—would come skittering forward, crushing us . . . before the eighty-eight-thousand-pound fuel-laden plane burst into flames. In all my years of adventuring—canoeing and kayaking the Arctic's wildest rivers, scaling twenty-thou-sand-foot peaks, dogsledding across the Arctic, then to the North Pole and across Greenland—I had never been this frightened. To reinforce my fears, I could overhear a Soviet mechanic, crouched nearby, whisper aloud, "St. Peter, here we come."

As we neared the landing strip we expected the pilots to touch-and-go, in order to test the conditions of the runway, to assess whether it was slick blue ice, or slushy, wet snow. But heavy clouds draped the base, and the touch-and-go was scratched. Our Soviet teammate, Victor Boyarsky, positioned just beyond the cockpit door, shouted out our altitude as we descended. "Eight thousand meters . . . seven thousand me-ters . . . five thousand meters."

Our landing on King George, home to eight scientific bases representing eight different countries and to the launching pad to the mainland of Antarctica, would mark the end of an ardu-ous ten-day trip. The thankful irony of our arrival was that we almost had not taken off. Engine trouble in Minneapolis had nearly delayed our departure by weeks, threatening to end the expedition before it began. We had scurried about, searching for alternatives to the broken-down Soviet plane, alternatives that ran the gamut from renting space on cargo planes to booking commercial flights as far south as Punta Arenas. Meanwhile, the Russian mechanics worked twenty-four-hour days, desperately attempting to jury rig a broken fuel pump. At one point they suggested we limp to Havana on three engines, but we—and the Federal Aviation Administration—balked at that suggestion, fearful of being delayed there for who knew how long. As if by magic, and truly at the last minute, the mechanics managed to patch the break, and we took off on schedule, rumbling out of the Twin Cities on our 10,700-mile flight as the sun set over the Mississippi River.

Now, for the first time in ten days, absolute silence ruled the cabin and we were requested by the crew to take our seats, even though there were enough for only two thirds of us. I scanned the aircraft to see if I was the only one exhibiting obvious signs of fright and recognized fear in the eyes of each of my teammates, except for the calm Japanese Keizo Funatsu, who was peacefully asleep. Jean-Louis leaned against the windowless wall, listening to Dire Straits on his Walkman, nervously pulling at his fingers. Rubber-faced Englishman Geoff Somers, the only one of the six of us who had traveled on foot in Antarctica before, stared straight ahead, his eyes transfixed on the back of the seat before him. He was recounting to Chinese glaciologist Qin Dahe the last time he was this frightened, thirty years back, just before being "thrashed" in boarding school for failing a spelling test. Dahe listened intently, his hands wrapped tightly around both armrests. Victor, usually the emotional pillar of our sextet, grimaced and sweated as he monitored our drop. "Three thousand meters . . . twenty-five hundred meters . . . two thousand meters."

As a team—minus Dahe, who had joined us just five months ago—we had already faced a handful of tense situations together. In the spring of 1988 we'd made a first-ever south-to-north traverse of Greenland; sixteen hundred miles in sixty-two days. We had traveled by dogsled and learned from each other's methods for surviving in some of the world's most brutal conditions. We had compromised on everything from diet to tent shape, disagreed only a few times, and returned true friends. Now, on the eve of beginning one of the world's last great adventures—we intended over the next seven months to ski and dogsled nearly four thousand miles across the breadth of the harshest wilderness on Earth—I hoped the three years of formidable planning, fund-raising, handwringing and pressing the flesh that had gone into this spectacle would not end in an ignominious, flaming heap off to the side of an icy runway.

At 250 meters above Antarctica, a place I had dreamed about crossing since I was a young boy, the Ilyushin's landing gear shuddered noisily into place. "One hundred seventy meters . . . one hundred meters," Victor shouted over the whine of hydraulics, his grip on the cockpit door tightening. Around me people were smoking (despite the barrels of fuel just feet away), praying and holding hands. A few made a final grasp for seat belts, which were either nonexistent or broken. As we dropped, the roar of the engines echoed back at us off the ice, creating a deafening din. Without warning the lights in the cabin went off. Our fear was now masked in blackness.

The scenario, as potentially humorous as it was dangerous, brought back a dream I'd had shortly before departing for Antarctica. At the time I attributed it to the nonstop, roller coaster of twenty-hour days that preceded our takeoff. In the dream I was running on a diving board and suddenly I stopped, to see where I was. I could feel people watching me and I panicked. My only option was to keep running down the board. I woke up drenched in perspiration. The dream was not hard to analyze, since for these past few months I'd been incapable of thinking of either success or failure, only of plunging ahead.

The plane hit the ice with an explosion of sound: the engines reversed madly, and the twenty-foot-tall side cargo doors crashed open—apparently some kind of Ilyushin braking system—and within seconds the stifling, dank compartment was filled with blinding light and blowing snow, trailed by the smell of burning kerosene. I expected a wall of flames to come rushing in behind.

It was noisy, bright and cold as the plane snowplowed down the runway, which we had hit prematurely, and the plane's front wheel carved a foot-deep trench in the rock-hard ice as we skidded, wiping out a string of landing lights before coming to a halt at the far end of the four-thousand-foot-long slick. The dogs were howling, and I opened my eyes; our gear strained at the cloth webbing that kept it from burying us. Later, watching videotapes of the landing, the Soviet pilots grinned thin smiles of relief and satisfaction. The nose wheel had hit first, and the plane's fuel-laden wings had drooped dangerously close to the ground. If just the tip of one of those straining wings had touched the surface, the plane would have flipped and cartwheeled down the runway, exploding in a ball of flames. Few aircraft could have withstood such a thumping, and the pilots knew it. In fact, when they arrived back in Moscow they would be awarded medals for their "heroism"—and the Ilyushin would be scrapped, never to fly again.

There were applause and cheers as a rush of relief pinned us in our seats. The thought of dying had weighed on us all as we descended. As we stepped off the plane and touched our soles to the ice of Antarctica, I grabbed Jean-Louis by the forearms and we broke into simultaneous smiles. "We have arrived," he proclaimed. "This is Antarctica." For the moment we were safe.

JULY 26

The morning dawned a bright and balmy 30°, tropical for Antarctica. We had been warned that a front was heading our way, carrying cold and storms, and that weather here this time of year—midwinter on the continent—tended to come in waves of three: three good days, three days of storms, and so on. Our primary objective was to get onto the mainland, and then worry about the conditions to come.

We would be shuttled by Twin Otter, the two-engine turboprop that is the workhorse of the Arctic and Antarctic, to our starting point near a long buried and barely exposed mountain peak named Seals Nunatak. Compared to the Ilyushin these eighteen-seaters were luxurious, if vastly smaller. At least they had windows.

Jean-Louis and I were on the third Twin Otter to fly. The first had gone last night and carried three employees of Adventure Network, the Vancouver-based air charter company that would be providing us support during the first two-thousand-mile leg of our trek. Geoff and Dahe went on the second plane, which left early this morning full of equipment and dogs. Victor and Keizo would trail with whatever gear remained. A fifth plane would carry a French film crew, Films d'Ici, and a crew from ABC Sports headed by announcer Bob Beattie. As we loaded our plane, my loyal lead dog Tim—still tied to his sixty-pound crate—dragged the wooden box across the runway. He did not want to be left behind.

Crammed among men and gear, the dogs were showing signs of tiring of the long trip south. They were thirsty, hungry and ready to run. Once the Twin Otter began its rocking motion as it hurried down the runway, the dogs calmed. Most had been in these small planes before and were familiar with the smell of sleds and equipment. Instinctively they knew there was big adventure awaiting at the end of this ride.

Jean-Louis and I were wedged into seats in the far back of the plane, between my two most faithful companions and lead dogs, Sam and Tim. The plane had been carefully packed, based on the experience I had gathered during many such trips over the years shuttling dogs and gear around the Arctic. The back half of the compartment, its seats removed, was loaded with dogs and a twelve-foot-long sled; the front half was jammed floor to ceiling with gear. The goal was to keep the dogs out of the cockpit. I'd learned that lesson well in 1982, heading for Resolute in the Northwest Territories, when we'd left little gear between the dogs and pilots, and a massive ten-dog brawl had erupted in midair. Three of the hounds ended up in the laps of the pilot and copilot, which seemed funny at the time but was in fact life-threatening.

The weather when we took off was absolutely perfect and we could see nothing but blue sky out the tiny windows. It was just a thirty-five-minute jump from King George to the tip of the Antarctic Peninsula, plenty of time to soak up the scenery below, which was essentially ocean littered with brash ice and icebergs the size of city blocks. Above, the sun shone brightly and a rainbow stretched to our right. Sam stared keenly out one window; Tim, his nose on my shoulder, peered out another. Panda, all 110 pounds of him, tried to crawl onto my lap. As Jean-Louis and I peeked over the dogs the tip of Antarctica, a landmass bigger than China and India combined, slowly came into view.

It had been twenty-four years since I last touched down south of the equator. I'd come in June 1965 with a group of twenty climbers—the curiously named Iowa Mountaineering Club—to scale three first ascents over twenty thousand feet in the Cordillera Blanca mountains northwest of Lima, Peru. I was twenty, and had hitchhiked to Miami from Minneapolis to catch the prop plane south. It was that expedition that cured me for good of any desire to devote more time to climbing; two of my teammates fell to their deaths. Since then my travels —and my knowledge of the wilderness—had been forged in the North, where I came to understand, and came to terms with, nature. I learned through years of exploring the Northwest Territories and the Arctic by dogsled and skis that while nature could be kind and beautiful, it was always the master. Many times I was dwarfed by its immenseness, silenced by its powers, threatened by its potential brutality. Over the years I learned perhaps the most important lesson any adventurer can, that in order to survive nature's harshest lessons you must recognize and give in to its power. You can't treat nature with cockiness, because it can't be "beaten" or controlled; the best you can hope is that you learn to adapt to what it dishes out, learn to use your ingenuity to survive its most brutal conditions. Failure in these conditions—which generally means death—is most often a result of being overconfident.

In 1985 I traveled five thousand miles by dogsled, most of them alone, from the Minnesota/Canada border to Point Barrow, Alaska. In 1986, with seven teammates and fifty dogs, I reached the North Pole after a grueling fifty-six-day "unsupported" trek; we had carried everything we needed from the beginning of the trip, and our success marked the first time the Pole had been reached without resupply. I knew all along that those experiences would someday bring me to Antarctica. Now, flying over the iceberg-laden Weddell Sea, the biggest adventure of my life was about to begin.

What I saw below filled me with a mixture of peace and apprehension. While I was looking forward to the quiet, simple life that such travel affords, the responsibility of making sure the six of us survived the rugged four-thousand-mile crossing rested heavily on me. The confidence I had in our ability came from knowing that each of the six of us was willing to adapt to whatever this place had in store.

To the south I could barely pick out the peaks of mountains, mountains I knew jutted three thousand feet into the air. They lined the peninsula's coast for hundreds of miles. Leading up to them was a two-mile-wide sheet of snow and ice, preceded by the blue of the sea. It was a picture of purity, similar to many I had seen in the picture books and slide presentations of the men who had come to Antarctica before us.

Like most, my impressions of Antarctica had been formed by such photographs; it was these majestic coastlines, snow-peaked mountains, fields of ice and snow, penguins and seals that said "Antarctica" to me. But in truth those scenes represent just 2 percent of this massive, unforgiving continent. Only a handful of men have ever penetrated Antarctica's interior—

Norwegian Roald Amundsen, Englishman Robert Falcon
Scott, Australian Douglas Mawson, a few others. No one had
even considered the nearly four-thousand-mile route we were
to attempt. While most of the areas we would cross had been
mapped, no one had ever traveled them in the seasons we
would. We knew little about the weather we would face, despite days of laborious research, because records of weather in
these areas during the winter months are rare. For much of
our traverse we would be operating primarily on assumptions.

"Could there be a place more desperately silent or more
hopelessly deserted?" Frederick Cook, one of the first to lay
eyes on the continent, wondered in his diary. I had long been
curious how Cook could use words like "desperate" and
"hopeless" to describe what I envisioned as a wondrous frontier. Or how Robert Scott, before succumbing to the brutal
cold and dying eleven miles from safety in 1912, could have
called Antarctica "an awful place." From the air it looked pristine, beautiful, awe-inspiring. Jean-Louis likes to call Antarctica "the world's fiancée," because everyone wants to get to
know her, everyone wants to protect her, everyone wants her
to remain a virgin. It was hard from this vantage point to
envision the monster that we knew Antarctica could be, boasting temperatures of −100°, winds up to two hundred miles per
hour, windchills that are barely calculable.

We had come to Antarctica for many and complex reasons.
First, of course, there was the adventure. We hoped to be the
first team ever to cross Antarctica by dogsled, though we were
hardly the first to have such dreams. Ernest Shackleton had set
sail from England aboard the *Endurance* in 1914 on his third
expedition to Antarctica (this one called the Imperial Trans-
Antarctic Expedition) with a similar goal. But the *Endurance*
was crushed by the ice pack that protects the continent, before
it ever reached the mainland. Shackleton and his men spent
fifteen months in small lifeboats struggling over ice floes and
frigid seas to save their lives. In modern times, two shorter
north-south traverses had been made by British expeditions

riding motorized vehicles—Vivian Fuchs and Edmund Hillary drove Sno-cats in 1957–58, and Ranulf Fiennes and two companions crossed on snowmobiles in 1981.

I was first drawn to Antarctica as a boy reading *National Geographic* during the International Geophysical Year of 1957–58. Spread after spread detailed the lives of the men in the scientific camps and recounted the traverse of Fuchs and Hillary. I was interested in the men and their lives, but I was even more intrigued by how they related to and dealt with this wild environment. I wondered how they got there, how they survived. My eyes dwelled on pictures of crevasses and mountains, and I recognized the adventures they hid. I knew then that Antarctica was a place I had to see.

It was a dream I kept close to my heart for the next thirty years. But that we were now minutes from landing on the continent was the result of a one-in-a-million meeting in the middle of the frozen Arctic Ocean, when the path of my expedition to the North Pole crossed that of Jean-Louis, who was skiing solo toward the same destination. We sat that night in a tent and drank tea and talked about our shared dream of going next to Antarctica. We exchanged phone numbers there on the ice, and after successfully reaching the North Pole we assembled this International Trans-Antarctica Expedition. While the North Pole trip for each of us was a personal best, this was to be much different. It was an effort in part to help preserve and protect one of Earth's last frontiers by drawing attention to it. A vastly unexplored wilderness—brutal, not yet harnessed or exploited—we believe Antarctica must be protected from humankind's greed.

We also hope to show that six men from six different cultures with little in common other than a passion for cold places could work together toward a common goal and succeed. We know there will be struggles and disagreements and that it will not be an easy trip. But if we can work out a system for traveling, a method for living under some of the cruelest conditions on the planet, our success might serve as an example for nations and humankind alike.

Our route will take us nearly four thousand miles, from the tip of the Antarctic Peninsula, past the Ellsworth and Thiel mountain ranges to the South Pole, then across the so-called area of inaccessibility and on to the Soviet bases of Vostok and Mirnyy on the far eastern edge of the continent. Neither the peninsula nor the 750-mile area of inaccessibility has been crossed on foot. What we can predict about the weather and snow conditions in either place is extremely limited. As advanced as technology has become since Amundsen became the first to reach the South Pole in 1911, there are many things about Antarctica we would not know until we stepped into the middle of it.

From the beginning we saw Trans-Antarctica as more than just another adventure. Over the past twenty-five years I've watched the North, and the people who live there, change unalterably. I've seen the wilderness shrink and become more polluted. My fervent hope is that the future does not hold the same for the bottom of the world as it has for the top; that humankind's role in Antarctica will be that of protector, not despoiler.

While Antarctica's role on Earth is vast and mysterious, most people think of it as a kind of cold hell anchoring the bottom of the globe. But the continent's link to global climatic and weather systems makes it the best barometer we have of the planet's future. The seas that surround it provide key nutrients to the rest of the world's oceans. Two thirds of the world's seals, a million whales, over 80 million penguins, and millions of other sea birds and fish call the deep seas that surround Antarctica home. Most important, Antarctica is a critical base for scientific study of the environmental problems that threaten the Earth.

Despite such an important status, ongoing negotiations could change and severely damage Antarctica's future. The international treaty that governs the continent was amended in

1991; the treaty's twenty-six signatory nations (and others that would like to have a say in the continent's destiny) debated the future of the oil and minerals that *allegedly* lie buried below its icy crust. Some estimate that 50 billion barrels of black gold permeate the rock and ice down under; others are convinced there are untapped fields of coal, copper, iron, uranium, plutonium and a variety of precious metals buried here. Representatives of nations from the United States to India debated whether and how to apportion the rights to drill for those resources, if they are proven to exist. Ultimately, they agreed to a fifty-year ban on oil and mineral exploration. Hopefully, by drawing some of the world's focus to the seventh continent during our expedition—especially by engaging the curiosity of the world's children—we will help illustrate why Antarctica is a valuable place that deserves preservation, not exploitation.

Below us the Weddell Sea was now dotted with icebergs of myriad shapes—tabular, domed, blocky, pyramidal, jagged. They are chunks broken off from the thousand-year-old glaciers that rise majestically from the shoreline, walls of sheer blue creased by frozen rivers of ice and riddled with deep crevasses. An engaging yellow light bathed the scene in a softness that is Antarctica's greatest illusion. To my right the gradient shadows of pink/red/rose painted the sky, but the prominent color of the landscape spread below was white—the pure, unadulterated, radiant white of snow and ice. From this vantage point how could we possibly predict that within sixty days we would not only understand what had prompted Scott to curse this as a godforsaken hell but sympathize with the wishes he and his men shared: to die, and die quickly, to get beyond the pain that Antarctica can inflict on warm-blooded creatures.

JULY

JEAN-LOUIS,
I PRESUME?

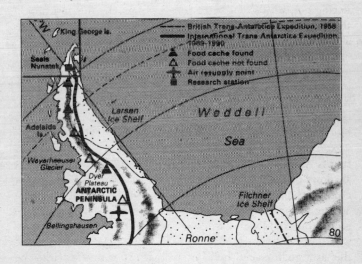

JULY 27, DAY 1

We have camped close to the ice shelf, and when I crawl out of my tent at seven-thirty this morning, a bit frazzled from the long, confined days of traveling south, I am surrounded by piles of boxes and gear, sleds and howling dogs. No vast panorama greets us from this first encampment; tall, jagged peaks of ice and snow are on one side, the Weddell Sea on the other. The temperature is 10°.

Perusing the disorder around me that will soon be organized into three distinct traveling units reminds me of the first expeditions I took, and how much things have changed. As recently as 1985, when I headed out the back door of the Homestead, my compound outside Ely, Minnesota, for a five-thousand-mile dogsled journey to Alaska, two friends drove me to nearby Lake Katatogama in a dilapidated pickup truck. Just me, eleven dogs, and Lloyd Gilbertson, who would accompany me for the first thousand miles. I remember looking back as we sledded away, waving to our friends. No champagne, no film crews, fewer headaches. We just took off, not telling anyone when we left or when we returned; in those days it was truly adventure for adventure's sake.

The expanse—and expense—of our coming adventure may be best illustrated by the effort that went into simply getting to Antarctica the food and fuel necessary for our seven-month traverse.

Even Amundsen and Scott set out caches of food and fuel; no one could attempt a journey to the South Pole or farther without them. The biggest advantage we have over our predecessors here, of course, is airplanes. Six months ago Geoff

Somers and Adventure Network laid out twelve caches across the first half of our traverse; they were interspersed at 150- to 400-mile intervals across the 2,000 miles from our first camp to the South Pole. They made the drops by Twin Otter; each cache contained a twelve-hundred- to two-thousand-pound plywood box stuffed with two weeks' worth of human food, dog food, white gas for cookstoves and kerosene for lamps. At the beginning of the 800-mile-long peninsula, where we'll see stormy, slow-moving days, the caches are closer together; from the end of the peninsula to the South Pole they are stretched farther apart. Marked by nine-foot-tall aluminum poles and blue flags, we hope they are not buried under drifted snow.

Our food was broken down a year ago into bags containing rations for 10 days. More than 5 tons of food, some donated, some purchased, was divvied up: 150 pounds of dried potatoes, 300 pounds of oatmeal, 145 pounds of popcorn, 250 pounds of salmon, 150 pounds of sardines, 40 pounds of wild rice, 450 pounds of egg noodles, 1,250 pounds of Land O Lakes cheese, 500 pounds of Canada Boy powdered milk, 50 pounds of sunflower seeds, 600 pounds of French Meadow granola, 150 pounds of bread, 700 pounds of butter, 450 pounds of Hershey's chocolate, 25 pounds of coffee, 114 pounds of dried vegetables and fruits, 5,000 Shaklee "Energy Bars," 150 pounds of Bear Creek nuts and fruit, 300 pounds of peanut butter, 150 pounds of pilot biscuits, 375 pounds of soup mix, 2,070 cups of Swiss Miss hot chocolate. Once separated, the packages were stuffed carefully into corrugated cardboard boxes designed to fit squarely on our sleds.

From the Twin Cities the food traveled by eighteen-wheeler to Baltimore, where it was transferred to the Polish Ocean Lines *Pulaski*, which in October 1988 crossed the Atlantic to the port of Le Havre, France. There it was loaded onto the Soviet icebreaker *Academic Federov*, which sailed to King George Island. Besides the separated foodstuffs, we shipped 400 fifty-gallon drums of white gas and 30,000 pounds of dog food. Unloaded at their base of Bellingshausen, the Russians prepared the boxes for the caches. What supplies remained on the *Federov* were then sailed to the base of Mirnyy, to be cached by Soviet tractor-train over the eight-hundred-mile stretch from Mirnyy to the Russian base of Vostok.

As we traveled, gear was to be carefully packed on three handmade, twelve-foot-long wooden sleds. Each carried an average of six boxes of dog food, four boxes of human food, a tent and four duffel bags. Keizo's and my sleds (named respectively after Japanese adventurer Naomi Uemerura and Roald Amundsen) were modeled after the Eskimo Komateks, made of spruce or ash, with plastic runners, curved handholds, and a ladderlike base. Geoff's sled (named for his hero Robert Falcon Scott) was modeled after those of Norwegian Fridtjof Nansen, the early Arctic explorer. The difference between the two designs is slight: the Komateks are less flexible and a bit heavier; the Nansen's frame rides higher off the ice, making it slightly more maneuverable and more susceptible to tipping due to its higher load.

The sleds will be pulled the four thousand miles by the real heroes of the expedition, the dogs: three teams of twelve (plus four that we'd left behind as "reserves" in Punta Arenas, should we need them) culled from more than seventy we'd trained over the past three years at the Homestead. Of the thirty-six that had made the cut, nine were leased from the respected Krabloonik Kennels in Snowmass, Colorado; five were the last descendants of Admiral Richard Byrd's breed used in his Antarctica expeditions; the rest were from my own particular polar husky breed that I've been refining the past ten years.

We knew this was going to be a trip to test the stamina, endurance, spirit and strength of the strongest animal, so the dogs' training was perhaps more rigorous than our own. For three years they had hauled cement, rock, sand, wood and supplies into the Homestead. In the early winter of 1988 they helped drag five hundred latrines into Boundary Water Canoe

Area campsites just north of the Homestead for the U.S. Forest Service and then capped their training with the sixteen-hundred-mile traverse of Greenland. The key components we considered when making the final selection were the dogs' strength and spirit. Our lives depend on these hounds—without them the expedition would be impossible—and we needed them to be tough, loyal and determined. These are not "racing" dogs like the kind that run the Iditarod and other such "sprints"; these are big, heavily muscled dogs (the average weight on my team is ninety pounds). They have got to be tough because they're going to be hauling a thousand-pound sled ten hours a day in temperatures down to −50° and below, every day for the next seven months. Protected by a double coat—a thick, dense outer layer and an oily, fuzzy down layer that lies close to the skin—they actually feel quite at home in these conditions.

My team (Sam, Tim, Ray, Buffy, Panda, Zap Junior, Hank, Yeager, Tommy, Chuchi, Bly and Gordie) is made up completely of dogs I bred. Keizo calls them the "Yankee" team, because they are wild and strong, and often hard to control. Geoff's dozen, a mix of Homestead dogs and a couple of the leased Krabloonik dogs (Soda Pop, Spinner, Sawyer, Huck, Chewbakie, Kaviaq, Floppy, Jocky, Jewbak, Pup and Jimmy) is led by the only female we'd brought to Antarctica, named Thule. Geoff's is a much more "British" team: well behaved, they respond quickly to his command. Keizo's team is the unruliest of the three, comprised of the five Antarctic dogs and seven from the Homestead (Bjorn, Kutan, Odin, Monty, Herbie, Rodan, Kuka, Arrow, Aukluk, Chinook, Casper and Kinta). While we expected Keizo's Zenlike calm to transfer to his dog handling, he turned out to be equal part samurai tactician and soft touch when it came to disciplining his team. His dogs, unfortunately, have learned well in the past three years how to "handle" him.

*   *   *

The expedition was officially launched at noon, under untypically balmy skies. Geoff set out first, while I wrapped up a stand-up interview with ABC, during which the carefully planned takeoff ran hilariously amok. Bob Beattie was going to make an on-camera farewell as Victor released the ice anchor that held my frantically tugging dogs, who were desperate to chase after Geoff's already bounding sled. The force of my dogs' exuberance bent the anchor at a ninety-degree angle and pulled it out of the ice, launching the steel projectile at an unsuspecting Beattie's head. Fortunately it missed, but just by inches; if it had struck him, it would have killed him.

Needless to say, my dogs, sled and I went flying by Beattie as he was in midsentence. Poor Victor was caught completely off guard and had to sprint for over a mile to catch up to me and my rampaging team. In all the excitement Keizo's team went into a frenzy and, breaking loose, ran full speed into and over the half dozen reporters who'd gathered to record our start. Cameras literally went flying and a number of people were knocked off their feet.

We traveled just four miles to our first cache; it had been placed that close purposely because we knew that we needed to break in the dogs, ourselves and our traveling system slowly. For the first few weeks the sun will be out fewer than eight hours a day. (By the end of October we will have twenty-four-hour daylight.) We made camp, cooked dinner, then—since these warm nights were the last we would see until sometime next March—I sat outside my tent, trying to figure out the stars in this "upside-down" sky. I've studied constellations since I was a boy and usually can pick out dozens on a bright night up north. Here I could make out only the teapot in Sagittarius, Corvus the Crow, and Aquila the Eagle, but it was not easy. After all these years of heading north, I realized I had seven long months ahead to retrain myself to think south.

JULY 28, DAY 2

At day's end I was skiing alongside the rear sled, the setting sun silhouetting the two teams ahead of me. In the background the rugged mountains of the peninsula dwarfed our colorful entourage of men, dogs and sleds. The billowing steam resulting from the rhythmic breathing of the dogs blends into the plumes of snow that are silently, majestically being driven off the distant mountaintops by hurricane-force winds. At that moment my dream of crossing Antarctica crystallized.

It was fate—and coincidence—that had brought us here. Running across Jean-Louis's ski tracks on the way to the North Pole, in the middle of the Arctic Ocean, a frozen jumble of ice ridges covering an area the size of the United States, was the biggest coincidence of both our lives. That we each harbored the dream of crossing Antarctica was fate.

Ironically it was shortly after conceiving the unsupported trip to the North Pole, in 1983, that I realized if it was successful it would be my ticket to Antarctica. Until then crossing Antarctica seemed logistically impossible; it was too far away, too expensive to reach, too complicated to organize. But I knew if we reached the North Pole—the first confirmed unsupported trek, since Robert Peary's claim is still being debated—I would be able to put together the team, the money and support network to go to Antarctica.

But I pushed my Antarctica dreams to the back of my mind throughout the planning of the North Pole try, until just a couple of days before we actually set off. On the way to our starting point, twenty miles west of Ward Hunt Island, we had flown into the Eureka Weather Station on Ellesmere Island and were stuck there in bad weather for three days. Stranded at the same weather station was Ran Fiennes, the Englishman who had crossed Antarctica by snowmobile in 1981. He had a map of Antarctica with him, and we sat that night and talked and I mapped a potential route—the longest, most difficult imaginable—across the continent.

While I sat with Fiennes, two of my teammates, Bob McKerrow and Ann Bancroft, were stuck behind in Resolute, where they met Jean-Louis. When my teammates finally caught up with us, McKerrow told me I should try to meet Etienne someday, that we were "a lot alike." At the time we all doubted that Jean-Louis would make the North Pole. I had only heard of him, and I questioned his stamina, since he had attempted a similar effort the year before and had ended it just twenty miles out, claiming a leg injury. As a result I wrote him off; these days there are a lot of people who set out for the Pole unprepared, and I'd lumped him in with them. Then to our surprise, when we were two hundred miles out and halfway to the North Pole, we ran across his ski tracks. It was a bitterly cold (−55°) and windy day, but we were traveling anyway. I was paralleling a huge ridge of ice and snow, mushing the dogs, shouting as loudly as I could, when my sled veered to the right, at a sharp thirty-degree angle. I looked up; twenty yards ahead of me was a man. I stopped the dogs and walked up to him. "Jean-Louis, I presume?" I asked "Will?" he answered, and we embraced.

The soft-spoken Frenchman and I talked for a few minutes before the others gathered around us, and the first thing I told him was that I did not feel competitive toward him, even if we were in a sense in a race to the Pole, though making very different trips. He was alone, pulling a six-pound Kevlar sled, and was to be resupplied by air five times. I was traveling with seven others and fifty dogs pulling thousand-pound sleds loaded with everything it would take to reach the Pole. Too often when modern-day explorers meet there is a tension, a kind of "I-don't-want-this-guy-stealing-my-show" attitude. I hoped he would make the Pole, and he felt the same toward us.

He said he was going to stay in his tent that day, so we suggested that he stop if he passed our camp the next morning and we would talk more. Curled inside my sleeping bag at daybreak the following morning, I heard him come into camp, whispering loudly "Will? Will? Will?" I poked my head outside the tent I shared with three others and invited him in for some tea (because of our unsupported goal, I could not accept anything from him, even tea); then we moved to my coleader Paul Schurke's tent for breakfast. Jean-Louis was so hungry he ate the burned remains of a pan of fried oatmeal that was to be fed to the dogs.

We both decided to travel that day and agreed to meet again that night. Ten hours later, camped and sheltered from the frigid night air, he and I talked about our dreams, our lives, our goals, our philosophies—and about Antarctica. He was considering skiing across Antarctica; I preferred the old-fashioned way, by dog. But I liked the notion of including a doctor on any such team (Jean-Louis practices sports medicine in Paris). Most important, though, despite the differences in our hoped-for modes of travel, I recognized in Jean-Louis a "mature" adventurer, not someone who was still searching for himself. We'd both done enough "personal" adventures and agreed that if we were to undertake an expedition in Antarctica it needed to include a consciousness-raising component. That's when we talked about using the expedition to draw world attention to Antarctica and the treaty that governs it, in an effort to make the traverse a truly global "event," rather than just a personal best.

We agreed that night that any such crossing would require Soviet support, since they have the only permanent bases in the eastern half of the continent. But that was as specific as our planning got. We exchanged phone numbers, and the next morning he was off before us, skiing across a patch of thinly frozen sea ice. I was very concerned for him; I thought he might perish on his way to the North Pole, and I very much wanted to see him again, alive.

Looking back today on that chance meeting, it seems much more fate than coincidence. If my team had taken the opposite side of just one of the hundreds of thirty-foot-high pressure ridges we had labored over for thirty days, we would never have crossed his tracks. Just the day before we met him we were caught in a violent storm and wove back and forth along a chaotic macramé of a trail that mysteriously led me to Jean-Louis.

Back home, after we each successfully reached the North Pole in May 1986, we talked occasionally by phone about an Antarctic trip, but only in general terms. At that point I wasn't sure we'd even travel together, but *I* was proceeding with a plan to cross Antarctica. That summer I traveled to the Scott Polar Research Institute in Cambridge, England, and began researching the Earth's most unforgiving continent. I wanted to know all I could about its geography, weather and exploration history. I met with a handful of experienced Englishmen who had been there, many with the vaunted British Antarctic Survey (BAS), including two of England's best-known Arctic and Antarctic explorers, Vivian Fuchs and Wally Herbert. In the fall I lined up my first sponsor commitments, from Hill's Pet Products, DuPont, Kodak, Minnesota Power and the Blandin Corporation, and by early 1987 I had paper commitments for $1 million. But still Jean-Louis and I had not sat down together, except for that solitary night in a frigid nylon tent in the middle of the Arctic Ocean.

Until early in 1987 I thought the trip would include Paul Schurke; we had in fact announced when we reached the North Pole that "our" next expedition would be to Antarctica. But while I was doing my research on Antarctica in late 1986, Paul was doing some of his own, including talking to the National Science Foundation (NSF) in Washington, the agency that administers America's scientific programs on the continent. We both knew the NSF does not encourage, in fact vigorously discourages, private expeditions to Antarctica. (It contends it does not want its scientific bases and personnel to be called upon to rescue any private expedition gone awry.) So I was hardly surprised when Paul came to me at my cabin at the Homestead and explained that the NSF had told him the route I'd picked out, especially if traveled during the seasons we planned, was impossible. We discussed the pros and cons of the expedition for the next few weeks. I needed Paul's full commitment, and he was obviously torn—by lecturing, a growing family, and a seed of doubt planted by the NSF. I worried that he would hinder my efforts, and in January we agreed we could not work together any longer.

In May 1987 Jean-Louis came to Ely for five days and laid out the traverse as he saw it, which included building a $2 million ice-worthy research ship that would sail us down to Antarctica and pick us up at the Soviet base of Mirnyy when we were done. He had already contacted the Soviet Arctic and Antarctic Research Institute—the Soviet equivalent of the NSF—and in three weeks planned to travel to Moscow and Leningrad to line up support and hopefully arrange for a Soviet teammate to join us. Jean-Louis, ever the diplomat, had come to Ely counting on my saying yes to both the ship and his initial diplomatic forays, and I did. In fact, the only real surprise I had during his visit was his size; I'd seen him only in full polar regalia, and I now realized this famous French "polar man," now known on the streets of Paris as "the doctor who skied to the North Pole," was even smaller than I, at five feet seven, 135 pounds. If you were to spot the pair of us on the street you might guess we were soccer players, or even jockeys, but few would peg us as "explorers."

After Jean-Louis returned to Paris I was confident we would be able to pull off our dream, even though we had nowhere near the $8 million we estimated it would cost to assemble a team of men and dogs, buy supplies, build a ship and arrange an array of international logistical support.

We proceeded quickly. By the time Jean-Louis first came to Ely I had already hired a business manager for the expedition, Cathy deMoll. Based in St. Paul, she would wear many hats, serving as chief negotiator with our financing sponsors and overseeing offices in both the U.S. and France charged with dealing with the media as well as organizing an educational component to the expedition (providing teachers and school-children with information and materials about our traverse and

Antarctica, so they could follow us as we crossed). I'd also hired a trainer for the dogs, John Stetson, and a manager for the Homestead, where we would train, Dave Sheild. Later that summer I traveled to Denmark to start making arrangements for our "training" expedition in Greenland and began the process of selecting the other four members of the team.

JULY 30, DAY 4

I finally had a solid night of restful sleep, my first in Antarctica. It helped clear my mind of the complexities that have ensnared it these past months, hopefully lightening my mental load as we prepare for the physical challenge to come. Hopefully, too, the clear skies and physical workouts will ease an as yet undiagnosed problem with my eyes, which causes horrific headaches. Several doctors attributed the headaches to the organizational stress of the expedition, and each suggested what I needed was a rest. For now the problem is still a daily irritation, a constant reminder of how fragile and complicated our bodies are.

The weather remains extremely conciliatory; lows in the teens to 20°, partly cloudy and nearly calm. No one expected this kind of welcome to Antarctica, but no one is complaining. For this first week we are averaging just ten miles a day, and I don't think it has quite dawned on us yet exactly what we are getting ourselves into. We know the next two months will bring storms, but we can only guess at their severity. We know we will see dangerous crevasse fields soon; in fact the second day out we crossed a one-hundred-foot-deep crack in the ice, as wide as three dog teams. We are expected at the South Pole early in December, Mirnyy by the first of March.

Since Shackleton's dream of crossing Antarctica by dogsled was crushed in the ice pack of the Weddell Sea in 1915, Antarctica has been flown over and snowmobiled across, but no one has attempted to venture coast to coast on skis.

Most exploration of this place prior to the nineteenth century was accidental: ships blown off course discovered the first penguins and icebergs. In 1773 English explorer James Cook took the first of three voyages, in which he came within seventy-five miles of the continent. But after much exploration of the ice sheets that surrounded the continent he was convinced that there could be no firm landmass and thus no reason for further exploration. The first man to actually see the continent was a Soviet, Thaddeus von Bellingshausen, who sailed south in search of the Pole aboard two ships, the *Vostok* and the *Mirnyi*, in 1820.

In the early 1800s, American, British and Russian sealers were the first to actually land on the continent. But because their sealing was illegal few accounts of their findings exist; considerable doubt remains as to who actually did what first. Thereafter, nationalist pride encouraged further exploration. The discovery in 1831 of the North Magnetic Pole spawned new interest in the south, and James Ross of Great Britain, Dumont d'Urville of France and Charles Wilkes of the United States almost simultaneously launched expeditions seeking the South Magnetic Pole. None were successful, though they did manage to map an abundance of previously uncharted territory in the South Polar seas. But despite their mappings, arguments continued over whether or not the ice shelves actually shielded a continent. The debate led to a dulling of enthusiasm for continued exploration, and it wasn't until 1898 that another Antarctic expedition was mounted, this one by a Belgian sailor named Adrien de Gerlache. Included were Poles, Romanians, Americans, and a twenty-six-year-old Norwegian named Roald Amundsen. They became the first men ever to spend a winter in Antarctica, when their ship, the *Belgica*, was frozen in the ice for thirteen long months.

In 1901 an unlikely hero led a British expedition to the continent. As a young man, Robert Falcon Scott was sickly and

shy. Despite this, he asked to join the Royal Navy expedition
to the Antarctic and was unexpectedly named its leader. More
scientist than adventurer, Scott managed to lead the expedition
to within 463 miles of the South Pole.

One member of Scott's team—twenty-year-old Ernest
Shackleton—was sent home with scurvy. Disappointed by his
failure, Shackleton became obsessed with conquering Antarctica. Handsome and charismatic, he quickly raised the funds
necessary to lead his own expedition, and using ponies and
dogs, in 1908 he passed Scott's record, coming within ninety-
seven nautical miles of the geographic pole; four months later,
a team of three, including Douglas Mawson, discovered the
South Magnetic Pole.

Scott returned to Antarctica in 1911, determined to reach
the geographic South Pole. While en route to Antarctica he
learned that the Norwegian Amundsen was also heading for
the Pole, and a race was on. (The North Pole had long been
Amundsen's goal, but Admiral Robert Peary had beaten him
there, so his attentions turned south.) Amundsen began the
"race" sixty-nine miles closer to the Pole than Scott and set
out thirteen days earlier, with fifty-nine dogs. Executing a perfectly laid "attack" and aided by good weather, Amundsen and
four companions reached the Pole on December 14, 1911.
When Scott's five-man party reached the Pole on January 17,
1912—they'd started out with ponies and dogs but ended up
man-hauling their sleds most of the way—they discovered a
tent and a note left behind by the Norwegians. Though hor-
rifically disappointed, Scott spent three days at the Pole "geo-
logising," despite knowing that bad weather and a lack of food
were sure to haunt him on his team's eight-hundred-mile
march back to safety. All five were to die on the return, Scott
and two companions pinned down by a vicious blizzard just
eleven miles from a cache laden with lifesaving food and fuel.

Those years were filled with history-making Antarctic expeditions. At the same time Scott and Amundsen were racing
for the Pole, the Australian Mawson set out with two men and

eighteen dogs to do some mapping in the name of his home-land. After several weeks of travel, one man, six dogs and a sled containing human and dog food, a heavy-canvas tent, clothes, sleeping bags, shovels and ice axes were lost in a crevasse. Two weeks later Mawson's remaining travelmate froze to death. On his own, Mawson trudged 320 miles back to safety, surviving several drops into crevasses, near starvation, and poisoning from unknowingly ingesting lethal amounts of vitamin A in the dogs' livers he'd eaten to stay alive. When he arrived back in camp the men awaiting his return hardly recognized him—many of his teeth had fallen out, as had all of his hair, and hunks of skin had fallen from his face.

By the time Shackleton's *Endurance* sank in 1915, the conti-nent's coastlines were well mapped. But the interior remained, and to a large extent remains today, a mystery, broached just a handful of times overland. Fuchs and Hillary traveled 2,158 miles in six twelve-thousand-pound Sno-cats pulling heavy sledges loaded with gear in the austral summer of 1957–58. Fiennes—who circumnavigated the globe by ship, snowmobile and on foot during a three-year stretch from 1979 to 1982—snowmobiled 2,254 miles across Antarctica in 1981. Until now, no one has ever even attempted to dogsled and ski across the continent.

The route we will travel is essentially the same one I picked out with Fiennes in Eureka in the spring of 1986. Experts, including Fuchs, assured me the trip was too risky, but I am used to people saying "you'll never make it." Across the Arctic I have pulled my dogsled into small Eskimo villages, hundreds of miles from the nearest road, and the inhabitants rarely thought I'd reach the next encampment. I'd studied this route carefully for three years and was comforted by a few things Fuchs could not know, about our logistics, the ability of our dogs and the confidence I had that we could ski twenty to twenty-five miles a day.

But the key to convincing myself that this trip was achiev-able were words from the lips of Giles Kershaw, the most experienced pilot in both the Arctic and Antarctic. We met in San Diego in mid-1987 to discuss the possibility of Adventure Network, the air charter company he'd cofounded, helping us lay our caches across Antarctica. Giles studied our route on a map, told me he had flown over much of it, and assured me we could make it. Given Giles's confidence, I was convinced that if we could raise the necessary money, keep the team on good terms, and stay on the good sides of a dozen different governments, the actual traverse would be the easy part.

Antarctica contains many of the uncharted spots left on the Earth's map that have long fascinated me. The stretch from the Ellsworth Mountains to the South Pole has never been crossed in November. (Both Amundsen and Scott traveled to the Pole from the opposite side of the continent.) The area of inaccessibility has been crossed overland just once, by Russian tractor in 1958. Totally flat, like a giant silver dollar, this stretch of the traverse is difficult and expensive to reach by air, so laying caches and being rescued are nearly impossible.

We will be traveling in Antarctica's late winter all the way down the 800-mile peninsula. By the time we reach the Ellsworth Mountains in late October, spring should be on its way; by the time we reach the South Pole, hopefully in early December, it will be Antarctic summer. While it would have been preferable for us to leave four to six weeks later than we did, to avoid the worst of winter, we could then never possibly have reached the other side before March 1, when winter will come roaring back in our faces off the Indian Ocean. The only way for us to complete the crossing is by beginning and ending in Antarctica's worst conditions.

For the first three months we will climb, slowly, from sea level to an altitude near ten thousand feet. Until past the South Pole, north-northeast winds will blow in our faces, up to eighty miles per hour. Temperatures should average between −30° and −40°. Windchills on the worst days will reach −100°. If we make it past the Pole and across the area of inaccessibility, then we'll run into the coldest place on Earth, near the Soviet base of Vostok.

From Vostok to our final destination 750 miles away at Mirnyy, winter will be back. Temperatures will drop below −60° and we will descend very quickly from the twelve-thousand-foot plateau to sea level, meeting supercold, very moist air propelled by gusting winds of up to 200 miles per hour. If the weather as we near Mirnyy is good—meaning −40°, winds of 20 miles per hour—we could make the last 200–300 miles in a week. If it's bad, we could be pinned down just like Scott and his men, unable to travel and just miles from safety. What we are undertaking is an endurance trip; daily hardship over seven grueling months, under extreme pressure—from sponsors, governments and our own dreams and commitments—to reach the other side of the continent.

We decided on an international team, six men from six different countries, from the very onset and sought out mature, easygoing adventurers. Not supermen, but experienced men in their late thirties or early forties, men who were no longer searching for "identity." (Keizo, at thirty-two, is the exception.) I would have preferred all single men, because they generally leave behind fewer responsibilities about which to worry, like wives and children; but the two team members who were selected by their governments, Dahe and Victor, are both married and each has one son.

We will need to compromise and adapt if we are to make it across; a rift between men in such conditions is my worst nightmare. Jean-Louis likes to say that we are each "the ambassador of our own country." None of us can get over the fact that less than two generations ago our ancestors were on opposite sides of various battlefields and today here we are mounting a struggle of our own, but not against one another.

Everyone has a specific job. Geoff was brought on because he knew the peninsula well, having spent three and a half years here as a guide with the British Antarctic Survey. He is one of the best dog handlers I've ever met. Victor was a sound choice, both for his representation of the Soviet Union and his meteorological studies; he'd also experienced the worst conditions in Antarctica, having spent two winters based at Vostok. Keizo, from Osaka, is an excellent dog handler; Dahe, an esteemed glaciologist. While we get along well so far, I remain convinced that the biggest challenge we face is concluding this adventure as friends.

JULY 31, DAY 5

The surface conditions these first few days have been lightning fast, and the dogs, their wild spirits awoken, have been impossible to slow. Even before we emerge from our tents in the morning they are yapping and barking, tugging at their necklines, anxious to get moving. We have no brakes on the sleds, no means of slowing them down except by shouting, so once they break the sled loose from the crusted ice at the start of each day the otherwise pristine scene quickly becomes a chaos of drivers shouting, cursing, and digging their mukluk heels into the rock-hard ice in a frantic effort to gain some control over the wild dogs. This morning, with Victor out ahead on skis, my sled followed by Keizo's shot down the hill, catching our point man and quickly leaving him in a cloud of powder. Behind us Dahe fell from the sled he was steering, creasing the ice with his elbows as he went down. Geoff, the firmest disciplinarian among us, managed to keep his dogs from engaging in the chase. But that the dogs are so rambunctious is hardly surprising; this is what they've trained for the past three years. They yearn to be harnessed, to pull. Thankfully, by day's end they mellow and for now sleep soundly.

One early problem is that Dahe has not yet mastered dog driving or skiing. He falls many times a day, and each time he does, the rest of us twinge out of sympathy and responsibility. Though he has been based in Antarctica twice, he never learned to ski. (Not many Chinese ever learn, even those who work here year after year.) He tells us that his previous cold-weather travels have been luxurious by comparison to this; in the Himalayas he and his science mates had porters to carry their gear, and when he worked with an Australian research team here in Antarctica they traveled by tractor-trains, with hot running water and electric blankets.

When we heard that Dahe would join us, we weren't overly concerned about his lack of skiing skills. He is a very serious scientist and a valuable addition to the team; we were sure he'd pick up skiing soon after we got on the ice. My confidence had been bolstered shortly after he arrived for his first visit to the Homestead in February 1989. On a two-day training run into the Boundary Waters I gave Dahe the reins to the heavy work-sled in deep snow and dense woods, though I knew he'd never run a dog team. He took them without complaint, and at day's end, despite sweating through his insulated parka and obviously worn out, he smiled and said thanks for the education.

In these first few days he has impressed us all with his determination and patience, yet it is painfully obvious that he lacks the one ingredient necessary to ski: coordination. Over the years I've taught more than a thousand beginners how to ski, but I've never seen anyone as helpless as Dahe. He did not grow up playing sports, and his motor coordination does not come naturally. We purposely assigned him to share a tent with Geoff for the first six weeks, because we knew the rigid Englishman would teach, and watch out for, our new Chinese friend.

As we neared camp today Dahe became surprisingly angry and frustrated with himself, but he took it out on the dogs, yelling and cursing at them in Chinese. We'd never seen this kind of outburst from the otherwise humble scientist. I felt so sorry for him that as we unpacked our sleds I pulled a tin of French candies from my lunch box, opened them, and held them out for him to choose from. He smiled, but we exchanged no words as he withdrew a single piece and slipped it into his mouth.

MILES TRAVELED: 39

MILES TO THE SOUTH POLE: 1,958

AUGUST

IT'S ANTARCTICA

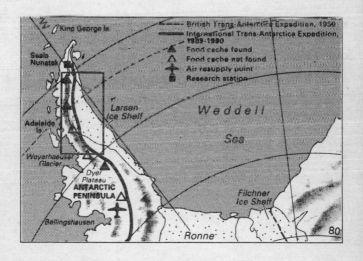

AUGUST 2, DAY 7

Today was as fine a travel day as we're likely to see for the next seven months, our longest so far. We covered fifteen miles in four hours over fast surfaces, under windless blue skies. The temperature dropped to −20°, our coldest yet. It feels, finally, as if the expedition has begun, the warmup over.

The morning began with a debate over exactly where we were. Jean-Louis and Geoff are the designated navigators, but the maps we will use during this first leg are just small jet navigation charts, which lack fine detail. It has become apparent quickly that the scale here will take some getting used to: Cape Disappointment, which we were aiming for and which appeared to be fifty miles away, was in fact just twenty miles ahead. The confusion was understandable; several times this first week we found ourselves carried away with the continent's vastness and grandeur. Given Antarctica's clear air we half expected to be able to see two hundred miles away.

The good conditions came as a surprise; last night a heavy wind blew until nine o'clock, when it leveled off at sixty miles per hour, gusting steadily off the mountains we have been paralleling for the past week. As it picked up steam the dogs grew irritated, and all night long they rustled and growled at each other. This is predictable, given that the surface is too hard for them to dig into and bury themselves for protection. Instead, they are subjected to the full brunt of the wind, which whips snow through the air like projectiles. By comparison, on clear, cold nights the dogs stay absolutely still all night long. They curl up in tight, frosted balls, their tails covering their noses. To get up to snarl at their neighbors means losing precious heat. On the coldest mornings they remain locked in this protective position even as we pack the sleds, their eyes darting back and forth watching us, patiently waiting to be harnessed to run another day.

It was −12° when we stopped, five miles southeast of Cape Disappointment. The cold air is surprisingly stimulating, and it is hard to go into the tent tonight. Instead I find myself dragging out my chores—unpacking the sled, untangling gang lines, feeding the dogs. For now the nights are very long, which means long hours getting used to tent life. The sun sets at three-fifteen in the afternoon, and by six o'clock it is pitch-black. We don't see first light until eight-thirty the next morning. When I finally enter the tent I leave the door unzipped to the dark night, so I can still see the twinkling southern stars. When Victor finishes his weather observations and crawls inside, the hatches are tightened down, a candle is lit, and the second burner of the stove turned on for heat. Inside our nylon shelters we polar men crouch at the foot of our sleeping bags and work the ice out of our mukluk lashings. The door is zipped tight, sealing off the cold. I stir supper, and we chat in simple English about the adventure of the day. This is a good life, though I often think about what an unusual sight it would be if someone stumbled by accident upon our camp.

Victor turns up the stove for our major chore of each evening: melting snow for dinner and tomorrow's thermoses. Each day we will melt enough snow to make four gallons of water per tent, a task that takes several hours. The ceiling of our oval-shaped dome looks like a mass of spaghetti, with lines crisscrossing above our heads to hold aloft everything from mukluks to sleeping bags, placed there to be dried by the heat rising from our cookstove. It is a comfortable, if confining, space, eight feet long by six feet wide and four and a half feet at its tallest peak. Since the sun sets long before we crawl into our tents, it is always dark when we are inside, though our light sources are various: outside, because it is a calm night, a kerosene Coleman lamp burns; on our heads we wear headlamps; and a tall, Chilean-made candle burns between us. The other tents use their kerosene lamps inside, but Victor and I have passed a "clean air" act, disallowing the nasty-smelling fuel in our tent. The inner walls of our nylon home are always frosted from floor to ceiling; as the tent warms, the frost melts and drips on us and everything else. Moisture is the bane of this life, almost more of a problem than the cold.

The floor of the tent is equally chaotic. Our sleeping bags are separated by two three-by-two-foot-long wooden boxes. The yellow one holds our personal gear, the green one keeps the stove and cooking utensils. Just inside the entryway sits a large empty cardboard dog food box that serves as both garbage can and table. On either side of the entryway are smaller boxes: the black one contains breakfast materials and serves as Victor's chair, the red one holds supper materials. The colors are necessary to help simplify packing and unpacking the sled; such delineation is essential when the wind is blowing over fifty miles per hour and you can't see your hand in front of your face.

I like to keep my "home" on the ice simple, and Victor and I share a similar domestic style—messy but clean. Jean-Louis and Geoff, on the other hand, are quite the opposite. Their tents, reflecting their personalities, are meticulous and orderly. Both are what we call "brushers": as they enter the tent they carefully stop to brush off all the snow that has gathered on their clothes and mukluks. Dahe is a "brusher" too.

I have brought along some distinctly nonadventuresome details to make this place a bit more cheery. On top of our "table" sits a woven green placemat and large cloth napkins. When I switch teammates—three times before the end of the trip—I'll break out new mats and napkins. This is going to be home for the next six months, and because it is always damp, close and stale smelling I've found over the years that such simple pleasures can make life in these otherwise primitive conditions more bearable.

We refined most of our traveling systems when we tra-

versed Greenland, including refining a novel system for packing our garbage. Every five days each tent gets a new, recently
emptied dog food box, which serves as our table and stove-
holder. The first thing we do is cut holes at either end, into
which go tea bags, onion skins, leftovers—we've dubbed it our
"mailbox." After five days we dump the contents into a plastic
bag, which we carry on the sled until it can be flown out. It is a
special night when we have a clean "mailbox" in the tent.

Keeping ourselves clean is more of a challenge. We will
bathe only sporadically during the next seven months, and
then it will be quickly. Victor has developed a penchant for
early-morning snow showers; he goes out barefoot and nude
into whatever conditions he finds and scrubs up with snow. So
far such baths have been limited, though, due to the extremely
hard surfaces. For the rest of us, bathing is confined to a small
washcloth and a few ounces of lukewarm water.

As for cooking, I handle the evening meal and Victor makes
breakfast. Each morning, promptly at six o'clock, he lights the
stove and heats water for oatmeal, about the only breakfast
option we have. For dinner my options are a bit less limited.
Tonight, for example, we're having a delectable meal of noodles and pemmican (a cold-weather staple, made of dried meat
and lard), topped by an unidentified red powder, which I think
is dehydrated tomatoes. For auxiliary taste I soaked the whole
mess in melted cheese and butter and threw in the leftover
soup from the night before.

AUGUST 3, DAY 8

It is still dark when we leave the tent at 7:30 a.m., and we must
carry lanterns or wear headlamps to see. This dark period is
good for now, because it forces short travel days and long
relaxed evenings. To truly understand the Arctic and Antarctic
I think you have to enter in the darkness of winter, because it
is only by experiencing these places at their blackest that you

can appreciate their summers. I cherish this slow, dark time but am already anticipating the days when the light of the southern skies lengthens, indicating the first hint of the austral spring. There is something about the return of the sun and its long, pastel-colored dawns that excites my spirit like nothing else.

This morning fantastic clouds rose from the west. High, wispy stratocumulus, they glow, backlit by the rising sun. The same clouds will return in the evening and remain visible in the clear, dark sky long past dark. The temperature is 2°.

On our left is the Larsen Ice Shelf, a four-hundred-foot-thick slab of melted glacier that extends up to a hundred miles into the Weddell Sea. Every few years a giant section of this shelf breaks off and becomes ocean-bound, joining thousands of other tabular, hundred-foot long icebergs that fill the bay and eventually float into warmer waters and disappear. To our right is the continuous barrier of the Antarctic Peninsula, a massive mountain range that stretches as far north and south as the eye can see. We will hug these mountains for three hundred miles, until we take a hard right and climb almost straight up the Weyerhaeuser Glacier to the top of the Dyer Plateau, six thousand feet above sea level. That plateau will take us to the interior of the continent.

When we set out ten days ago it was with a gnawing apprehension about the unknowns that lay ahead. While it goes unspoken, each of us questions whether or not we'll make it across the continent. As the days roll by, that apprehension is slowly dissolving. I imagine it is a feeling similar to having tamed a wild horse to a point where you have just received its trust, but are still not certain it might not rear back, throw you to the ground, then stomp you for good measure. None of us think we can "tame" Antarctica—we just hope we can survive the ride.

Each day we're seeing increased evidence of our biggest danger during this first month of travel: deep, mysterious fissures in the ice called crevasses. Caused by the folding and buckling of ice sheets as the glaciers melt and shift, crevasses are literally "faults" in the surface that can be 30 feet wide and 150 feet deep. These are the deepest on Earth, and they line the perimeters of Antarctica like protective moats.

Among us Geoff has had the most experience with crevasses, having dogsledded up and down much of the peninsula and more recently having studied thousands of reports by the British Antarctic Survey teams made over the past thirty years. Three times during his Antarctic career Geoff's partner, a man to whom he was roped, has fallen into a crevasse, one dangling upside down for fifteen minutes before he could be rescued. Because of his experience Geoff will guide us through this area, a big responsibility, especially since he is convinced that the one failing we have as a team is crevasse rescue.

"Crevasses are nothing to be taken lightly," I overheard him reminding Dahe this morning before we set out. "Sometimes you can see them ahead of you, maybe detect a slight shadow that gives them away. But usually you can't see them from a distance. If the area ahead looks suspicious at all, two men—both roped to the sled—must go carefully to the front of the sled and probe the terrain with a ski pole. If the pole vanishes into very thin snow, there is most likely a crevasse beneath it.

"The first lesson is don't go wandering off on your own. Always stay roped up, and keep one hand on your sled at all times. If you are walking to the front dog of your team, don't walk along the side of the dogs: straddle the central rope so if you fall through you've at least got a chance of grabbing on to something.

"A crevasse has a theoretical maximum depth of one hundred fifty feet. But if you fall in, it's not the depth that will kill you, it's the narrowing of the crevasse. When you land you'll be crushed between two ice walls, incapable of moving. The worst case is to have your sled fall in a crevasse, especially bad news if you're roped to it."

After a week on the ice our systems are gradually becoming

refined; for example, I know exactly how my sled is to be packed and unpacked each day. It is an art not dissimilar from successfully packing the trunk of your car before a vacation, and efficiency is the key. The fewer ropes, knots and hassles the better, for each day you pack and unpack in bitter cold. I have a system in which four lengths of rope secure the whole load. Using carabiners as S hooks to weave the rope from one side of the sled to the other, I cinch each length up and secure it with mountain-climbing Jumars. I'm able to tie the whole load without taking my gloves off, a necessity in nasty weather. The goal in all of our camp chores is to reduce efforts to the simplest of tasks.

Tonight as we made camp an incredible windstorm began, whipped upward of sixty miles per hour. Outside, a few of the dogs cried from the stinging snow. Inside, we prayed the tents hold.

AUGUST 4, DAY 9

"It's okay, Gordie, it's okay. It's okay, kiddo, it's going to be okay." Gordie—my gentle 110-pound veteran—is unfortunately covered with a thin coat of fur and he suffers more than his thick-coated brothers in these brutal winds. He was crying this morning when we woke, and I talked to him through the tent wall first thing, hoping the sound of my voice would soothe his discomfort.

When we took off it was 20° and calm. We packed the sleds without gloves, but by lunch the winds had started to whip again and by midafternoon we were traveling in our first real storm. By three o'clock the winds had reached seventy-five miles per hour, forcing us to stop and put up camp.

We needed a storm to get our blood, and ingenuity, flowing. Believe me, it takes both to put up a tent in seventy-five-mile-per-hour winds. Victor and I struggled desperately with our dome: our mukluks slipped on the icy surface, and to walk upwind required an ice ax as a cane. If you stopped walking even for a second the wind blew you backward. Driving tent stakes into the rock-hard ice required patience and a good whack with the ax; shoveling snow onto the ground flaps—specially designed so we could weight down the tent during just such winds—was a nightmare. But it was a good drill: we discovered that the metal grommets through which we lashed down the tent fly had already ripped out and that hammering tent stakes into solid ice seriously risked cutting the thin, nylon fly with the ax head.

Slight equipment failures are typical at the outset of any expedition, and by comparison to our predecessors we are extremely well-prepared. Turn-of-the-century polar explorers hardly had it this good; Shackleton's men slept in reindeer-skin sleeping bags. I've never been this well outfitted before myself. I remember in 1979 going out for a month-long trek into Canada wearing army surplus gear. Four years later, on a dogsled journey to Alaska, I couldn't afford a radio and was short on dogs. The Salvation Army pants I wore cost me two dollars; the jacket, three dollars. The only thing I had plenty of was bacon, which I used to trade with the Indians for sled dogs as I traveled north.

Here our lives are dominated by zippers and Velcro, and the clothes we wear every day are not that dissimilar in their technology and construction from space suits (not surprising since we were set to walk across the planet's highest, windiest, coldest land). Our clothing system was manufactured by North Face, using DuPont insulation and Gore-Tex fabric, and the designing process had taken months. We wanted to take every precaution for dealing with these "spacelike" conditions, right down to the colors we chose (purple, teal and orange, chosen for their psychologically pleasing tones).

The "uniforms" were designed with personal preferences in mind; for example, some of us liked drop-seat pants, others one-piece suits. Essentially I dress the same every day: Thermax long underwear; stretch pile pants and shirt; a stretch pile pullover; and one of a variety of Gore-Tex shells over top and bottom, depending on the temperatures. (We have one-piece suits, anoraks, and heavy, insulated parkas to choose from.) On my feet I wear wool Hollofil socks, wool midthigh duffles, and moosehide-and-Gore-Tex mukluks, designed by my ex-wife, Patti. To protect my hands, most vulnerable to cold, I wear a wool wristlet that covers from my forearm to over my wrist and then giant beaver-skin mitts consisting of a pile liner and a Gore-Tex outershell. On my head is a Gore-Tex-and-pile hat and the hood from my jacket, which is lined by a fur ruff.

No matter what outer jacket I wear, I always keep the exact same things in my pockets each day: in the right pocket a face mask, a headband and a thin pair of Thermax gloves; in the left pocket a small pair of pliers and a tube of sun block. In an inside chest pocket I carry a compass and a small waterproof container of matches.

Our navigators are using two different systems. Geoff prefers the old-fashioned ways of compasses, watches and the sextant; Jean-Louis relies on a high-tech satellite system. I'm glad we have both, as a means of checks and balances. Each morning Geoff emerges from his tent having studied the maps and pictures of the areas he took last January when he helped place the caches. He gives Victor, who on most days skis out front of the sleds as a reference for the dogs, an indication by compass of the day's direction. At day's end, if Jean-Louis is able to make radio contact with our Punta Arenas base camp, we verify the exact latitude and longitude of where we camped the day before, which gives us a rough idea of where we've set up camp.

We are able to get that satellite location by carrying a battery-operated transmitter that broadcasts a constant signal. Our signal is picked up by a U.S. orbiting National Oceanic and Atmospheric Administration (NOAA) satellite and transmitted to the Argos Processing Center at Toulouse, France.

From there our latitude and longitude are relayed via Paris or
St. Paul to the Punta Arenas base camp, where Adventure Network keeps an office and where our ship, the *UAP*, is docked;
Criquet deMarlive, one of the ship's four crewmen and for
twenty years a friend of Jean-Louis's, and John Stetson are our
point men there. Occasionally Geoff argues that the satellite
position is off, but that has yet to be proved. The only problem
with the satellite system is that it cannot be relied on during
stormy conditions; if we cannot make radio contact, which we
know in the coming months will become more and more infrequent, the satellite information is worthless to us.

As suddenly as the storm began this afternoon, it stopped
early in the evening. Snuggled in our tents, the instantaneous
calm perked our ears. Out of the clear night came the sound of
a flute playing an oddly familiar tune, similar to the theme
song from *The Good, the Bad and the Ugly*. I looked outside, half
expecting Clint Eastwood to be staring down at me. Instead,
there was Keizo, humming on the loon whistle he had brought
to remind the dogs of home. It took me instantly back to a fall
day at the Homestead, but the dogs seemed oblivious, wisely
preferring to stay huddled beneath their blankets of blown
snow.

AUGUST 5, DAY 10

Today is the first time we will write in our journals, "No progress." The winds are back, causing ground blizzards and zero
visibility. Given the crevasses that mine this area we can't risk
navigating blindly, so the decision is made to take the day off. I
wish we deserved it, but our bodies are not really tired from
the meager mileage we have covered thus far. At noon Geoff,
antsy to be on the move, crawled into our tent and we had a
peek at a map of Antarctica. Victor pointed out Vostok, three
thousand miles from where we sit.

This is the kind of weather we expected on the peninsula.

Twenty yards in front of me I can barely make out the silhou-ette of a dog team, snaked in the shadowy near distance like a string of pearly black rosary beads. Unfortunately the blowing snow is not covering the dogs, so they're again bearing the full brunt of the storm. Once every few hours the storm will stop, abruptly, then explode again. When Victor talks about the storm he keeps reminding us that "it's Antarctica," meaning this could go on for hours—or days.

After dinner Jean-Louis tried to make radio contact, a chore he will handle throughout the expedition. Simply ready-ing the radio for operation is a monumental chore, especially on stormy days like this. The antenna runs out the tent door where the zippers come together, to two skis stuck upright in the ice and anchored with ice axes. The radio is a French military-made multiband Thomson. It weighs ten pounds and is carried in a black wooden box that rarely leaves Jean-Louis's sight. Its receiver, covered by a plastic bag to protect it from moisture, resembles a telephone receiver. Inside the tent a speaker suspended from the ceiling allows others to hear the conversation. Often Jean-Louis will spend hours trying to es-tablish radio contact; during storms it is difficult to reach *any-one*, at either our base camp or any of the Antarctic bases. Even when contact is established, the reception is often awful and sounds like ducks quacking. But Jean-Louis enjoys the chal-lenge of the radio. It gives him something to do each night, and when clear contact is made he engages in lengthy chats in French with Criquet, catching up on news of the outside world, which he, more than the rest of us, craves.

A veteran of mountain climbing, around-the-world sailing and now polar adventures, Jean-Louis is highly regarded in the expeditioning world. He crewed in the 1976 Tall Ships Race on the *Bel Espoir*, then raced around the world in the biannual Whitbred Race, aboard the *Pen Duick 6*, in 1978. He has climbed in Patagonia twice, including the first crossing of the Hielo Continental from the Pacific Ocean to the FitzRoy Range; sailed and climbed along the coast of Greenland and twice climbed in the Himalayas, including the northwest ridge of Mount Everest. But on those expeditions he was always the team physician, one of several mates. It wasn't until his successful solo to the North Pole that he earned his stripes as an adventurer.

Unassuming, quick-witted, an accomplished jazz pianist and eternal bon vivant, Jean-Louis is our "quiet leader" and diplomatic liaison. The last is a necessary skill if we are to pull off an international expedition (on a continent governed by the mutual agreement of thirty-nine nations). He also brought to the expedition a $2 million pledge from his longtime sponsor UAP (Union des Assurances de Paris), France's second-largest insurance company, which went into building the 135-foot aluminum-hulled ship Jean-Louis designed and named for her sponsor. His relationship with UAP goes back to his first, unsuccessful trip to the North Pole in 1985; they gave him $100,000 for that effort, and when he failed he returned $80,000. Such manners are not typical of failed expeditions—caveat emptor is the general rule of thumb when it comes to such sponsorship—and UAP's executives were so shocked, and pleased, by his consideration that when he launched what would be his successful sixty-three-day trip in 1986, they gave him $400,000.

He was born in Vielmur, a small town in southern France ("far from the mountains, and the sea, and the cold," he laughs), in 1946. His father and grandfather were tailors. First interested in "mechanical" school, he later went to medical school and moved to Paris. Though he practiced medicine right out of school, specializing in nutrition and sports medicine, he recoiled from the nine-to-five of an office, preferring the more loosely structured life of a "professional" expedition physician. "I like to be free, I like to move where I want, go when I want," he had told me in that tent in the middle of the Arctic Ocean. "My definition of the word 'adventure' is to 'invent life.' That's my advice to everyone: 'Invent your life. Be happy. Do what you want to do.' " In Paris, though he can afford better, he lives in a $250-a-month, sixth-floor walk-up, furnished sparely with a plank of wood serving as a table. He has always "invested" anything he earns in his next adventure.

AUGUST 6, DAY 11

The storm intensified in the middle of the night, and when Victor left the tent at seven-thirty this morning to record his weather observations he shouted back simply, "It's bad." Visibility is less than five feet. Again the storm would stop, abruptly, and when everyone's attention was drawn outside . . . *Wham!* the wind exploded back, gripping the tent in its teeth and creating the already too familiar sound of whining guylines and snapping nylon. Safe inside, for now, we spent the day writing, talking, thinking and listening to the storm.

Waiting at this stage doesn't threaten our schedule. Rather, our biggest mistake would be to get ahead of schedule and travel farther along the peninsula while it is still in the grip of winter. The best pace for now is slow and steady. I don't think the dogs are ready for the really serious conditions that currently wrack the peninsula's plateau: temperatures down to −50°, winds up to one hundred miles per hour. Where we're camped, despite being socked in by wind, the temperatures remain mild, with lows of −10°. When these winds subside we will try to make the most mileage we can, but we can't count on that happening anytime soon. Again Victor reminds me, "It's Antarctica."

All day long we move restlessly between tents, as much for the exercise as for companionship, but we walk cautiously. These are frightening conditions, the kind that can blow a nylon tent away in seconds or whisk a man off his feet. Victor had a close call early this morning, almost getting lost in the whiteout coming back from making his weather observations. He fell, knocking his headlamp off, and when he got to his feet he could see no reference point—no tents, no dogs, nothing—

despite being only ten yards from Jean-Louis and Keizo's tent. When he told me this story we agreed that, just as at home, most dangers lie close by.

One good thing about these days off is that they give our trio of scientists time to prepare the various research projects they will conduct across the continent. Though their research, whether coming at the end of a long day of travel or midday during a miserable storm, is sometimes seen as a cruel hardship in these extreme conditions, Victor, Dahe and Jean-Louis are committed to their studies.

Victor makes his weather observations three times a day, recording barometric pressure, air temperature and humidity, and wind speed and direction. In September and October he will take daily measurements of the atmospheric ozone; the measuring device is a heavy state-of-the-art but temperamental Soviet-made contraption. It is in those months that the ozone shield above Antarctica is at its thinnest, and we hope that Victor's studies will gather evidence of this year's depletion from ground-level vantage points never before recorded.

Dahe, who has done glaciological research in other parts of Antarctica as well as the Himalayas, will collect snow samples for oxygen isotope and chemical analysis from here to Mirnyy. His strength and patience will be severely tested as he digs five- to six-foot-deep pits twice per degree, or about every thirty miles, and scrapes and bottles hundreds of snow samples to measure the evidence of pollution in the ice. The ice of the area of inaccessibility has never been sampled, and Dahe's peers around the world are anxiously awaiting his findings.

"I have made a promise to myself to not skip any day," Dahe told me when we first arrived. "If we ski slow, it could be several days between diggings. If we ski fast, I must dig every day. If we ski thirty miles in one day—a very hard day—I must still dig. If it is soft snow, it will take thirty to forty minutes. If it is hard, one hour. If it is very hard, one and a half hours, with an ice ax. It will often be difficult, but this is my life, this is why I am here, to explore the truth about Antarctica's glaciers and their impact on the environment. I know one thing, though, if my wife asked me to work this hard at home, I would say no."

As for Jean-Louis, he is committed to the psychological and physiological studies he will conduct throughout the expedition, especially the urine study. A bluntly named "piss jug" is the dominant feature of Jean-Louis's tent, hanging over the Coleman stove and labeled in simple English: "Please give me your twenty-four-hour urine for science. Jean-Louis." Each day a different one of us carries the plastic bottle and empties his bladder into it for twenty-four hours. Jean-Louis thaws it and removes a half-ounce sample, which he will send home as part of a stress test he is conducting for the European Space Agency.

The collection of the urine samples has already proved a hassle. Last night Victor slept with his specimen inside the jacket he wore to bed, hoping to turn an unfrozen specimen over to Jean-Louis in the morning. Unfortunately, sometime during the night the top came off the bottle and that day's experiment spilled into his pocket and all over his sleeping bag.

Jean-Louis is also taking the temperature of both dog and man and conducting weekly psychological tests for the European Space Agency. They are interested primarily in how an international team works together, because they must select ten European astronauts for a space station they hope to launch in the late nineties. The test requires us every Friday to answer fifteen questions, using a sliding scale from one to nine. The questions range from "How are you today?" and "Do you miss your family?" to "Do you feel you are going to make it?" and "Do you agree with the goals of the leadership?" So far, Geoff is refusing to take the psychological tests, claiming he can't see their value. Dahe, on the other hand, gladly answers the questions, but with the same response to each one, a middle-of-the-road "Four." (In the U.S., NASA has requested

that we confer with them upon our return about the success or
failure of our "consumables"—our diet.)

AUGUST 7, DAY 12

The winds stopped at two o'clock this morning and the dogs
immediately began barking and snarling, as is their wont after
a storm has subsided. Their restlessness made sleep difficult, so
I was forced to go outside in my underwear and enforce some
law and order by swinging a ski pole in circles over my head. It
was worth the effort—the dogs quieted and the stars were
spectacular.

Of the six of us only Geoff is really familiar with these
southern skies, once having lived under them for thirty-three
consecutive months. I first met Geoff at his home in the pic-
turesque town of Keswick in England's Lake District in the
summer of 1987. Conservative, shy, fastidious, rigid, and pos-
sessed of a quick-but-dry British wit, he was working as a car-
penter, just home from his second Antarctic tour, where he
had worked as a guide and dog handler accompanying scientists surveying the peninsula. He had heard of our expedition
from a friend, though not specifically of me or Jean-Louis, and
had sent out letters trying to track down its organizers. One of
his letters found its way to Ely, and after spending some time
with him I knew I'd met the navigator and guide to lead us
across the crevasse-strewn peninsula.

Born in Sudan, Geoff was sent off by his father, a doctor, to
strict boarding schools starting at age seven. On his summers
off as a teenager he and his brother Chris traveled the world,
from England to Australia and many ports in between. His
first job was working as an Outward Bound instructor in
Africa, followed by similar stints in England and British Co-
lumbia. When he first heard of our planned traverse he was
landlocked in the mountains of Borneo, on a month-long trek
through the jungle with a pair of friends. When we met he had

readily admitted a skepticism for commercially funded expeditions; joining Trans-Antarctica, with all the media attention and sponsorship hoopla we endured, had been an eye-opener for him. On more than one occasion during the months that led up to our arrival in Antarctica, the demands of both media and sponsors irritated Geoff; thankfully, most of the time he kept any grievances to himself.

"When I first heard of the trip, I considered it strictly an adventure, something I wanted to do for myself" is how Geoff describes his initial interest. "It wasn't until much later that I fully understood that this was not an expedition for me but for everyone involved with it, everyone following it." His fascination with Antarctica goes back to 1972, when he first saw photographs taken by a veteran British Antarctic Survey guide. The following day Geoff wrote away for an application to join the renowned outfit. When it arrived he realized he had nowhere near the climbing, dog handling or survival skills required, so he spent the next six years getting them—and then filled out the same, now yellowed application he'd sent away for. "I think that impressed them," he laughs.

In his forty-two months on the Antarctic Peninsula he'd camped 400 nights away from the shelter of the British base Rothera and learned to travel here the same way the British had been doing it for the previous thirty years. Everything they did was highly organized and efficient, allowing little room for spontaneity or change. This training led to the biggest problem Geoff would have on our expedition; his rigid "there's-only-one-way-to-do-things-and-that's-my-way" inflexibility was not always a comfortable fit with the changing demands of a seven-month-long adventure. He had admitted to me that on previous adventures his inflexible ways had earned him a reputation as a "troublemaker." "I take life perhaps too seriously sometimes," he'd confessed, "but I don't think there's necessarily anything wrong with that." But we were embarking on a long trip that involved many unknowns, and I hoped his rigidness could be bent just a little, for his sake and ours. He was hardly the first Englishman to "suffer" his way across Antarctica, though. Roland Huntford, writing in *Scott and Amundsen*, claimed "polar exploration was a moral source of suffering. [And] one aspect of the English was to equate suffering with achievement." As well as I thought I knew Geoff, there was always a hint of secretiveness to him; for example, it wasn't until knowing him for three years that we learned he spoke fluent French.

AUGUST 8, DAY 13

Nine p.m., on the radio with John Stetson, in Punta Arenas:

Will: "We had a pretty rough day, broke up both the Komatek sleds."

Stetson: "How'd you do that?"

Will: "Well . . . it wasn't too hard. We were descending a steep mountainside laced with blue ice and snowdrifts and we picked up tremendous speeds, faster than I've ever traveled on a sled. Unfortunately, my sled spun sideways, hit the drifts, and split a runner. Victor was roped to the sled, and when it crashed he went sailing over the top. Luckily he didn't get crushed by the sled as it rolled. A similar accident broke a runner on Keizo's sled, almost simultaneously."

Stetson: "That's bad news. What's the plan?"

Will: "Right now by lashing the broken runner on Keizo's sled it is usable. But the broken runner on my sled is beyond repair, so tomorrow I'm going to cut it in half and fashion two six-foot-long 'peewee' sleds. The worst thing is the whole debacle could have been avoided if we'd just looped ropes and carabiners around the runners as we descended, as brakes, like affixing chains to your car tires on a mountain road. But we never thought it would be this slick."

Stetson: "Should I plan on sending the spare Komatek in whenever the film crew is able to visit you?"

Will: "That's a go, John, we'll definitely need it later on.

The area we're in now is a minefield of crevasses; very, very dangerous. In fact there's a fifty-foot-deep crevasse right in front of Jean-Louis's tent. I'm not sure how these peewee sleds will do in this area. Hopefully by the end of the day tomorrow we'll be off this incline and back onto the flats. Over and out."

It was a physically rigorous day, and everyone needed a good night's rest. Tomorrow I'm afraid will be spent solely on repairs. But for the second night in a row I was up at two o'clock, disciplining Keizo's dogs, always a painful task but especially when it's another man's team. It is hard if you've never traveled by dogsled to understand just how torturous being woken from a dead sleep by a barking dog can be. But imagine that you've fallen asleep when vicious barking between two or more beasts breaks out. You try to ignore it, try to relax, fall back asleep, and then they're back, growling and snarling. It's like somebody dropping a stack of encyclopedias next to your head, over and over, and some nights it goes on for hours.

After being so awoken fifteen times in the early morning, you begin to take it personally and start trying to weed out the culprit, by the sound of the growl. This night, unfortunately, I wasn't able to discern which hound was my adversary, so I crawled out of my tent in my long underwear and shouted directly into each dog's face. The light in Geoff's tent was on too, so I knew I wasn't the only one being driven mad by this barking. I wasn't sure how Keizo was managing to sleep through this, but I'll have a talk with him in the morning about his sound sleep. We're rolling out of the bag at five forty-five these mornings, so it's important to get a good night's rest. Of course, once the dogs quieted down I still couldn't fall back asleep.

AUGUST 9, DAY 14

We spent today on repairs, thankfully under clear skies and mild temperatures of –10°. It was good for us to work together as a group on a single project; that's a rarity, since usually we are each responsible for different tasks.

My biggest regret about breaking up the sleds is that both accidents could have been prevented. Keizo had put brakes on his sled earlier in the day but took them off because they were slowing him down. The real shame was that each of the sleds was the result of hundreds of hours of craftsmanship. Because of the jury-rigged sleds we would also have to travel lighter and cut back on the extra food and gas we were carrying. Victor and I lost any sense of order we had in our packing system when our sled crashed. It was like taking your home and dumping the contents into the street; now we were forced to find a new place, and order, for everything.

Repairs were completed by late afternoon and I huddled alone inside my tent, sipping tea and reading up on the history of this place we would soon know intimately.

Ever since the first bases were built in Antarctica in the late 1950s science has been the prime work here, yet surprisingly little is known about Antarctica's geographical history, due chiefly to the inhospitable conditions that rule much of the year. The most widely believed theory is that Antarctica was joined some 200 million years ago to the supercontinent Gondwanaland, which then included South America, Africa, India and Australia. Antarctica was then a fertile land, a warm and gentle continent covered with swamps, pine forests and tropical jungles of massive ferns. Fig trees and sequoia grew during the time of the dinosaur. Penguins stood nearly as tall as humans. But since Antarctica holds no fossils of mammals, it must have pulled away from Africa and South America about 50 million years ago and settled over the South Pole, far from the sun's direct rays.

No one knows for sure what changed the climate, but the

changes were cataclysmic. Until this century the far south has been inhabited only by some truly indomitable life-forms. Varieties of mosses and lichens and two rare flowering plants make up the totality of its flora. The only land animals to survive the cruel conditions are mites, springtails, lice and midges. But the ice cap contains a wealth of scientific clues. From the Antarctic ice sheet scientists and explorers in the past have recovered more than six thousand meteorite fragments, many of which are unique types, and they reveal much about Antarctica's geological and environmental history.

Although just a small percentage of Antarctica has been explored for minerals, finds have been noteworthy. The Transantarctic Mountains contain perhaps the world's largest formation of low-grade coal. Concentrations of copper, molybdenum and other minerals—including gold, silver, manganese, cobalt and platinum—are thought to riddle the rock beneath the peninsula. The Dufek Massif area, once linked to southern Africa, is thought to contain deposits of chromium and platinum. Offshore, the Ross, Bellingshausen and Weddell seas may overlie substantial oil and gas deposits. It is these riches that many First and Third World countries would today love to exploit.

The continent is divided into regions known as East and West Antarctica (though every direction leading from the South Pole is actually north). West Antarctica, where we began, is anchored by the spectacular Ellsworth Mountains. Vinson Massif, the highest peak in the Ellsworths, rises 16,066 feet. The peaks of other mountains poke through across this region, rising to various heights, and their exposures are known as "nunataks."

The slow accumulation of snow over millions of years created an ice cap more than one mile thick, covering all but 2 percent of the continent. During the winter months, the sea ice extends beyond the Antarctic landmass to cover an additional 11-million-square-mile area, reaching thicknesses of between three and six feet. The ice flows continuously from the high elevations to the sea, then splits off to form icebergs as big as Rhode Island. Today 90 percent of the world's ice and 70 percent of the world's fresh water is contained in the 15-million-year-old ice cap.

Paradoxically, Antarctica's glaciers account for both the desolation of the interior and the profusion of marine life in the surrounding seas. Essentially a mass of densely packed snow, glaciers take hundreds of years to form. The snowflakes fall on the surface of the ice sheet in the form of hexagonal crystals, but within days their delicate extremities disappear. Gradually the snow crystals become rounded, forming into a layer of grains, trapping air pockets between them. As more snow falls, weighing down heavily on this layer, the air spaces become smaller and smaller until the grains cannot be packed down any more. Under continuing pressure, due to the weight of the snow above, the grains of snow change their size and shape, allowing the air spaces to become even smaller and more isolated and making the snow less permeable to air. Gradually all the air spaces are closed off and the material becomes impermeable. At this point it becomes true glacier ice.

The continent's frozen inland reaches are arid, sterile plains, receiving just two inches of precipitation a year. Only lichens, mosses and a few species of insects survive there. But the coasts are another matter: by cooling the waters of the southern Pacific, Atlantic and Indian oceans, which meet in a ring called the Antarctic Convergence, the ice fosters unusually fertile seas. The incessant, turbulent mixing of warm waters from more northerly latitudes with icy currents from the Pole thrust plankton, algae and microorganisms up toward the surface. And pack ice extending hundreds of miles beyond the shore suspends algae through the winter, then releases them, in astonishing numbers, upon melting. Together, these rich sources of nutrients feed billions of Antarctic krill, which in turn nourish perhaps 65 million penguins and 35 million seals, as well as 300 species of sponges, 126 kinds of fish, and whales of every description. Antarctic seas may be nearly frozen, but they teem with life.

AUGUST 10, DAY 15

This morning when we exited our tents we were anxious to get back on the trail, but visibility is marginal. While we are all in a hurry to get down off this hill and onto some flat ice, an image sticks in our minds that encourages us to proceed with caution. Two days ago, when I went to check on Keizo's broken sled I passed over a collapsed snow bridge and a gaping, hundred-foot chasm below. That maw, more than anything we've yet seen, reminded me of the realities facing us for the next thousand miles. So we sat still for a while this morning, hoping the winds would die down. This is a time when the maturity and experience of the team comes into play; none of us is brash—or foolish—enough to challenge Antarctica's dangers thoughtlessly. It's better to sacrifice time than a life.

While we waited we tried to find small tasks to keep us busy, like sewing and repairing gear. I changed my underwear and took a sponge bath. By ten o'clock the skies began to clear, at eleven o'clock we were outside packing the sleds, and at one o'clock we left, in a fog. Geoff went first, then Keizo, followed by my pygmy six-foot-long sled and then Victor, on what he has laughingly dubbed his "poor boy" sled. I had divided my dog team into two, and they pulled our jury-rigged contraptions through visibility of just three hundred feet.

As we descended, fresh snow slowed us down. Today, we had taken the precaution of lashing on brakes—a rope with rings and carabiners tied around each runner. Though the increased drag created by the brakes makes the dogs pull harder and slows us down, it increases our confidence despite the dwindling visibility. Even with the better grip on the ice the brakes provided, the dogs were so anxious to run that halfway down the slope I tied a rope to the gang line they are hitched to and jumped atop the sled like a stagecoach driver. When we threatened to go too fast, I jumped off, dragging on the rope and yelling, "Whoa, dogs. Whoa, dogs. Stop. Whoa. Sit. Sit, goddamnit. Whoa. Stop. Stop," which usually gets the required results.

Victor "found" a sizable crevasse late in the afternoon. It was too dangerous an area to walk without being roped to the sled, but Victor's dogs kept getting tangled and he would unclip himself, walk to the front of the team, and work to free the iced-up lines. On one such effort he failed to heed one of Geoff's first instructions, which is always to straddle the center rope as you move forward. Near his lead dog Victor fell in a deep crevasse, catching himself only by his outstretched elbows. A solitary orange line attached to the sled lay within reach of his searching hand, and he was able to pull himself out as quickly as he'd plunged in, as if his toes had touched ice-cold water. I caught up with him as he crawled out of the hole, and peered down into the dark abyss. Though we were nonchalant about his fall, he was literally inches from a tumble that would most likely have crushed his legs and hips.

An hour later we were on the flats of the Larsen Ice Shelf. We made camp in temperatures of −2° and the moon appeared, promising better weather for tomorrow.

AUGUST 11, DAY 16

This morning as we hitched the dogs Jean-Louis and I stopped and scanned the crystal-clear horizon. The moon we'd watched rise last night lingered in the southern sky. "Sometimes I feel like we are on the moon, and that is the Earth," he said, pointing to the glowing orb.

The sunrise that followed bathed the ice in lime green, a hue neither of us had ever seen in the sky before. A sun pillar —a cylindrical shaft of sunlight that appeared to connect the sun directly to the ice, a phenomenon we would see across the continent—grew as the sun rose. We stood, awestruck. I had never seen such radiance. In front of us our tents and Geoff, rousting his dogs, stood out in stark silhouette against the pastel sky. This is one of the reasons we'd come to Antarctica, to witness for ourselves its grandeur, its majesty. "This is purity, a first-class vacation," smiled Jean-Louis. Keizo joined in our reverie. "Beautiful mountains, beautiful moon, beautiful sunrise," he whispered. We found ourselves unable to move, halted by the sheer awesomeness of this place. It was as if we had front-row seats in a natural temple. We were safe, on schedule, well fed and warmed by moderate temperatures. The vista before us added to our serenity, and we drank it in, knowing that in the weeks to come, as the sun climbed higher each day, its brightness would wash out much of this aural beauty.

As we watched the sun rise, the dogs began to crawl from beneath their blankets of snow. Generally they wait until we are out of the tent before moving, and Sam is always the first dog up. "They smell like a good sleep," said Keizo, recognizing the aroma of their damp fur. Shaking their chains and yawning, each began the morning with a lengthy pee. When Geoff approached, Jean-Louis inquired when he expected we would find our second cache. "Oh, it is just around the corner, I assume," Geoff smiled. Our hope was to find it by midday, near Churchill Peninsula, and then keep on traveling.

Once on the trail it took us three hours to travel up what at first glimpse seemed like just a slight incline interspersed with blue ice and deep drifts. We pushed uphill all morning, the otherworldly lime green light dancing on the snow-covered mountainside. The moon dominated the horizon until long past noon.

About one o'clock we found the Churchill cache and posed for a group snapshot before opening it. Geoff used his ice ax to pry the lid off the four-by-four-foot box, and it was as if we were eight years old again, waiting for a giant birthday present to be revealed. Once the box was cracked we hauled out the cardboard boxes from inside, searching first for the one containing the "treats": soon a bottle of brandy was being passed around, as we unpacked tins of dried fruit, popcorn and dried chicken.

It took us over an hour to pack up our sleds; my stubby six-footer could barely handle its additional weight of boxes and duffels. Victor's "poor boy" also gained five hundred pounds of human and dog food, and the heavy, awkward loads promised an afternoon of thrills and reckless driving as we descended from the ridge where the cache was located.

At two-thirty Geoff led us off, over a slope of blue ice into a thicket of fog. I stood at the back of the pack and watched the others drop down the hill, and it was a fantastic moment: dogs and men racing down the slopes, clear strata above, the air filled with shouts of "Whoaaa . . . Whoaaa." Victor had a wild, out-of-control ride on his stubby sled and ended up tumbling to the ground, then chasing his team to the bottom on foot.

The afterglow of the sun allowed us to travel beyond our usual stopping time, and shortly after five o'clock we entered the thickest portion of the clouds that had hugged the coastline all day. Immediately we were plunged into darkness, as if someone had arbitrarily turned off the lights. Within five minutes visibility dropped to zero.

In such conditions watching out for crevasses became frighteningly impossible. But we were innately developing a sixth sense for their danger. I kept a constant eye on the dogs' paws; when they punched through the snow it was a sure indicator of fragile crust ahead. The fear wasn't only of falling in a crevasse, though; if you stepped into a small crack and tripped, the dogs were just wild enough they might drag you to injury. After two weeks on the ice they were responding better to our voice commands, but getting them to come to a stop immediately in these crevasse-strewn areas was a must.

AUGUST 13, DAY 18

Antarctica's identity is starting to reveal itself to us, and it feels
distinctly feminine. We are seeing everything here for the first
time: each shard of ice has an individual beauty, like cut glass,
and the air here is heavy with sensuality, whether it is dry or
moist. Often we are enveloped in a silence so complete the
quiet draws attention to itself. Each day offers a new, if dis-
creet, glimpse of Antarctica's mystery, usually just enough of a
glimpse to set a mood for the day. Today's was celebratory. At
noon we crossed the Antarctic Circle and stopped to toast with
a bottle of half-frozen, slushy brandy the continent we are still
just getting to know. We all hope this spectacle continues to
reveal itself the length of the peninsula.

This afternoon became bitterly cold, the coldest of the trip
so far. I made the mistake of not having my face mask handy, a
mistake I won't make again soon. The cold wind penetrated
the zippers at my throat, chilling my chest and numbing my
chin. In an effort to stave off the chill I alternated between
skiing until either my feet or face got cold, then running
alongside the sled to warm up. The only way to warm up more
quickly is to have to break up a dogfight, when temperatures
can go from near freezing to boiling over in a matter of seconds.

Several factors contribute to the cold here. First, the continent's location at the polar region means it receives fewer direct rays (darkness is a constant from the middle of March
through September); second, its high continental elevation;
third, due to the perpetual ice sheet covering it the majority of
the continent is highly reflective and doesn't absorb warmth.
The coldest temperatures on Earth were recorded near Vostok
on July 21, 1983: −128.6°; winter temperatures at the South
Pole average −70°.

But wind rather than temperature is the most influential
element of the climate. Antarctica is shaped like a bottle cap,
sloping gently from the interior plateaus down to the coast. As

the elevation drops and the air warms, the gusting winds—
known as katabatics (from the Greek *katabasis*, for descent)—
grow stronger, up to two hundred miles per hour. Katabatics
can come up without notice and may last a few minutes or
several days, turning pleasant travel into a survival test. "They
can hurl heavy objects into the air, and blow men from their
feet," wrote explorer Douglas Mawson's biographer, Lennard
Bickel. "Born in high solitudes, they pick up snowflakes, ice
crystals, and frozen pellets, compacted like hail, all of which,
blown in the wind, become abrasive material that can polish
rough metal to brilliant sheen and scour the wood from between the grains when they are left exposed for a winter."

We will travel many days in whiteout conditions, created
when light reflects and refracts both from the snow surface and
from a thick cloud ceiling. Traveling in such conditions has
been compared to walking blindfolded down a street lined
with open manholes. Surface definition is lost because there
are no shadows; the horizon disappears as the white surface
blends into the white clouded sky. Along with cold, wind and
whiteouts, the daily irritants we put up with are frostbite, snow
blindness, sunburn, altitude sickness and hypothermia. While
we hardly welcome these, we expected them. If we wanted to
avoid them, we'd have gone to Cancún and sat on the beach
for half a year.

These conditions demand that we be fastidious in caring for
our clothing at night. Moisture is our mortal enemy; drying is
our savior. The colder it gets, the harder it is to rid your
clothes of dampness, from long underwear to parkas. At −30°
you begin to notice the moisture you'd ignored before, as it
dampens your insulating layers and allows the cold to seep to
the bone. Tonight we devoted ourselves for the first time to an
extensive evening of drying. We strung all of our wet clothing
in the nets and one-eighth-inch rope that crisscross the ceiling
of our tent, and pumped up both burners on the stove. Even
our sleeping bags were suspended in the air, prompting Victor,
after gazing at the chaotic scene above our heads, to speak, as

he often does, whole paragraphs with one word: "Adventure," he said.

We had a relaxing night, warmed by a fine hot meal of rice, cheese and meat. Two candles flickered and danced between us, reflecting off the bright orange biscuit box that serves as their holder. Even in this otherwise primitive setting candles lend a touch of elegance. Though I'm sure Emily Post would not approve of our table setting—spent sardine cans, bent knives, metal cups, and a plastic bottle filled with burned matches—it is comfortable.

While I cook, Victor works on various minor ailments that the cold is beginning to inflict on all of us. He spreads vitamin E oil on his feet to soften his blistered skin. "Sometimes I don't feel the big 'finger' on my feet," he says, meaning his big toe, of course. "Sometimes they lose 'sensibility,' and at night I feel they are no [sic] my fingers. Maybe they are just a little frozen." He also has deep cuts in his thumbs parallel to the nails. The skin has cracked from the dry cold, and each morning he religiously wraps them with tape.

Victor's membership on the team—he was "assigned" the "job" by his superiors at the Soviet Arctic and Antarctic Research Institute (AARI) in Leningrad—came via a circuitous route. While Jean-Louis and I knew that having a Soviet team member was crucial, we were not sure how our asking would be received in Moscow, the country's political base, or Leningrad, where its scientific community is headquartered.

Initially, Jean-Louis hoped to include another Soviet, Dmitry Shparo, who had already led an expedition to the North Pole. But Shparo was regarded as a privateer of sorts in the Soviet Union. In the past he had organized, raised money and traveled outside the realm of official Sovietdom, without the approval of many politicians, and with a blatant disdain for scientists. We valued Shparo's experience, but were concerned that in Antarctica, where every move is government-controlled, his inclusion would not be deemed "correct" by the Soviet leadership.

Jean-Louis was invited to the Soviet Union by the AARI, and flew to Moscow in May 1987, expecting to meet Shparo and others. When he arrived at the airport on a Saturday evening, Shparo was there, holding a sign with his name on it. But before Jean-Louis could grasp Shparo's hand in greeting, he was interrupted by two men he did not know, Konstantin Zeitsev, a senior official with the Arctic Antarctic Marine Department, and Victor Boyarsky, a physicist with the AARI. Within minutes the pair convinced Jean-Louis that they were there to escort him, and, though confused, Jean-Louis agreed to go with them. As they left the airport, Shparo approached and insisted he be allowed to speak with Jean-Louis in private, a request his escorts refused. (Shparo would later write an article for a Soviet newspaper, detailing how Jean-Louis had been "kidnapped" by the Soviet Antarctic Expedition. In a further irony, my North Pole partner Paul Schurke would team with Shparo in the winter of 1988–89 to travel with a dozen Americans, Soviets and Eskimos by dogsled and boat from the Soviet Union to Alaska, across the Bering Strait.)

The next morning Jean-Louis laid out our plan to a gathering of Soviets that included Zeitsev, Victor and three of their comrades, including the chief of the Soviet's Arctic Antarctic Marine Department. They quickly expressed their desire to be a player, as long as several guarantees could be made: that the project have a strong scientific component; that approval from the U.S. National Science Foundation and the Expéditions Polares Françaises be obtained; that a rescue program be planned for the entire traverse; and that a boat for security, communications and independence on the expedition be part of the planning. They encouraged Jean-Louis to travel immediately with Victor to Leningrad, to meet there with the head of the Polar Geographic Department, the chief of the Arctic and Antarctic Research Institute in Leningrad and others familiar with the Soviet programs in Antarctica. (The ensuing train ride to Leningrad turned into one of the expedition's first experiments in international cooperation. Since Victor spoke no English or French—he'd studied German in school—he and Jean-Louis communicated only by rudimentary hand signals.) At a successful meeting in Leningrad, Jean-Louis was impressed by the Soviets' enthusiasm, as well as their suggestion that the name of the expedition be Trans-Antarctica and include the word International. In return for our including Victor on the team, the Soviets promised they would carry our caches by ship to Antarctica, provide support and rescue across the eastern half of the continent, drop fuel at the South Pole (an idea we dismissed at the time) and open their bases to us.

We immediately judged Victor a sound choice. Physically robust, eternally cheerful and friendly, he'd been to Antarctica four times since 1973, working as a meteorologist and radioglaciologist. "The committee asked me to join Trans-Antarctica for several reasons," says Victor today. "First, I am married, which meant I was both stable and would be sure and return to the Soviet Union. Second, I had experience in Antarctica. Third, I was the right age and in good health."

"Nobody in the Soviet Union believed the project could be done," he told us when he first came to the Homestead in March 1988 and began his crash course in English and dogsledding. "I tried to believe it was serious, but I had been to Antarctica before and I could not believe anyone would try to cross it." He was also a little stunned to be part of an international team, since prior to joining us he had had virtually no contact with anyone but Soviets.

His favorite books as a boy were by Jack London, his hero the great Norwegian Arctic explorer Fridtjof Nansen, and he dreamed of being a seaman like his father. But he was turned down by the Soviet Navy (his eyes were bad, they said) so instead studied to be a radio operator, eventually going to work for the Arctic and Antarctic Research Institute in Leningrad. Rather than becoming a seaman, he became a "polar man," which more than satisfied his desire for adventure.

Always bursting with energy, Victor's mind seems crammed full of memory chips. Here on the ice he keeps weather data in his head for days, then records it, accurately. He composes and memorizes long poems as he skis, then recites them verbatim at week's end in long radio conversations with friends stationed at Soviet Antarctic bases. He has proved to be the ballast on the team; rock steady, always ready for the next move, never complaining. His generosity and love of life are his biggest assets. "Without humor, we will not make it across Antarctica," he is fond of reminding us.

Fortunately for us, he was able to convince the two women in his life back home that joining us was the right thing to do, for neither approved. Natasha, his wife of sixteen years, was already a long-suffering "polar wife," and she was not anxious for him to be gone again; when a Soviet man goes to Antarctica it is often for a year at a time. "I was very, very perturbed when it was reported to me that he was going," she told me when we first met. "But nobody is asking me about it. The family somehow always takes a back seat; work, work, work comes first, the family is by and by." While the expedition was a dream come true for Victor, he would miss his wife and fifteen-year-old son Stas.

Victor's mother was also "apprehensive" when he told her he was going back to Antarctica. But she remained convinced that since the Soviets were involved in planning the expedition it would assuredly "come apart." When it became apparent that the trek would in fact begin, she said good-bye to her only son with a mixture of sadness and pride.

Before we blew out the candles this night, Victor sang softly in Russian, as he would on many nights to come. Tonight I asked him to translate the beautiful song he was humming. He explained, "It is about people who are like polar adventurers, people who prefer to go far away, who don't like to sit around all the time at home. The song is about people like us, who are getting older, and we don't have the time to just watch. People who haven't time to look behind . . . just ahead."

AUGUST 16, DAY 21

We are now plowing through a foot of soft snow, which makes
for long days and minimal forward progress; today we covered
just twelve miles. In an attempt to find solid snow for water I
had to dig down three feet before reaching hard-packed surfaces. Obviously this is a pocket of calm winds and heavy snow
accumulation, indicative of what's ahead for the next hundred
miles. Geoff is already worried that our next cache—at Three
Slice, fifty miles ahead—may very well be buried under deep
snows.

Thankfully we expected such conditions and the resulting
slow travel, so there is no sense of urgency. Once we top the
Weyerhaeuser Glacier, another two hundred miles or fourteen
days away, the winds should pick up, helping to smooth the
surfaces, and our travel days will lengthen due to increased
daylight. We hope to reach our first real destination—Patriot
Hills, at the foot of the Ellsworth Mountains, where Adventure Network has a temporary encampment—by October 15.

Tonight I prepared a particularly tasty three-course meal:
bread, which I made in a small Teflon pan on the Coleman
stove, pemmican soup, a heavy-duty chili-meat-and-cheese
casserole, plus a box of Russian pilot biscuits. The last, unfortunately, taste of white gas, which spilled accidentally into the
box they are carried in. But they are too valuable a commodity
to throw out, so we put up with the hint of petroleum that
accompanies each bite.

AUGUST 19, DAY 24

I was having the strangest dream, the first to take me away
from Antarctica since we arrived, when Victor woke me with
his morning salutation of "Weel, Weel, get up." In the dream I
was in a place of intermingled snow and green leaves and soft,
summery winds. Elephants were staked out on the lawn of a

country home, and I was surrounded by a team of good, loving, well-behaved dogs. The reality I woke to hardly seemed more real; Victor was attempting to thaw a tube of toothpaste by holding the end of it in his cup of hot water, a sign that it's colder than –40°. (It is also a sign that he is using Russian toothpaste; Colgate, we've discovered, doesn't freeze until –60°.) That he is brushing his teeth every day is something new for Victor, and Dahe too. Both had very bad teeth when they first came to the Homestead—Dahe's were literally rotting in his mouth—and we were concerned that in this constant cold they might create medical problems during the traverse. So we arranged for them to visit the Duluth Dental Clinic for complete overhauls last February. Dahe had eleven teeth pulled and is breaking in his first set of dentures. Dental hygiene is obviously not high on the list of young Soviets or Chinese.

I find that personal hygiene is easier here than at home, because living in these conditions you develop a routine that rarely changes. First thing every morning I pull a frozen lump that is my washcloth out of a plastic bag, drop it into a big metal cup, and pour hot water over it. Once it is thawed and warmed, washing, even with just a few ounces of water, is one of the highlights of the day.

The morning began in a fog, which disappeared by noon. Rising against the blue green sky, we could see rolling mountains twenty miles to the west. Gargantuan winds whipped across their peaks, blowing clouds of snow up their near vertical slopes and then thousands of feet into the air above their summits. I watched this phenomenon from a distance, bathed in the clear, calm skies of early morning. What struck me was the silent power of those winds. I felt as if I were watching a TV program with the sound turned off. Having done my stint as a mountain climber, I knew what it was like up on those high ridges. The most frightening thing about this picture, though, was that we would be in those clouds soon. For the moment I felt safe, yet awed by the brutal cold winds and wet that lay ahead.

The snow deepened as we traveled, and as an aid to the dogs Dahe, Victor and Jean-Louis skied ahead to break a trail. After lunch the wind began to blow into our faces. Dahe was leading and was soon engulfed by the billowing storm. By two o'clock the winds were registering sixty-five miles per hour. Directly in front of me I could see the gusts blowing Geoff's half-ton sled off the trail. Visibility was near zero.

Geoff pulled his team to a stop, and we gathered to make a decision on whether to camp or continue. The thought of setting up our tents in these winds (windchill was –70°) was no more appealing than continuing to travel. We stood in a tight circle and pondered our options. I suggested continuing, hopeful that the winds might die down, but after ten minutes we voted to stop for the day.

Our domed tents, modified North Face Himalayan Hotels, were designed so that their six long poles remain in the sleeves and in theory they should just pop up. But sixty-five-mile-per-hour winds test even the best theories. While I prefer domes, especially in storms, they can be hellish to erect in blowing conditions. The procedure is to first stake the tent down on the windward side; in theory it should then pop up like a sail in a fresh breeze. Today Geoff came over to help Victor and me, and everything was going smoothly—we had the main body up and the fly almost snapped into place—when a gust caught us off guard, sending our happy home flying into the air toward the Weddell Sea. The three of us made a stupendous flying tackle: Geoff leaped into the air and landed on top of the tent, I shoestringed the lower poles, and Victor made an angled lunge and caught the downwind poles. Without this spontaneous group effort we would have certainly lost the tent. As we crawled inside, Victor muttered, "Welcome to Miami Beach."

Geoff had brought a different design of tent, a specially modified pyramid made in England, similar to the ones he'd used with the BAS. Pyramids had their origins in the sealing industry; when the hunters came ashore they stuck four oars in the sand and draped a canvas over them. While the pyramid is slightly easier to put up in bad conditions, it is not as secure a shelter in storms simply because the floor is not attached to the tent body. If Geoff's tent were to be blown away while he was inside, he would be left lying in the storm in his underwear, with all his possessions—parkas, sleeping bag, mukluks —scattered to the wind.

AUGUST 20, DAY 25

Our days are beginning to take on a repetition. Up by six o'clock, outside by eight o'clock, on our way by nine o'clock. We stop for a half-hour lunch at one o'clock, and quitting time, for now, is four o'clock. Two hours of staking and feeding the dogs, setting up the tent and unpacking sleds follow; we're drying and cooking by six-thirty, and in our sleeping bags by eight. That means we spend five hours every day unpacking and packing, setting up and tearing down camp, and seven hours traveling. By the end of September we should have fourteen to fifteen hours of light per day, and we'll begin to travel longer days.

We broke camp this morning in strong winds that quickly saturated our clothing with blowing spindrift. The temperature was a mild and unexpected 2°, which caused most of us to overheat, adding perspiration to the melting snow gathered around our necks and faces. By late morning the winds had died down, and it turned into the most pleasant day of the expedition. Just before lunch we topped a large knoll and could see that it was the first of an increasingly larger series of rolling troughs and crests. This, we soon came to learn, was an indication that we were nearing mountains or steep slopes.

Ahead of us, in fact, lay a long stretch of mountains. For the past week I had observed them closely as we neared. In the morning their peaks generally stood out clearly against the horizon; by eleven o'clock the winds and blowing snow picked up, and by afternoon gigantic storm clouds erased the peaks from sight. It was an ominous sign.

Just before halting for lunch we noticed Geoff stopped in the lead, his body prone to the ground in an awkward position. Dahe, one hand firmly grasping the sled, signaled with the other for us to come quickly. As I neared their sled I understood the predicament: Geoff was struggling with a tug line that dropped straight down through the ice, and a dog dangled from the end of it, swinging wildly in a deep crevasse. Keizo and I stopped our sleds and gave our dogs firm commands to sit and stay. Grabbing ropes and carabiners we cautiously ran to Geoff's side, arriving just as he began to indicate that he was losing his grip on the dog. Confused at first over what role each of us should play—Dahe, for example, was alternately helping and photographing—it became apparent that we lacked an orderly rescue system.

Actually three dogs had fallen into the crevasse. Two dangled from their harnesses, but Spinner had fallen out of his and landed on a ledge twenty-five feet down. Luckily for him he had "chosen" the perfect place to land, because on either side of the narrow sill that held him the blue void widened as it dropped into blackness. We quickly pulled the two harnessed dogs to safety, relieving Geoff's strain, but it took ten long minutes to set up a belay system for Jean-Louis, who would drop into the crevasse and put a spare harness around Spinner, who was frozen in terror.

Once we lowered Jean-Louis down inside the crevasse, he had a hard time getting the harness on the frightened dog in such narrow confines. Once he managed, the pair was pulled to safety quickly. The aftermath—untangling the snarls in the rest of Geoff's team, repacking rescue gear—took an hour. As we struggled to straighten out his team, a windstorm swept up, dropping the windchill and freezing our exposed fingers. To make the job more difficult, because we were in the midst of a heavily crevassed area, we did all of this patience-demanding work with our skis on.

Finally untangled, Geoff's team dashed over the treacherous snow bridge. All around we could see signs of deep crevasses. Antarctica had just given us a gentle slap in the face, to remind us not to get too comfortable here. We spent lunch talking about our rescue system and how it had to be refined. If it had been a man instead of Spinner, we would have to have worked more quickly. Dahe joked soberly that "when the dogs fall in the crevasse, it keeps them honest." The same could be said for man: any expedition involves confronting a series of unknowns, and this morning we'd been challenged by one of the most serious Antarctica has to offer. Our ability to adapt, and survive, these unknowns was a true test of whether or not we deserved to succeed in the crossing.

We arrived by midafternoon where the Three Slice cache was *supposed* to be. Placed last January in the middle of a three-mile-wide valley between opposing mountains, its marker, a nine-foot aluminum pole topped by a blue flag, was nowhere in sight. We suspected immediately that the cache was buried, because in this expanse, with the sun going down, the shadow of the tall pole should have been easy to spot. But after searching on skis for an hour, Jean-Louis and Geoff returned to where we waited, shaking their heads solemnly. "It could be ten yards from us or a mile away," admitted Geoff.

A missing cache at this stage put us into an interesting, adventurous dilemma. We had ten days of dog food and two weeks of human food on the sleds and we would have to push ahead to the next cache, a hundred miles away at the top of the Weyerhaeuser Glacier. (There was a slim possibility that the film crew might visit us sometime in the next week, if the skies cleared, and if they did they could bring in any necessary resupplies.) While I hesitated to say it out loud, I had almost hoped for this situation. I prefer traveling light and fast, and I think we needed to test ourselves a little, before the conditions got any worse. The most rewarding adventures are ones that force you to improvise. Our combined experience in situations like this is our latent reserve; we needed to measure our collective ability to overcome whatever obstacles Antarctica threw in our path.

We decided to camp and then conduct a full-fledged search at nine o'clock the next morning. After a relaxing dinner Victor and I engaged in what has become the expedition's first ritual. The Chinese government generously provided us with hundreds of 10cc vials of a well-known homemade curative called Royal Jelly. Victor and I had already developed a habit of toasting each other with three vials a night (usually raising them to "good weather"). Dahe insisted if we drank Royal Jelly religiously it would keep our spirits and minds strong, and our health good. We debated constantly among ourselves whether the potion, which tasted like children's cough medicine, contained alcohol (it did not) or if it was an aphrodisiac (given the circumstances here, we hoped not).

As we laughed and talked I had a longing for something I knew I wouldn't see for the next half year. At that moment—legs crossed, my body squeezed into a corner of the tent, my head hitting the wet nylon above—I wanted a chair.

AUGUST 21, DAY 26

At nine o'clock it was obvious that we weren't going anywhere today. A violent windstorm made merely walking impossible. Though visibility was zero, Geoff and Victor went out on skis to search for the cache, but returned within a half hour, empty-handed. We took compass readings, then compared our current Argos position to the sextant readings Geoff had made when the cache was placed, on hard-packed ice, last January. It was especially frustrating knowing the cache was nearby. Geoff dug out Polaroids he'd taken when he and Adventure Network placed the cache, and we tried to verify any landmarks—hills, hummocks, ripples, anything that might give us a clue to where the cache was buried. He even got out his 35mm camera and tried, by looking through the lens, to match a view to the Polaroids. But nothing worked and visibility worsened. We decided to stay put for the day and search again the following morning. But we agreed that if Three Slice didn't surface quickly, we would make a dash for the next cache.

We took advantage of the day off and had a lengthy, overdue team meeting in Jean-Louis and Keizo's tent, our first of the expedition. We went over rescue procedures and equipment repair, practiced safety knots, and discussed sledding techniques and tent arrangements. By eleven o'clock our legs were getting too cramped to continue socializing, so we headed back to our respective tents. It turned into a pleasant day, though we spent most of it inside; Victor sang from a Russian songbook; on a tablet of paper I designed doors, windows and stonework for a building I plan to construct at the Homestead when—and if—we return.

Geoff was feeling extremely guilty about the missing cache. Last night he told us he barely slept, and when he did he dreamed about the cache, dreaming that squirrels had eaten it. He remembered, too, that when he and the Adventure Network pilot had landed here the pilot was short on fuel, the weather was worsening, and he hadn't wanted to spend a lot of time carefully situating the cache. His haste was obvious now, since the cache had been left in an area of known high snow accumulation.

"My general rule was 'If we can see a mountain, we can find the cache,'" Geoff explained this morning. "In the past I've been able to pick out a silver pole from a hundred yards away on a totally flat plateau. That had been good for my confidence. But I had never laid caches before in places with these kinds of conditions."

AUGUST 22, DAY 27

It is dark this morning, darker than usual because we are already rationing our candles and the batteries that operate our headlamps. As a result, it is very hard to see the oatmeal I know is in the bowl in front of me. The winds, local katabatics blowing sixty miles per hour, are typical of what's to come for the next two months.

It took us nearly two hours to dig our tents and sleds out from underneath the drifted snow; then we searched for the cache for another hour before deciding to travel on. We have eight days' food for the dogs, twelve for the men, and the next cache is one hundred miles from here. On one hand not finding the cache is good, because we will be able to travel faster and safer with our lighter sleds. The downside is that we will be forced to travel whenever, no matter how cold or windy it is. In truth, if we weren't short on supplies we probably wouldn't travel today, since visibility is about twenty feet.

We left in a white haze, and Geoff's lead sled nearly vanished in the clouds as his well-rested dogs took off south, up the valley. Keizo followed, and my dogs howled and strained at the lines, anxious to pull. On command—"Hup, hup, hup"— my team, led by Tim and Sam, raced for where Geoff's tent had been, to inspect the site with quick passing sniffs. With my depth of field limited by the whiteout I did not see the ramp of snow left behind, and my stubby sled went careening up it, crashing onto its side and wedging itself squarely into the barren spot where Geoff's tent had stood. Victor helped me dig it out, but the crash exacted a payment, a bruise the size of a small grapefruit on my right thigh.

After righting my sled we raced into the fog, the dogs finding the trail by the scent of the team that preceded us. The wind was strong and surface conditions near perfect: hardpacked with just a trace of freshly fallen snow, which made for smooth gliding. By lunch we had made 6.5 miles, and Stubbs Pass lay directly ahead.

After lunch it took us nearly three hours to march up the incline, to 1,300 feet above sea level. The dogs kept a strong, willing pace. Cresting the top of the pass we looked down into yet another valley, which meant yet another potentially dangerous descent. But the view was spectacular; on each side of us were mountain ranges as far as we could see. Our route stretched ahead, into the unknown, and I felt a bit like what the pioneers must have felt when they first crossed the Rockies.

The dogs tugged anxiously at their harnesses as we tied every available rope around the runners as brakes, then let them have their heads. The descent was wild; without brakes it would have been suicide. We wound down the slope for an hour, four thundering specks dwarfed by majestic mountains and glaciers. The clouds above us changed from gray to yellow to orange as we dropped, and we made camp on a hill at the southern foot of the pass.

AUGUST 23, DAY 28

We began the day in the middle of a crevasse field, and the dogs' paws punched through the crust repeatedly, revealing deep, blue fissures beneath the surface. All morning I kept an eye on the sled in front of me, while focusing the majority of my attention on my team's paws. The dogs are heavier per square inch than we are on skis, which is why they are continually breaking through and we are gliding over the crusted snow. While our twelve-foot-long sleds are probably lengthy enough to avoid dropping into a crevasse, that is not the case with the stubby peewees Victor and I are steering.

Despite the tense watch, we shared an optimistic mood. We talked among ourselves as we made camp: Keizo and Geoff stringing out their dogs, Dahe drilling for snow samples, Jean-Louis spreading his radio's antenna, Victor writing down wind speed and temperature. The lengthening daylight stretched the mood well into night, and from inside our tent I could hear the others talking about the day. Songs, in French, Russian, English, Japanese and Chinese, filtered through the tent walls before lights out.

AUGUST 24, DAY 29

We exited the tents a little past seven o'clock this morning, an hour earlier than usual, in order to get a head start. Jean-Louis had heard on the radio last night that an Adventure Network plane was at the British base of Rothera four hundred miles away on Adelaide Island, with the three-man French film crew and a new sled aboard. He had arranged for us to meet them fourteen miles from where we were camped.

We traveled without incident until we reached the foot of the glacier, when once again Geoff's sled came to an abrupt halt. From one hundred feet behind I could see him prone, inspecting what we now knew by instinct to be a crevasse with a dog dangling in it. This time it was Huck, and he too had fallen out of his harness, dropping nearly seventy feet onto a narrow ledge.

I hurried to the crevasse and began to clear snow from its edge, and Huck whined as the falling snow rained upon him. We methodically set up our belay system, and the rescue came off without a hitch. Geoff and Jean-Louis handled the technical side of the belay, constantly questioning and requestioning each other's moves, a necessary safety precaution. I was roped to an anchor point and served as the communicator between the crevasse and Victor and Keizo, who manned the other end of the rope, which was attached to the second sled. This time Geoff descended by rope down to Huck, wrapped a harness around him, and we winched the pair of them up in eight-foot increments. As Huck neared the lip of the crevasse I called out his name and he shot me a quick, one-eyed glance. His body was petrified and his legs stuck straight out. Once on terra firma, the old hound shook hard and then acted as if nothing had happened. We disassembled the rescue site—coiled ropes, unburied anchors, packed up ice axes—and were quickly on the move again.

After lunch we were lulled into a sense of near somnolence by the calm, crevasseless conditions. I was daydreaming about meeting the plane in a few hours, when there was a big commotion among my dogs. Looking to the front and left of my sled I could see only four dogs where there should have been six. The black main line and orange tug line speared straight down into a big blue hole from which I could hear the frightened crying of dogs.

I was alone and moved carefully to the front of my stubby sled. Dropping to my stomach, I crawled toward the edge of the crevasse cautiously, in case there was an overhanging ledge or other hidden danger that might carry me down into its depths too. Sam and Yeager had fallen twenty-five feet down; Sam was safe on a ledge but Yeager was spread-eagled, his paws dug into either side of the crevasse, holding him upright. Both were still in their harnesses, but whimpering and quivering. I leaned way over the lip and tried to comfort the dogs. The others had by now gathered around me and grabbed my feet. I was in an awkward upside-down position, and with bare fingers I untangled lines and clips and readied the dogs to be pulled out by hand. Yeager's frightened pleas encouraged me to work with urgency. Hand over hand I pulled the two ninety-pound dogs slowly up the wall of the crevasse.

The strength did not come solely from a rush of adrenaline, it came from my heart as well. When I realized the crying and pleading from deep inside the crevasse were Yeager and Sam, two of my best dogs, I was moved, and frightened, beyond words. These were faithful friends; both had been to the North Pole, and we had spent many days together, survived many tough times. Now, in a twist of fate, I needed to pull them to safety. When I got them to solid ground there was little pause for thanks, or ceremony. I gave them each a hug, untangled their lines and clipped them back in with their running mates, and we were off. It was a good, and necessary, reminder of how too often we take the dogs for granted, seeing them as mere engines rather than the loyal friends they are. As I watched Sam and Yeager, helpless in the crevasse, I recognized their mortality and vowed to myself to be sure to give my old pals a good rub more often.

For the rest of the afternoon Jean-Louis and I roped ourselves to the front of the lead sled and led the dogs through the crevasse fields. A rope around my waist was tied to Jean-Louis, who skied carefully 120 feet ahead. A second rope stretched behind me to my sled. I skied alongside Sam and gave him stern "Sloooow" commands. If the dogs got too excited and indicated they were about to take off, I skied into the middle of them, essentially herding them to a stop. The biggest trick for me was keeping the pair of ropes out from underneath the sled's runners and the dogs' feet. This was a technique I had used many times when soloing in the Arctic. The dogs catch on quickly to the rhythm, and my veterans appreciate my becoming "part of the team."

Because of the crevasses the plane couldn't land nearby; instead the film crew and the new sled were dropped several miles from our planned meeting site. By six thirty we were in our tents, cracking open vials of Royal Jelly, toasting to a safe journey and inspecting a shipment of Chilean meat, a treat brought in by the film crew. While appreciated, and cosmetically appetizing, the meat tasted like shoe leather. So much for the treat. . . .

AUGUST 25, DAY 30

Before we left this morning there was a quiet, heated argument between Geoff and Jean-Louis. Geoff's anger was directed at the film crew, specifically at the extra gear we had to carry now that they had joined us. "Too much, too much," he said when-

ever the three-man crew was around. Their presence always
made him surly and short-tempered. He often refused to be
interviewed by them and was sluggish to participate when they
wanted any kind of group shot. He had explained his attitude
to me in the past, saying that he didn't understand why filming
our expedition was necessary and that their presence only
slowed us up. Usually Jean-Louis ignored Geoff's complaining, but this morning he got into it, verbally, with him,
questioning Geoff about the rationality of his anger. The film-
makers were friends of ours, Jean-Louis argued, not enemies,
and they were vastly experienced in these kinds of conditions.
Welcome them, he implored. Don't be so angry.

"Look," said Geoff, "more dogs have been killed in this
part of Antarctica than in any other area of the entire continent. It is strewn with crevasses. So naturally I am very, very
concerned about the safety of the team, both dogs and men."

Jean-Louis responded quietly to his fellow navigator's concerns. "Everybody's concerned, Geoff. I don't understand why
you feel you are more concerned than everybody else. Perhaps
because you know more about crevasse rescue, that's why you
are concerned. That is good. But that changes nothing. We
know it is going to be dangerous, but what would you have us
do? We could fly home now; that would solve it. Or we go
across this glacier as carefully as we can. No one sees this as a
picnic, Geoff. We all understand the dangers."

Geoff's inflexibility had surfaced. It was both learned and
innate, I think, but no matter from where it stemmed it was
often a cause for consternation. In Greenland we had moved
up our pickup date by four days early in the sixty-two-day trip,
and it took Geoff a week to readjust his inner clock. He stewed
then, just as he was stewing now.

So far in Antarctica we had all gotten along well. We had
agreed that it helped that we came from different countries: we
weren't competing for attention back home; we were in a sense
"ambassadors" from our respective nations. One of this team's
strengths was our differences, our blending of a wide variety of

experience. The blend usually was a help: Jean-Louis and I kept us moving ahead, and Geoff's cautious ways always reminded us to be careful. But as we headed into the unforgiving interior of Antarctica, communication was paramount; we couldn't allow any irritation with one another to fester. For that reason, Geoff and Jean-Louis's early-morning verbal sparring was healthy: it got any frustrations out in the open.

When we finally rolled out, the scenery again overwhelmed us. We had camped on a low crest between two valleys, and as the sun rose in the north they were both kept in the shadows while the mountain peaks that overlooked them were slowly illuminated by the bright light. Each crevasse and ice river on the jagged slopes stood out in fine definition and in stark contrast to the dark, smooth valleys of snow below. We had a reprieve from the cold—it was 7°—and as we traveled we kept pace with the rising sun, so that we saw its low-arcing rise many times, each turning the sky a variant of yellows and purples. A calmness shrouded our sleds as we "hupped" the dogs forward.

The day passed uneventfully until midafternoon, when Buffy, one of my dogs, fell into a crevasse. I was sledding along at a fast pace when the dog closest to my sled—in the "wheel" position—disappeared, and the sled rammed to a stop. I unroped myself from the sled and cautiously crept up to the hole.

I was alone, punching at the snow every foot to reveal any soft spots. Convinced that I was on firm ice I focused my attention on poor Buffy, who hung head down, swinging over the bottomless abyss like a pendulum, ten feet below the surface. He was crying but not yet in a panic. I talked to him to settle him down. "It's okay, Buff, it's okay, kiddo, I've got you."

Victor came up and lay flat on the opposite side of the crevasse, and, holding on to the edge of the fissure, grabbed the line that held Buffy. But because of the overhang, and because the tug line was caught underneath the sled's runner, we couldn't pull him out. I fumbled and stretched, trying to reach my knife so I could cut the tug line, but it was buried deep inside my insulated parka. I was dangling a dog in one hand, grappling with zippers and Velcro with the other, threatening to drop into the crevasse myself. Once I reached my knife I flipped it to Victor, who had both hands free. He slashed the line as I tugged Buffy out of the crevasse. A small cut on his lip was the only indication he'd fallen. Once again, Antarctica had been kind to us.

As I hugged Buffy, Jean-Louis came over and patted him on the head. "It's like walking on eggs here," he said. "There are so many crevasses, one every ten meters. And we are only seeing maybe ten percent of them."

AUGUST 26, DAY 31

Whiteout conditions greeted us when we emerged from our tents, compounded by six inches of fresh, fluffy snow. As we set off, Jean-Louis was barely visible ahead of me; in the strobe-light effect created by the blowing snow he looked like an animated flip-card character, coming and going from sight. The large drifts that surrounded us made it difficult to keep the sleds upright. Keeping them on the trail was made even more difficult because we had to stay tied to them, for this was still crevasse country. All day it was a struggle to keep the sleds upright and on the trail, akin to a ten-hour wrestling match.

All day long, too, the dogs were confused by the eeriness of hearing their own barks echoing off the cliffs that now rose up to the west. Delayed by seven or eight seconds, their barks would come bouncing back at them, causing them to stop in their tracks, growl, and search the horizon for other beasts.

We were headed for Mobiloil Inlet, a passageway known as the ramp to the Antarctic continent. The ramp would lead us up, to the top of the Weyerhaeuser Glacier. By midafternoon the veil of low clouds and light snow lifted to reveal that we were now surrounded on three sides by mountains and were heading into a boxed canyon. For a moment Antarctica again offered us a glimpse of her most intimate side. Snow covered the rugged peaks, turning them soft and gentle. Sunset brought candy-colored hues of yellow and violet, which played on the distant ranges that marked the boundaries of Antarctica's mainland. The weather was surprisingly warm, but as the cloud blanket vanished temperatures began to drop. In the hour it took to set up camp, the temperature fell twenty degrees; by the time the first stars made their appearance it was −30°.

Antarctica has taught us one thing our first month here: never trust it. It will reveal its most intimate side to you one day, then the next unleash a violent storm that makes you wish you were anywhere but here. There is no match on the planet for the mood swings Antarctica is famous for. A wind out of the south when it's −30° causes us to suffer and curse the place; the next night a majestic sunset lulls us into thinking it is our friend; the following morning violent winds are back, reminding us of our fragility, reminding us that Antarctica could take our lives in a second.

AUGUST 27, DAY 32

I rolled over at the usual time—five forty-five—and five minutes later Victor was up lighting the stove and crashing about as I buried my head back inside my sleeping bag. When I heard the familiar hiss of the Coleman burner going, I poked my head out to be met with a handshake from Victor. "Happy Birthday, Weel," he shouted far too loudly for this early in the day, and handed me a long, thin box. Inside was a twenty-four-hour watch and a wonderful rhyming poem, which he proceeded to read aloud. Birthdays are very important occasions for Victor (we would each celebrate one during the crossing, and five of us received a similar gift and poem from Victor),

and he had talked since the beginning of the trip about mine
and the party we would have. He is outside now as I write,
creaking and crunching away in the dark as he takes his
weather observations and shouts *"Dobroye utra"* ("Good morning") to the other tents. My real present today is the friendship
of the five men I am with and the fact that we are safe in
Mobiloil Inlet.

The day passed in a fairyland mood of delicate lighting and
soft surfaces as we traveled on. It snowed all day long, and by
day's end nearly twelve inches of new powder had piled up.
While the new snow was beautiful, the dogs paid for the visual
rhapsody with an exacting day, straining to tug our heavy sleds
through the mounting accumulation.

By camp time we had gained an elevation of 1,000 feet,
which gave us our first opportunity to look back at where we'd
come from. To the east, toward the Weddell Sea, a low bank of
clouds indicated that a storm was heading our way. We hoped
that as we climbed higher the fog that had accompanied us
these past few weeks would disappear, mostly because it was a
navigational nuisance.

Tonight we had a party in our tent, the first time in a month
the six of us had met together in one shelter for a meal. We sat
three men on a sleeping bag, and I placed an extra Science
Diet box between us to extend our table, which held bread,
pâté, cheese, chocolate, sardines and cigars. We had saved up
brandy and wine and whiskey for the occasion, which led to
much singing, in several tongues. It was a wonderful birthday,
and I taped the whole shebang for posterity. Victor was at his
most jovial, drinking copious amounts of anything, smoking a
small cigar, and singing like a canary. Even the teetotaling
Geoff had a drink and patiently sat through the cigar smoke
and the songs.

Midway through the party Jean-Louis slipped away to make
radio contact. He came back with a message from my parents,
the candles dancing in the fresh night air that trailed him into
the tent. "Your father says that forty-five years ago on this

same day," Jean-Louis said, "they had a big party in *his* tent in Guam during World War Two, with fifty gallons of alcohol. All because he had received a telegram saying he had his second son." We toasted my parents with Royal Jelly. It was a great birthday, camped on the ice of Antarctica. It felt like home.

AUGUST 29, DAY 34

We traveled the full day in a whiteout, only our teal, orange and purple windsuits breaking the milky view. My sled was in the lead all day, and I skied alongside, plowing through the foot-deep snow and encouraging the dogs to keep pulling. With visibility this poor I was more concerned than usual about losing the sled in one of the big holes we continued to pass routinely. In the most crevasse-riddled areas I dropped a loop of climbing rope tied around my waist over the upright on the handlebars, giving myself an option: if I fell into a crevasse and the sled didn't, I would dangle from the loop attached to the handlebars. If the sled went in and I didn't, I could easily separate myself by flicking the rope away. The dogs pulled hard until eleven o'clock, when they began to drag and then stop.

It is hard work driving a dog team uphill in deep snow, and few people these days can truly comprehend the rigors of sled-mushing, especially in conditions like these. There is little romantic about it. You must shout continuously at the top of your voice, barking commands like a quarterback. When the dogs are mired in deep snow, you are constantly straining at the back of the line to help them coordinate a lunge. By day's end, you are all exhausted. Hundreds of times in the past I have been in situations where the dogs and I were completely worn out, none of us knowing where the energy to pull and push again would come from. Many times in the Arctic if I had given up—on myself or the dogs—we would not have survived. The only thing that keeps you going is that you have no choice.

I have been in similar conditions, and worse, in the Arctic and seen stronger men than I give in to nature, beaten down by the cold, or deep snow. Because of my years of experience traveling in conditions like these, when I get into a dangerous situation my mind and spirit go into a kind of peaceful "overdrive." I find myself traveling more calmly and observantly than usual; I don't allow anger or frustration to absorb me. An inner strength results from this calm approach, and I try as best I can to achieve a peaceful coexistence with my surroundings. I actually *enjoy* the test of such hardship, for both its challenge and its reward.

Traveling in these conditions is 70 percent mental. I know others look at this way of life—putting up with temperatures of –50°, camping in the snow, skiing twenty-five miles a day— as eccentric, or worse. What separates me from most men is that I rarely see boundaries, or limits. If I want to do something, I do it. As a result, there is no profound answer as to why I love this kind of life, or why I want to cross Antarctica. I simply want to.

AUGUST 31, DAY 36

The weather lifted a little as we broke camp, and by the sign of the rounded, windblown snow domes to the south it is obvious we are nearing the top of the Dyer Plateau. While Antarctica is virtually a desert, some areas, including parts of the peninsula we will soon be crossing, receive more than fifty inches of precipitation a year, sometimes in dumps of two and three feet overnight.

Shortly after we set out, the skies cleared enough so we could look back down the length of the Weyerhaeuser Glacier. Behind us stretched a range of jagged peaks and steep walls topped with hanging glaciers, many of which we had passed these last few days without seeing, due to the whiteouts. We were now at an elevation of 6,000 feet. As our caravan slowly closed in on the top of the glacier the surfaces became more solid. The foot of snow we'd been slogging through dissipated and revealed a crusty surface below. By ten o'clock, the surfaces were hard enough to support the full weight of a skier. By eleven o'clock the dogs were no longer breaking through the surface. By noon our sleds, for the first time in ten days, glided across firm surfaces of ice and snow.

At our twelve-thirty break the six of us huddled together on the leeward side of my sled; the wind filled the air with a fine, powdery drift that covered everything, including our clothes, our thermos cups and the inside of our mouths as we bit into our frozen lunches. It was a miserable break. Blowing snow melted on our faces, sending a chill into the warmer, protected areas of our chests. The hot tea and soup hardly staved off the cold, little more than fuel to keep our furnaces stoked. At first it looked like a local storm, one that would pass quickly; swirling snow blew across the flat surfaces ahead, but patches of blue sky above gave us optimism.

After lunch a low fog blotted out the sled ahead and obliterated the tiny black silhouettes that were my teammates. These were very dangerous conditions. The tracks of the sled in front of you were covered immediately, which meant we had to stay almost on top of each other or risk being separated. We had a simple rule of thumb in such conditions: if you can't see the sled in front of or behind you, stop until you can. If the conditions continue, set up a tent. Stay warm. It may take days for the winds to subside, but if everyone follows the same rule, we'll all be safe. The last thing you want to do in these conditions is wander around blindly looking for a teammate or sled.

We set up camp in a horrendous blowing storm, taking comfort only in the knowledge that tomorrow we would take our first "official" day off. Victor and I had a great multicourse meal of soup, toasted bread and a heavy-duty, high-octane concoction of meat poached in butter with a pound of cheese melted on as topping. We ate slowly, and I felt like a caveman as I ripped apart dripping, greasy meat with my fingers in the dim candlelight. The meal was improved by the fact that we were starving; the cold wind had sapped calories and energy from our bodies during an exhausting day of skiing. After our feast we lay back on our sleeping bags, like satisfied lions after a kill. We chatted and hummed and mumbled songs we knew only half the lyrics to. On occasion a spontaneous lull replaced the wind whistling through the guylines, singing its own lonesome rhyme. Gusts of wind snapped the tent walls, causing our candles to flicker and frost to shower down onto us. Outside in the blackness the dogs hunkered down under the blowing snow, anxious, too, for a long night's rest.

We had camped on a flat area near the top of the glacier, pinched between two peaks. The night was filled with the sounds of Antarctica's power. We could hear avalanches cracking off pieces of the hanging glaciers above us; the giant slabs then rumbled like thunder on their way down to the valley several hundred feet below. Ghostlike winds came and went: they hovered over our camp, poked around furtively, then moved on as quickly as they'd come up, leaving behind total stillness, only to be followed by another ten minutes later.

While I listened to the mysterious night sounds, I recalled a note of encouragement I had received a few years ago. During the struggle to raise money to go to the North Pole, we had an ardent supporter in Duluth, an eighty-five-year-old woman named Julia Marshall, whose family owned a hardware store. At a time we were desperate for cash, I remember getting a check in the mail from her for $5,000. Accompanying the check was a nearly illegible note, which took me four or five readings to decipher. It said simply, WE NEED ADVENTURE NOW. Those four words have been my coda these past twenty-five years, and a spirit I wish more people lived by today, in an era noted for complacency and retreat. Somehow, instinctively, I sensed we were going to see plenty of adventure in the weeks ahead.

MILES TRAVELED: 316

MILES TO THE SOUTH POLE: 1,681

SEPTEMBER

THE KINGDOM
OF BLIZZARDS

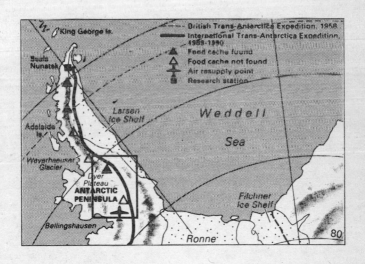

"Good morning, Victor."

"*Dobroye utra*, Weel."

The start of another day, this one to be spent tucked snugly inside, while driving snow and a fierce wind pelt the tent. A vicious winter storm is raging; even if we hadn't planned to take the day off we would have been forced to sit today. Visibility is zero and somewhere nearby in the whiteout lies our fourth cache.

We attempted to make the best of any day off, and I arranged a hair appointment a cut and wash for three-thirty. Both operations would be done with me hanging my upper torso out the door in the storm, while Victor hacked away, first with Swiss Army knife scissors, then with fingernail clippers. Doing the "mowing" outside was essential, because if a clump of hair were to get loose inside the tent we'd be finding evidence of it in our food for the next several weeks. Since I was shirtless in the −40° temperature, it was far too cold for perfectionism, and we moved quickly from the cut to the wash, with Mister Victor dumping hot water from a thermos over my head, mixing in soap, and scrubbing away. The rinse was performed by pouring a teakettle full of hot water over my head; the drying required me to hold my head over the Coleman stove for ten minutes. I patted myself down with some Russian cologne and I was a new explorer. It was a great feeling, after forty days of abstinence, and when we finished our home smelled like a French beauty parlor.

Victor postponed his appointment until his birthday, two weeks away. He has been absorbed all day by the repair of his ozone-measuring machine, which has been giving him trouble since the start of the expedition. The problem is simple; it refuses to work in cold temperatures, freezing up at 5°, a temperature we may see three times in the next six months. At four-thirty he finally took it outside to test his repair, flipped it on, and all I could hear was violent Russian cursing. Silence followed, as if he and the machine had been completely covered by a snowdrift. Then a burst of song broke the stillness, and I could make out the scuffle of dancing footsteps on the creaky, hard-packed snow. He was apparently having such success that soon he was singing individually to each of the dogs. Later, poking his head into the tent, an ear-to-ear smile across his bearded face, he said simply, "The ozone machine works."

The first month on the ice has proven a good shakedown, excellent preparation for the months ahead. In three weeks the long, dark days will be history, the crevasses will be mostly behind us, as will, hopefully, the unpredictable weather of the lower elevations. We are camped on the very edge of the plateau, six thousand feet above sea level, and between here and Vostok we will rise to over eleven thousand feet before descending to the sea next March. Everyone is eager to put in some long days, since each step takes us closer to the interior, which promises more stable weather and longer travel days. We are not off the hook by any means; storms like the one blowing today and head winds will continue for at least the next month. But increasingly we feel at home in Antarctica now, the apprehensions of the first few weeks slowly dissipating. As I lay back on my sleeping bag I am looking forward to the next half year on the ice.

SEPTEMBER 3, DAY 39

Today is our third straight stuck in our tents; we have been unable to travel due to the raging snowstorm that continues.

Yesterday we made several attempts to find the fourth cache but to no avail. We were able to make contact with the Twin Otter, still sitting at Rothera, and it went up to ascertain whether our fifth cache, at Lane Hills, could be seen from the air. If it is also buried, we are going to have to make some quick decisions, play some "cache poker." (The average cache contains 360 pounds of human food—60 pounds per man; 20 boxes of dog food—62 pounds, or 19 days' worth; white gas and kerosene.) If the Lane Hills cache is visible, one option is for pilot Henry Perks to "rob" food from it and airdrop it to us here. That cache would then be short, and we would have to count on pristine weather for the next two weeks if we were to find the following cache in time to keep the dogs, and us, fed.

Henry contacted us midafternoon to tell us he'd spotted the Lane Hills cache. Given the slow and strenuous progress we've made up the glacier, we gave him the okay to pick up seven boxes of dog food and three boxes of human food and bring them back to us. He will also take out the film crew, which has been stuck in the storm alongside us. This gives us ten days' rations, plenty to reach the remaining food at Lane Hills. We would have to ration stove fuel, though, which we're already short on.

"Il n'a jamais existé une grosse expédition comme ça." ("There has never been an expedition as big as this.") Jean-Louis muttered this often, especially when we engaged in the kind of logistical arithmetic necessary to keep us fed and moving. This long traverse of Antarctica—more than twice the distance anyone has ever traveled by dog on this continent—could never have been done eighty years ago. The distance is far too great for such a traverse to be accomplished with just a ground effort. Without radios and airplanes it would be impossible to lay out the necessary caches.

Shackleton's planned 1915 traverse along a north-to-south slice of the continent was to cover less than two thousand miles. He sent a team of men and dogs by ship to the opposite side of the continent from where the *Endurance* was to drop him, with the assignment of laying out the caches he and his men would need to complete the second half of the proposed journey. But Shackleton never reached the continent much less attempted the traverse, his ship crushed before he reached the mainland. The ten-man team that sailed on to lay caches could have had no idea what had befallen Shackleton. Three of them died during their attempt to lay out the supplies for the traverse that would never be attempted; the seven survivors were marooned for nearly two years, surviving on the supplies they'd brought for the caches and on seals they shot. Even if Shackleton had reached the mainland and set out on his traverse, he would likely have failed, and probably died, since there were no caches awaiting him.

Like Shackleton we knew we could never have attempted our traverse without laying out caches in advance. We were also well aware that our dependence on modern technologies made our attempt very much different from our predecessors', and we talked often about the incredible challenges they must have faced.

"For Scott, Amundsen and Shackleton it was impossible to be rescued. That was a big difference," said Jean-Louis this afternoon as he, Geoff and I waited to make radio contact with Punta Arenas. "But the biggest difference was that they discovered something. I would exchange our radio any day for the ability to discover. By comparison we have everything—Twin Otter, rescue possibilities, radio—and we have maps, we know exactly where we are going. The unknown made their trips very exciting and I would have preferred that. But today it is not possible.

"At the same time, carrying a radio doesn't change the temperatures or the wind speed," he added. "The conditions we are traveling in are the same, perhaps worse, than Amundsen and Scott endured. We will also, I am sure, spend long stretches, two weeks and more, without radio contact, when rescue will be impossible."

We all knew of Geoff's admiration for his countryman Scott, and wondered if he wouldn't have preferred to have been born a century earlier. "Yes, I would have joined Scott if I'd been alive," he admitted. "Three years ago I took a one-month trip into the jungle of Borneo with two friends. The route we took through dense jungle and over high mountains had never been traveled. We carried no radio, just went in one side and came out the other. If we had had an accident, we would have been finished. In some ways, I consider that trip more dangerous than this, despite its shorter length.

"But was I born a hundred years too late? No, because neither Scott nor Amundsen could ever have imagined a four-thousand-mile traverse. We are doing a much longer trip, sledding in more brutal conditions than they ever sledded. Aircraft is merely part of this expedition; without it this could not be done. Simple as that. Even Amundsen and Shackleton had resupplies, and they traveled with more men and more dogs."

At six we gathered in Geoff's tent for a logistical meeting. The biggest complaint, after three days of sitting, was that we had run out of toilet paper. The meeting was launched by Geoff, who told us he had not been sleeping at all due to the lost caches. He bore the full weight of their "disappearance," and Dahe confirmed his tentmate's anxiety. "Every morning at three o'clock, Geoff is waking up, tossing and turning." Ultimately, the fault rests with the Adventure Network pilot, whose bearing reading was apparently faulty.

"Enough said," concluded Geoff. "I apologize again and I'm confident we'll find the rest. There are five more, including the one at Patriot Hills."

The only consternation expressed as we talked on was that by our self-imposed schedule we were now a week behind. "That's okay," I reassured Jean-Louis. "We're still learning about this place. There is no hurry."

SEPTEMBER 4, DAY 40

It took us an hour and a half to dig out from under three days of snows and high winds. An inch-thick frost covered everything—skis, sled bags, boxes—and had to be brushed off. The sleds were drifted over, and all the lines and hardware frozen beneath hard-packed snow. The dogs' gang lines, tug lines, neck lines and the long stakeout that anchored them were buried. Sections of the dog lines were cased in six inches of ice, resulting from the melt that occurs when the dogs "nest" on top of them. Retrieving the dog lines intact thus required chopping through an ice plate; our shovels and shoulders got a good workout as we wrestled to free them.

The tents were nearly covered, and it took Victor thirty minutes to disassemble ours. The two-foot-long snow flaps that extend from the tent to anchor it must be dug out with caution. One careless lunge with the shovel could cause a sizable rip in the nylon, rendering the ground flaps useless.

At nine-thirty Geoff's team rolled out in the lead position, heading south. A misty snow fell and clouds hugged the surface. As expected the dogs were crazy to pull, but their wildness threatened to dump our heavy loads. The morning's battle was to try to contain them until they burned off their extra energy. For that reason alone we appreciated the deep snow, because it made the dogs work harder and slowed them down.

By late morning the surfaces leveled out and became harder packed, and the skies cleared. The parting clouds revealed a beautiful scene, resembling a white moonscape. The mountains that bordered us on both sides were drifted with deep snow. Even though the sky was clear, delicate ice crystals filled the air, and sunlight refracting off them created a sparkling display of visual phenomena: rainbows, arcs, pillars and halos. In front of our sleds the snow's surface was covered with colorful prisms, each reflecting the sunlight in a multicolored spectrum. In the distance a low fog hugged the horizon. All day—

we traveled nearly nineteen miles—we watched Antarctica's beauty unfold. Every time we topped a new crest, a different mountain view was displayed and the fog and ice crystals created a new light show. This was a region few men have seen at this time of year, and we sledded through it reverentially, quiet but for the rasping of the dogs and our own periodic shouting to encourage them. When we made camp the weather was calm, a mild −10°, and from the top of the knoll we were afforded a wondrous 360-degree view of the mountains that now surrounded us.

This was how we had pictured the peninsula. As we crawled into our tents, we were all convinced that finally the good weather had returned, for good.

SEPTEMBER 5, DAY 41

We put up camp tonight under the clearest skies we have had in two weeks. The temperature dropped fast and the wind was calm, promising a cold, still night. It was tempting to skip the chore of shoveling snow onto the tent's ground flaps, but in Antarctica you can't afford such chances. Sure enough, by nine o'clock the wind had picked up, and all night long it whistled through the guylines.

Three years ago when I first studied the map of the continent a trio of peaks named Faith, Hope and Charity—known cumulatively as the Eternity Range—caught my eye. As of yesterday, we were now paralleling the Eternities, and they would be our guideposts to the next cache. Yesterday we skied past Faith and tonight we camped parallel to Hope, its summit looming over us, above the clouds. Charity lay directly ahead, pointing to Lane Hills. As we set up camp, the trio of peaks dominated the eastern horizon and I watched them turn white to blue to violet, and then, as darkness covered us, they remained a distant shadow in the moonlight. These mountains

felt incredibly symbolic to me, not just because of their names
but because they served as our gateway to Antarctica's interior.

SEPTEMBER 6, DAY 42

This morning the wind and snow are blowing so hard we can't
see the other tents. I unzip the double-zipper system on the
inner and outer tent doors, and a cold blast of snow and fog
roars in. Looking up the line of my staked-out dogs I can see
only to the eighth of twelve. Our sled is completely covered
and it is bitterly cold, winds blowing over thirty miles per
hour. We have just spent three days stuck in our tents, and are
tired of the isolation, yet it looks as if we'll sit again today.
With only seven days of food left we can't afford to sit too
long, so after a quick meeting in Jean-Louis's tent we agree
that if the sun comes out enough at any time today to give us
our bearing, we should try to travel. The only good thing
about the conditions is that the wind is blowing across our
route, not in our faces.

As we wait, Victor again justifies his reputation as the
team's premiere oatmeal chef, serving up the most delicious
bowl of oatmeal I've ever tasted. I half jokingly am encouraging him to open an oatmeal shop when he gets home; every
time I mention it he laughs uproariously, trying to envision
"Victor's Oatmeal" in downtown Leningrad.

We designed our diet based on our training in Greenland,
consultations with nutritionists, and individual experience on
the trail. We had several goals: we needed plenty of fat and
calories to sustain arduous days of skiing and cold, as well as
lots of energy-providing carbohydrates. While we each had
preferences—I like lots of butter, Dahe loves sardines, Jean-
Louis savors lots of spices, Victor eats anything—we had arrived at a "team" diet, which we knew was going to get very
tiresome after seven months on the ice.

Each of us is rationed thirty-six ounces of food per day.

Breakfast is usually oatmeal (four ounces) and peanut butter (four ounces). Lunch includes six ounces of individually selected foods, like dried fruits, nuts, chocolate and high-energy bars. Dinner is butter (four ounces), spiced soup (six ounces), cheese (six ounces), and a choice of noodles, rice or potatoes (six ounces). For hors d'oeuvre there is four ounces of pemmican. We estimate that to maintain our body weight given the daily exercise—the equivalent of skiing a marathon each day—we'll need to eat an average of five thousand calories per day.

As for the dogs, they have their own special diet: two pounds a day of a specially formulated Science Diet Endurance, made for us by a team of nutritionists headed by Mark Morris at Hill's Pet Products in Topeka, Kansas. The high-energy, high-fat, high-nutrient "bricks" of food are the equivalent of fifty-seven hundred calories a day. (By comparison, the average fifty-pound pet eats fewer than eighteen hundred calories a day.)

We met again at noon and decided to try to travel. But just as we began to pack our sleds the swirling snow worsened and visibility dropped to zero. Jean-Louis suggested, and we all concurred, that it would be better to wait. This is a new travel pace for us; in Greenland we traveled forty-one out of forty-three days, averaging 28 miles per day. So far in Antarctica our best day has been 19.5 miles, and we've been stuck four out of the first six days of September.

So we wait, in our frosted, ice-covered tents, tiring already of the dark, dim light of the cave we call home. The interior walls are covered with beads of dampness; inches from my left shoulder the cold nylon flaps in the storm. By the middle of the afternoon the snow began to accumulate between the protective nylon fly that covers the tent and the tent itself, forming a concrete-hard igloolike shell around it. One night in Greenland under similar conditions Victor and I were buried inside our tent when it finally collapsed from the weight of snow gathered between the fly and the tent. When we woke we could barely move, and we dubbed that "The Night of Pompeii." Now we make certain no space exists between the ground and the tent fly; that's why we spend so much time each night securing the fly's ground flaps. The slightest opening in these blowing conditions can allow a potentially life-crushing wall of snow to build.

Perhaps the worst thing about being stuck inside is that every movement has to be calculated. If we so much as nudge the tent wall a shower of melting frost splashes onto us, our bags, our food, everything. You quickly develop a delicate/awkward way of moving inside the tent, because one false move—reaching for the teakettle, spooning stew, urinating—can mean a dousing. You also have to be cautious, for if you were to knock a full teapot of water onto a sleeping bag it would make for cold sleeping for days. Worst, all of these cautions must be observed in near total darkness, since only the narrow beam of your headlamp lights the space in front of you.

Darkness will be an impediment for only a few more weeks, though, as each day we gain fifteen minutes of light. The twenty-four-hour light to come will alter the mood of our interior life and help reduce the dampness inside the tents. Thankfully this is the tail end of winter we're traveling in, not the beginning, so this misery should be behind us within a month.

SEPTEMBER 7, DAY 43

The wind stopped blowing this morning at four-thirty and the penetrating silence snapped Victor and me out of our sleep. We decided unanimously yesterday that we must travel today, no matter the conditions. Dog food is dwindling and we have more than thirty-three hundred miles yet to go. We can't afford to sit around.

Due to the resulting urgency, last night six pairs of ears

were tuned in to the vagaries of the wind as we prayed it would die down. Though the snapping of nylon and the literal shaking of our tents is becoming a familiar lullaby, we each dreamed of quiet. When it came, early this morning, we awoke, thinking hurrah! the wind has stopped.

While we waited out the winds last night, I contemplated the possibility that they might not abate and we would be forced to travel in such violent conditions—winds gusting to fifty miles per hour, temperatures –40°, windchills of –70° and –80°, visibility zero. Despite our resolve to move, none of us was looking forward to such punishment. In weather like that it is impossible to shout commands to the dogs, too noisy for them to hear. Instead we rely on a lead skier to guide us and another man skiing between each sled as a visual guide to both dogs and man. In my mind I worked out a traveling order for the day: Victor would ski out front, I would be point sled, Jean-Louis skiing next, followed by Keizo's sled, Dahe skiing and Geoff's sled bringing up the rear.

We are not completely surprised by this weather, given the season (winter) and the elevation (6,500 feet). We are on top of the Dyer Plateau, literally "in the clouds" and subject to the results of clashing atmospheric conditions. The plateau is narrow at this point, about seventy miles wide. On the Pacific side strong winds and storms create low pressure systems; when they reach the top of the plateau they rapidly accelerate into katabatic winds as they descend into the deep glacial valleys that run to the Weddell Sea. Before we climbed to this height, while still skiing along the Larsen Ice Shelf, we would often see these low pressure storm clouds lining up in a row in the skies ahead, like 747s waiting to land at a big-city airport on a rainy evening, patiently waiting to unleash their might.

By eight o'clock this morning the storm returned, raging harder than ever, implying it might blow itself out. But that was merely a hope on our part, because there was absolutely no indication it would let up anytime soon. Still, we met outside in severe windchills to vote on whether we should risk traveling. As soon as we stood upright outside the tent door we realized the south wind blowing directly at us would make skiing impossible. So the decision was made to sit, again. Now we have only six days of food left for the dogs, and we are sixty miles from the Lane Hills cache. Late in the morning I met with Geoff and Jean-Louis to lay out a rationing plan, which included feeding the dogs our food if the blizzard persisted much longer. That was the most frightening aspect of these storms: they could last for weeks.

The storm worsened as we sat in Jean-Louis and Keizo's tent, and a large drift piled up in front of the door. The conversation revolved around the cache after Lane Hills, called Savan. It was supposed to have been placed twenty miles farther south at a rocky outcropping near Mt. Vang. But when it was put in last January a storm was approaching, forcing the pilot to alter the cache's location. Rather than sitting on a safe rock surface it sits in an area of heavy snowfall. Since we have already tapped into the Lane Hills cache, we can't afford to skip—or miss—Savan. My suggestion is that we change our daily schedule and in good weather start our days by six o'clock and travel for twelve hours. Geoff is concerned that such a plan will lead us deeper into the last of winter.

"Can it get much worse?" I said. "We've sat five of the past seven days."

"Maybe not worse, but it might continue," answered Geoff. "If we find the sixth cache, at Savan, we're back in the game, no problem, with ten days' food to spare. Slow, steady travel is the key here, not big mileage."

"But Savan is three weeks away," I counter, "hardly a sure thing."

Jean-Louis asked when we were expected at Patriot Hills, Adventure Network's base camp near the Ellsworth Mountains. As soon as the question was raised, Geoff proposed we start thinking now about skipping that planned stop, which included meeting a handful of reporters. His reasoning was double-edged: going to Patriot Hills would take us slightly off a straight line, but more important, Geoff would just as soon skip meeting the press. "I haven't worked out what the extra mileage is, but it is out of our way and could cost us up to a week's time," he rationalized.

As much as I knew the outside world was now planning on our arriving at Patriot Hills around October 20, I had to agree with Geoff that if we were slowed much more we would have to consider skirting Patriot Hills. "We need to pick a date," I suggested, "a last date for arriving at Patriot Hills—say October twenty-first. If we see that we won't make that, we must consider other routes."

Back in my tent I occupied myself baking corn bread and drawing. In these circumstances you become adept at killing time, whether by sewing, baking, drawing, watching your watch, or picking lint out of Velcro. Victor made a foray outside to check the ozone machine and do odd jobs but was swiftly forced back inside by the winds. He spent the rest of the afternoon attempting to dry his sleeping bag over the flame of the Coleman stove. We went to bed early, at eight o'clock, in order to save fuel. Overrested, I tossed and turned and tried to stay warm.

Victor and I had only two days of oatmeal left, so we had spent part of the day plotting how to bolster our breakfast stash. I had a plan: when we stopped at King George Island the Chinese at the Great Wall base had given us three chickens. We knew the other two teams had eaten theirs soon after we set off; we had saved ours, and figured now it was worth more than a fistful of cash. We fantasized about what we would barter for: oatmeal, dried milk, sugar, toilet paper, chocolate? As I tried to fall asleep, I was comforted knowing, for the moment, that we had chicken in the bank.

SEPTEMBER 8, DAY 44

The sun rose above Mt. Hope, framing its silhouette on our tent wall. As we crawled from our bags and started the stove, the mountain's shadow slid down the wall, revealing the brightness of a cold, clear day. When we left our tents it was –40° with an eight-mile-per-hour wind.

We were on our way by nine-fifteen. Mirages appeared to be "lifting" the mountains on the horizon off the surface, a result of differential heating of the snow and ice surface. It was our first sign that spring was coming, that the sun was making its first impact in months on Antarctica.

Ahead of me Keizo and Jean-Louis—in teal and orange, respectively—were cut in half by the mirage effect, their heads and shoulders hovering above the rest of their bodies. As we traveled through the rolling, frozen waves of ice, called sas-trugi, the mountains disappeared completely from sight as we dropped into the three-foot-deep dips, then reappeared as we crested them. It was like surfing, behind thousand-pound sleds.

SEPTEMBER 9, DAY 45

The winds returned at four o'clock this morning, and the temperature warmed from –40° to –25°. We were at least three days from the next cache, and had four days of dog food left. We could not afford to sit, so despite whiteout conditions we were off shortly after nine. As we moved south a stiff wind out of the northwest rose at our backs, and a wedge of ominous clouds gathered on the horizon ahead. We were lucky to break camp when we did in order to get a head start traveling into the teeth of yet another storm.

The dogs ran excitedly, pulling a light load and dashing into the blowing snow and mist. Visibility held all day at about fifty yards, and we moved carefully. Though the winds swept

the surface the dogs were able to pick up the trail of the sled
ahead and stay on course. We couldn't afford to be separated;
in the time it would take to regroup, the storm would be on
top of us. With a cross tailwind, Geoff shouted voice commands to Thule, enabling us to travel faster than usual, and in
a straight line. (With the wind in your face, it is impossible to
shout commands to the lead dogs, because they can't hear
you.) On his handlebars Geoff had mounted a floating navigational compass, which allowed him to monitor Thule's exact
direction. Between the two of them they have proven remarkable guides, allowing us to cover a record twenty-eight miles
today, four to five miles farther than we could have without
their leadership.

Traveling in a storm is never as bad when the wind is at
your back; it actually gives the sled and dogs a boost. The
surface conditions are generally excellent, because the loose
snow is blowing in the air rather than on the ground. But any
storm makes for an extremely isolated day. Conversation is
kept to an absolute minimum since it means turning your head
into the frosted crust of your parka and shouting at the top of
your lungs. It is generally not worth the effort unless it is
important. So your day is spent alone in your thoughts, peeking out of your frost-coated hood through the narrow slits of
your frozen face mask. Your field of view is narrow, and constant attention must be paid to the surface directly in front of
your skis, because avoiding steaming clumps of dog droppings
that bind the fish-scale surface of your skis is an absolute necessity. There is no time to stop, stoop, and scrape.

The key to traveling in these conditions is concentration;
the key to survival here is keeping your mind clear and focused
on the steps just ahead. Today's travel reminded me of an adventure I had in 1983, on a ridge above the Upper Mackenzie
River in the Northwest Territories. The temperature was −60°
and I was almost out of food. The corner of the map that
would have helped me find a trail had been torn off. I was

sledding across a slushy lake, stopping occasionally to peer through my binoculars, searching for a trail I knew was somewhere nearby, a trail that would take me to safety and food. Through the binoculars I spotted in the distance a trapper's stove on the edge of the lake; since it had no snow on it, I knew there must be a fresh trail nearby. I called the dogs to a stop. Focused, mistakenly, on the bank several hundred yards ahead of me, I left the dogs behind with the command to "Stay." But as I skied toward the stove, the slush beneath my skis began to soften, and quickly I was scampering over nearly open water. I barely retreated, and got back to my sled, where the dogs waited patiently. It had been close—another few strides and I would have dropped into the icy water. The mistake I'd made was not concentrating on what was directly in front of me; my mind and concentration were instead on the bank, and the stove. I had allowed my mind to race ahead, to the fresh trail and safety, when it needed to be kept firmly on the ice in front of me. That's what I like about being on the trail for several days or weeks; it allows your mind to clear, and such concentration then comes naturally. The experience on that slushy lake had saved me many other times, when I might have made similar life-endangering errors in judgment. I'm confident that lesson will also protect me—and my teammates —here.

SEPTEMBER 10, DAY 46

We woke this morning to the worst snowstorm I've ever seen. Winds gusted up to ninety miles per hour and the temperature was −40°, making for windchills of −150°. It was blowing so hard we had to shout to communicate *inside* the tent. Overnight a hard-packed layer of snow had built up between the fly and tent wall, which helped keep the temperatures inside warm but created a virtual "rain" inside. Everything was wet. Once again we had no option but to sit and wait, our sixth nontravel day in the past ten, still twenty-five miles from the Lane Hills cache. Jean-Louis's satellite message to Punta Arenas was simply "Windstorm. Tent okay. Be patient only."

Never before had I seen so much snow in the air during a storm. When you stepped outside the tent you were instantly coated with swirling white crystals, penetrating zippers, filling up pant cuffs and coating the inside of your mouth when you gulped for a breath. It was like being suffocated. Inside, the snow literally "sizzled" against the exterior tent walls, sounding like sleet, and it felt as if someone were outside throwing handfuls of wet snow as hard as he could against your shelter.

We have just three days of dog food left, and if this storm continues the dogs are going to suffer. We're already rationing their food, but the storms are sapping their strength. Due to the hard surfaces they are unable to bury themselves under a protective layer of snow at night, and the stinging, blowing snow is burrowing into their thick coats, chilling them further. The winds are so strong it is difficult for us even to get out to feed them, though most are savvy enough in these conditions not to eat, not even to move, but to preserve themselves, curled in a tight knot in one place.

On blizzard days we usually reassess the weather at noon. Geoff is always out of his tent first, to check the dogs, followed by Keizo, who is particularly antsy in storms. Victor assumes the role of messenger, relaying weather information from tent to tent. Jean-Louis and Dahe are usually the last to exit. No matter the conditions I force myself outside on the second day of a storm, and it is always a comfort to see your teammates. In storms like this we are never certain when we go to sleep that our own, or someone else's, tent might not blow away in the middle of the night.

Passing time in our tents is already becoming arduous. This morning I zip up my sleeping bag and dress warmly in insulated bibs and a tent sweater. I try to avoid staying in my bag during the day, since it can accumulate moisture that way and never dry completely. We try not to eat much, especially the second day we are tentbound, since we haven't done enough to work up an appetite and are running short of food. Luckily Victor and I enjoy each other's company. We talk back and forth, joke, sing, all in short spurts. We seldom have lengthy conversations, the kind you might have with someone who speaks the same language and shares the same culture. For me, talking with any of my teammates, except Geoff, requires concentration—to listen, to choose the right words and to enunciate clearly.

Before we crawl into our bags to sleep this night I engage in an established blizzard-day activity practiced religiously over my years of such travel: making popcorn. This is the first time I've done it in Antarctica, and it results in an unexpected bit of fun. Victor has never seen corn popped before. He is startled when it begins to pop, and insists on peeking under the lid of the pot to make sure everything's okay. "Boom, boom, boom!" He laughs and laughs.

"You don't have popcorn in the Soviet Union?" I ask.

"No!" he responds. He can't quit laughing. For once, Victor is speechless.

SEPTEMBER 11, DAY 47

Up early—the weather outside exactly the same as yesterday— I pick all the lint out of the Velcro on my sleeping bag. This is the very last "job" I had to do; there is nothing else to occupy time inside this tent today. So despite the seventy-five-mile-per-hour wind, Victor and I decide it is a good day to go visiting. But you have to prepare very seriously for even a short visit on such a day, for it is easy to get lost and freeze to death, twenty yards from your tent.

In 1976 Victor was traveling overland from Mirnyy to Vostok in a convoy of giant tractors (or "trax"), making a supply run, when it was halted by a storm similar to this. The "sleeping" car was separated from the "cook" car by 150 feet, and when Victor and a friend tried to move between them they found themselves lost in a blinding whiteout, just seconds after stepping outside. They wandered, ill dressed for such conditions, for an hour, searching on their hands and knees for safety.

"I was not very worried—at first," Victor remembers. "But within ten minutes I lost my hat, and my parka filled with snow. My friend couldn't see anything because his face was so badly covered with snow and ice and frostbite. We didn't have a rope, and the wind was so strong we could barely walk. Worse, no one knew we were out there, so there was no good in sitting and waiting for help to come." In their desperation they tried to dig under the snow, like the dogs, but the surface was too hard. By a miracle, Victor tripped over a black cable he had placed there the day before as part of a radiowave experiment, and they followed it to safety. Two days later, when the wind finally stopped, they could see that the cable was the only thing separating their camp and a string of deep crevasses.

Similarly, Dahe told of an incident that occurred while he was based in Antarctica in 1983, at Australia's Casey Station. A meteorologist went out to make a routine weather observation in a storm and quickly found himself lost between two buildings, no more than a hundred feet apart. He was found frozen to death the next morning, sixty feet from the building he'd left.

Those tales and others we'd heard were never far from our minds on stormy days. But Victor and I were intent on escaping our tent hell; once outside we first found our dogs' stakeout chain and then ran across several skis stuck upright in the snow ten yards apart that led us to Geoff's tent.

Inside we found that Jean-Louis and Keizo had had the same notion, so the six of us talked all morning long, primarily about what we had been thinking during the blizzard. The long waits during storms are something we don't talk about back home, but sitting on sleeping bags, wasting time, wondering how the dogs are faring, listening to the sounds of the storm beyond the tent walls are all major preoccupations of any polar traveler. While we sat, Jean-Louis typed out a message on a special alphanumeric keypad linked to the NOAA satellite. Such messages had to be short, since the system could relay a maximum of thirty-six characters. *"Tempête. Toujours blotti sous la tente."* ("Windstorm. Always huddled under the tent.") The message would be plucked from the satellite by the Argos center in Toulouse and relayed to St. Paul; we relied on this system during storms, mostly to let the outside world know we were still alive.

We each admitted to having been thinking these past few days about Robert Scott, who froze to death in his tent nearly the same distance from his cache as we are from Lane Hills. Scott and three of his men sat in a storm like this for nine days and simply ran out of food and heating fuel. They had made other mistakes that contributed to their demise, though: for one, the kerosene cached with their food had leaked and ruined valuable, strength-providing nourishment. They had also, inexplicably, lugged thirty-five pounds of rocks back from the South Pole, an effort that undoubtedly contributed to their weakness. But in the end what killed them was that the storm never let up.

"These are frightening days," admitted Geoff. "I'm never sure if my tent will be there in one or two seconds' time. Occasionally, the thought petrifies me, but it is like being a passenger in an airplane—you have no control. My worst, most nagging everyday fear is that we will lose someone in the whiteout.

"Yesterday Jean-Louis's tent was ten yards from mine, yet I could not see it. So it would be highly unlikely that I could find him if he were lost in such weather. I think about that often while the storm is blasting away. It makes me think that Antarctica doesn't want us here, and it is making every effort to remind us."

Jean-Louis agreed. "I feel like an asthmatic in these storms, unable to take a full breath. When the skies do clear, when you can see blue sky for the first time in days or weeks, it is like being able to breathe for the first time. You gasp and suck in fresh, clear air."

"The most difficult days for me," said Victor, "are when the head winds are strongest. It is hard enough to watch the compass as I ski out front, but I have to watch for crevasses as well, and I am constantly falling down because in these whiteouts there is no shadow, no contrast. You never know if the next step is a hole or a wall."

We have gained a great deal of respect already for the explorers who preceded us here, even though historians, journalists and movie producers have not always been kind to Scott and his men. But you must travel in their footsteps to understand what they endured. Being stuck in a storm, short on food and only twenty-five miles from a cache, truly sensitizes you to their experience and suffering.

Ten days ago we thought we could wait these storms out; now we realize that this bad weather might be with us for weeks, that we must keep moving. But despite conditions that might lead outsiders to think otherwise, our morale remains strong. No one is complaining; there is no talk of anything but going forward.

At nine o'clock, back in our respective tents, the wind stops and the dogs immediately go into song, a sign that the storm is at an end. All around camp we can hear the rattle of chains as the dogs emerge from their snowy retreats and begin to shake off their two-day blanket of snow. Inside our tents this is a now familiar sound, a sound of relief.

SEPTEMBER 12, DAY 48

The temperature is a balmy 10° when we meet this morning to shovel out the camp, and we strip off our jackets as we dig. Everything is buried under two feet of drifted snow, and it takes two hours to extricate ourselves.

When we finally depart, Danielle Nunatak appears to our left, rising like a rocky pyramid out of the ground-hugging fog ahead. After two days stuck in the tents we run as if it were a holiday. Our minds are relaxed, the dogs are excited. Our route south takes us along a subtle five-mile descent to the foot of Danielle, where solid surfaces and warmer temperatures will, hopefully, make for friction-free gliding. The wind is at our backs and it is a fine time for daydreams or easy conversations. Our hope is that we have lucked out; if we could maintain this pace we would reach the cache twenty-five miles away by five o'clock.

Behind us, to the north, Mt. Charity's peak stands out in sharp contrast to the blue sky, and we can see seventy miles back. But ahead, south, a white cloud hugging the surface draws closer, indicating that another storm is brewing. Beyond the fog we can see clear blue sky. The combination of warm temperatures and looming storm clouds, which usually means stormy weather, worries us and encourages us to try to pick up our already fast pace.

By lunch the winds pick up and clouds erase any hint of blue sky and warm temperatures. As Jean-Louis lights his routine after-lunch cigarette, our signal that it is time to depart, I remind Geoff to keep an eye on the back sleds, and that if for any reason we are separated to stop and wait for half an hour. If no one shows up, put up a tent. That is our standard operating procedure in whiteouts, though one we haven't yet used in Antarctica. As we depart the new storm swallows us in walls of gray clouds and snow. Visibility drops to twenty feet, and our eyes strain to keep track of the darkening specks of the sleds ahead. It is a bad sign when the faint silhouettes that are your teammates keep appearing and disappearing ahead of you, because it indicates that walls of blowing snow and intense winds separate you. The cold is intense, and conditions demand that your whole body keep on alert. I curl and uncurl my toes and fingers to keep them from freezing, and cock my head to avoid the wind. My nose drips continuously, and my goggles are fogged. No daydreaming now.

Within the first half hour past lunch, Keizo, running second, makes a wrong turn and Geoff's sled disappears from sight. I catch up with him and the four of us—Jean-Louis and Victor too—assess the situation. This is exactly what Geoff and I discussed at lunch. His sled's trail is already blown over and searching for it will be futile, so the four of us curl up into little balls and hug the leeward side of the sled, waiting for either the winds to die or for Geoff and Dahe to reappear. Fifteen minutes go by, and we agree it is too cold to sit outside, so we pitch the emergency dome tent I carry on my sled. It is two-thirty; we decide to wait until four o'clock. If by then there is still no sign of Geoff and Dahe we will make a permanent camp and wait for clearer weather.

Time passes slowly when you are cold and wet and waiting, and during the next hour and a half we keep thinking we hear voices just outside the tent. Again we find ourselves talking about Scott and his men and how at a certain moment on their desperate march back from the Pole they must have realized they weren't going to make it. Titus Oates, whose feet were badly frozen and whose injury had slowed the rest of the men down, finally left the tent one night, saying "I am going out. I will be a long while." Everyone knew he was going out to die, yet no one stopped him. Waiting in this emergency tent causes us to ponder how many times Scott and his men heard Oates's voice in the storm during their final days.

At three forty-five the wind lets up and we are preparing to go outside and make a decision on whether or not to make camp when we hear a voice. It is not a hallucination, it is Geoff.

When he and Dahe realized they were no longer being followed, they stopped too, and strung together all of the ropes they had on their sled. Geoff tied one end to the sled and the other around his waist, and began an extended circular sweep of the area hoping to run into us. It took him a full hour, but he finally found our tent.

"I thought I could hear dogs when we stopped," says Geoff, "but the sound plays tricks on you, doesn't it? We are only one hundred fifty feet away, and from the end of the rope I could see your tent clearly. I planted my ice ax at the end of the rope and then walked exactly forty-seven paces from it to your tent."

Since Geoff has staked out his dogs and set up a full camp, our hopes of continuing are dashed, even though the weather has cleared and calmed. As we put up our tents, a breathtaking display of white clouds set against the backdrop of an emerald green sky emerges from the trail of the storm. We are still fourteen miles from Lane Hills.

SEPTEMBER 13, DAY 49

Another day spent in our tents. Seventy-five-mile-per-hour winds buffeted our tents all day. Then unbelievably, at eleven o'clock at night, they *blew harder*, and temperatures dropped to −40°. I have never experienced winds like this, winds that blow at a constantly increasing rate all day long. They are horrific, and I'm surprised our tents are still standing. Now that we've witnessed these gusts, I can't imagine what the katabatics that blow up to two hundred miles per hour must be like.

It was a frightening day, not only for us but for the dogs. As we tossed in our sleeping bags, restless and bored, we could hear them whimpering. It was pathetic, yet there was nothing we could do to help. Even if it were safe to venture outside, which it was not, what could we do? The dogs are also crying because they are hungry; they have been on half rations the past few days, so their bodies are having an even harder time producing adequate heat to stave off this killer wind. We are down to our last day of dog food, and I lay awake last night praying for a break in the wind.

Few weather statistics exist for this area, because only a handful of parties have traveled here during September. Even the rugged British Antarctic Survey has now ruled out traveling on most of the peninsula during the month of September, because of the exact conditions we are now enduring. All we can hope is that this cycle of storms will break. If they do, we need to find the cache immediately. That will provide us with fifteen days of food, which used to seem like plenty, especially to cover the 212 miles to the next cache. But in this weather, fifteen days' worth seems barely enough.

My biggest mistake of the trip so far was not insisting that we travel the other day after we'd been separated. We made camp early, under clear skies—perfect traveling conditions. We could have sledded for three more hours and now been sitting within four miles of the cache.

The storms are teaching us lessons each day, though, little tricks that will help us make better mileage when we can travel. For example, after several mornings of digging for twenty minutes to unbury tug lines frozen under packed snow and ice, we now bunch them up above the surface, suspended on an ice ax or tripod. We have also learned to pitch our tents beyond any shadow the sled or dogs might cast. If the tent is isolated from those shadows it doesn't get heaped with the same large drifts as it does when either is parked nearby and serves as a ramp for the blowing snow. It is these small lessons, and our ability to constantly improvise and adapt, that will keep us going. It is also a reminder that small errors can spell disaster.

SEPTEMBER 14, DAY 50

Visibility was just 450 feet when we took off this morning, but we had to travel. We were down to literally ounces of dog food. The winds were across our back at forty miles per hour, and another storm was closing in. We weren't sure when we took off if we'd find the cache in a matter of hours, or days, but we felt better being on the move.

We are actually very efficient at traveling in this kind of visibility. We had many days like this in Greenland, and it was a perfect training ground. Now, with more than fifty days' experience in Antarctica, we've become a well-oiled sledding machine. Few dog teams have traveled in these conditions here; in fact, these are exactly the storms that turned Amundsen and his eight-man, eighty-six-dog team back from their first dash for the South Pole in September 1911. On that first try they made it only four days out, before retreating to Framheim, their base camp. They then waited until mid-October, the beginning of Antarctica's summer, and when they set out again temperatures were in the twenties.

The part of the Dyer Plateau on which we were sledding was thin and perfectly flat; it was as if we were skiing on a sixty-mile-wide boardwalk. The upper peaks of the Lane Hills stuck out of the plateau ahead of us like a rooster's comb. Its several hummocks were bumps on the horizon, interrupted by a single peak rising from the center. This was the reference point we were looking for, and we made a steep, fast ascent, five hundred feet up the side of the nunatak, to reach the cache. Geoff led the way up the hill as six pairs of eyes strained to the left and right, looking for a thin aluminum rod jutting out of the snow. As we climbed we rose above the blowing storm and gained a pristine view of the mountains that stretch for a hundred miles back to the northeast. All around us the surface was smoothly polished ice, evidence of the constant, powerful winds that whip this region every day.

The dogs ran excitedly, as if they knew we were on a cache hunt. My veterans know from experience that when their food is rationed it often means there is either a village, a resupply, or a cache nearby. They were hard to contain on this slick, crusted snow, and Victor and I tugged hard to restrain the sled, until Geoff veered sharply to the right and came to an abrupt stop. We followed within minutes to find the other two teams standing around a bamboo pole with a black flag, the signpost Henry Perks had left ten days ago when he came by plane and "robbed" from this cache. A few feet away, only two feet of Geoff's original nine-foot marker were exposed.

It was cold and windy so we spent little time celebrating. We unpacked three shovels from the sleds and within minutes Science Diet boxes were uncovered and stacked nearby. What a wonderful sight, all those red-and-white-labeled boxes—seventeen in all—piled high. The four-by-four-foot plywood box was opened next, unveiling its three boxes of ten days' worth of human food and a smaller box containing the "essentials" like toilet paper, powdered milk, hard candy and more Royal Jelly. The five gallons of kerosene planted with the cache were missing, so the digging continued. Once they were unburied we divvied up the take, stripped and repacked the sleds, and were off into blowing snow, heading south. The visibility held until six o'clock, when we came to a halt after twenty-three miles.

We slept warm, relieved to have the cache search behind us. The only thing that allowed us to find the cache with ease today was the momentary lull in the wind; it was almost as if Antarctica wanted this game to continue a little longer so she "allowed" us to find Lane Hills, which enabled us to keep moving.

So far we are averaging one travel day for every four storm days—not a good average. If that pace continues we will soon be far behind schedule. Jean-Louis reports that we should not expect any break in the weather for another two hundred miles. As a result of that forecast we have initiated a new policy: if we have a storm day and it clears at two or three the following morning, we will be up and moving. We must travel every hour possible.

SEPTEMBER 15, DAY 51

Victor hums loudly as he dresses after a snow shower in a temperature of −30°, readying to go back outside for the first of his daily weather observations. As he measures the wind speed and temperature he will also give a wake-up call to Jean-Louis and Keizo's tent and a friendly *dobroye utra* to Geoff and Dahe, who are always the first to rise.

Victor and I are together for only two more weeks, and already I sense I will miss his roll-with-the-punches stability. The only advice I will pass along to his next tentmate, Jean-Louis, is to watch him carefully whenever he starts cursing and hollering in Russian; it implies he is on the verge of breaking something out of frustration, be it a frozen tent pole, a stove that's not lighting properly, or a compass. Because of the language and cultural differences I'm never sure if he's really angry or just irritated. (I have the same problem with Jean-Louis, who can seem gruff at times, but I attribute those moods to my not understanding what he is saying as he walks away muttering.)

The way Victor forces and breaks things has become a running joke among us all, and I find myself keeping a constant eye on him, especially inside the tent. When I hear angry Russian cursing I look up to see what he is about to break and interrupt him with a simple "Victor?" He looks up, smirking like a schoolboy, and says, "Yes, I know. Be careful." Jean-Louis has nicknamed our Soviet friend *"la Touche Magique"*— the Magic Touch. Even Victor now jokes that he is "the Broken Man" and that the only items he's sure not to break "are big, heavy steel things."

We got a break in the weather today, and it was the first morning in two weeks we weren't buried under a foot of new snow. We traveled through a morning fog that gave way to clear skies and a south wind, and covered twenty-four miles, a good workout for dogs and men. For the first time in ten days we could see the mountains to the south, and a spectacular vista lay ahead. The peninsula has to be one of the most beautiful places on Earth—under calm, clear skies.

SEPTEMBER 16, DAY 52

The wind increased from the north as we broke camp, and by ten-thirty we could see only the now customary thirty feet ahead of us. Victor led on skis, I was the lead sled, followed by Jean-Louis and Keizo, then Geoff and Dahe. The wind at our backs nearly pushed us across the smooth surfaces; traveling alone in the Arctic with backwinds like this I have made forty to fifty miles in a day. Here, constantly being separated in the whiteout and forced to stop and search for each other, we'll be lucky to make twenty miles.

By eleven o'clock the winds were blowing more than fifty miles per hour, and Victor and my sled picked up tremendous speed. In these conditions it is difficult to tell when you are dropping in elevation, and without warning Victor vanished completely from sight. I struggled to control my dogs, who were running at breakneck speed, without a reference point. My eyes searched the horizon for my Russian friend, and suddenly he appeared at the bottom of a steep drop-off. He had skied over a 150-foot incline, and we were all coming fast right behind him. My sled slid sideways, nearly breaking the runners as I too dropped downhill; my dogs ran faster than their paws could carry them and we ended in a tangled jumble at Victor's feet.

My jaw dropped when I looked around: a third of a mile to our right was a series of cliffs that dropped down to a rocky pile. On our left was a string of deep crevasses. If we had come down on either side of this narrow river of ice—easy enough to do on a day when you could barely see to the front of your sled—the dogs would have been killed, the sled smashed to bits, and I would have been badly injured at best.

When the other two sleds appeared at the crown of the hill,

Keizo and Geoff dragging their full weight to slow the dogs, they stopped and put on brakes and carefully skidded down to join us. It had been a close call for Victor and me, but we didn't waste any time celebrating our good fortune; we simply sledded on.

All day as the visibility continued to dwindle, I wondered how we would find the pass that would lead us through the rocky range directly ahead of us. That concern was lessened when we discovered that by standing atop the sled and balancing carefully on tiptoes, you could gain a clear view of what was to come. The wind was directly behind us, racing up to sixty miles per hour, and we traveled with lightning speed over the hard-packed surface. Every mile or so we would stop and Jean-Louis would clamber atop Keizo's sled, peer into the distance, and we would adjust our route by his hand signals. Though the sun was out above the fog, sending filtered beams of light through the clouds like randomly placed klieg lights, we could see virtually nothing at ground level; as a precaution, we put brakes on each sled.

Throughout the afternoon we tried vainly to cajole Victor into slowing down, but he insisted the wind at his back made "going slow" impossible. The truth is that speed on skis thrills Victor, though it wreaked havoc on the pace of the sleds as the dogs tried to keep up. Many times during the afternoon we were separated; Victor would get far ahead and have to wait for us to catch up; then we would come racing out of the fog and nearly run him over, which inevitably tangled the dogs and caused more delay. Late in the afternoon Geoff's dog Sawyer collapsed from exhaustion and had to be tied on top of the sled. One of Sawyer's problems is his long hair; he looks like a musk ox and ice collects on his inner layer of fur, costing him insulation, thus warmth and strength. Eskimos always kill long-haired puppies for this reason, but we had taken Sawyer to Greenland and he had worked out well. Here it is another story. The poor dog is carrying more than forty pounds of ice and snow in his fur, and Geoff is having to take him into his tent each night to thaw him out. Sawyer will have to be sent out the next time we are visited by a plane.

Jean-Louis and I agreed at midafternoon that we had to make camp as soon as we reached reasonably flat ground, in part to end our daylong frustration with Victor. We continued cautiously until six o'clock, when eighty-two-mile-per-hour winds forced us to stop. Jean-Louis's satellite message tonight was "Tempest. Real adventure."

Tonight we celebrated the Magic Touch's thirty-ninth birthday—maybe that's why he was skiing so excitedly—and any frustrations we had with him during the day disappeared. I made a special meal of grilled cheese sandwiches and a cake made from bread mix, pecans, cinnamon, dehydrated blueberries and ten bottles of Royal Jelly. The party was warm but subdued; we are getting up at five-thirty tomorrow morning and face a long travel day in heavy wind, which put a damper on any extended celebrating. We managed to fortify ourselves, however, with a bottle of Russian cognac and two bottles of vodka. It was a nice get-together, affectionate and loving, and fit Victor's temperament to perfection.

SEPTEMBER 17, DAY 53

I woke with a sobering thought. Today, if we are lucky, we will pass the five-hundred-mile mark. We've been on the ice more than fifty days already, and we have thirty-three hundred miles to go. My mood isn't brightened when I pull out my *National Geographic* map of Antarctica and realize that in nearly two months we've traveled about four inches. We still have two feet to go.

We made twenty-two miles today, in zero visibility, with a thirty-seven-mile-per-hour wind in our faces. We lost sight of each other repeatedly and several times were forced to resort to dropping to all fours and searching the snow for the faint trail of the sled that went ahead. We have been locked in these same brutal conditions for fifteen days now, traveling through the equivalent of a cold desert sandstorm. "Sometimes I feel just like a dog," said Jean-Louis as we wrestled to put up his tent in seventy-four-mile-per-hour winds.

SEPTEMBER 20, DAY 56

We struggled across sixteen miles today, in the worst conditions we've seen yet. A monstrous storm blew up while we were stopped for lunch, carrying a tremendous amount of snow and drift. It was a strange sight, because despite all the blowing at ground level, the skies above were clear and bright.

Visibility dropped dangerously low, to only six feet, so Geoff and Keizo tried roping all three sleds together as a way to stay in each other's sight, but to no avail. Within five minutes a massive tangle convinced them of the futility of using ropes to counteract nature's power. If you faced the wind for just an instant, your eyelids froze shut, your nose and mouth filled with snow, and it felt as if you were suffocating and freezing simultaneously. Extra caution had to be taken, for when the frigid blast smacked you in the face, you reeled backward, temporarily losing your bearings. In these conditions, if you were to wander ten feet in the wrong direction you could easily get lost and perish. This was truly a "killer" storm.

Sixty-mile-per-hour winds forced us to stop and set up camp at three o'clock. As we tried to weight down the tents, the wind blew the snow from our shovels before it could be dumped. By eight o'clock gusts topped one hundred miles per hour and the tents were vibrating so violently we had to shout to communicate. Due to the strong winds outside, the vapor from our breath shimmied inside, an unsettling phenomenon. The snow washed up over the tent, covering us in a drift. And still the wind's speed increased. In his tent Jean-Louis was unable to make radio contact and instead tapped out a message to the satellite: "Extreme weather."

As the frost dripped on my head and shoulders, I thought back to the fifty-sixth day of our North Pole expedition, because that was the day we finished. Here, we were barely an eighth of the way home.

SEPTEMBER 21, DAY 57

Tentbound again, in what we're calling the Scott Uplands Blizzard. Amazingly, Jean-Louis got through to Punta Arenas tonight, and we understand that Hurricane Hugo is whipping the east coast of the U.S. with winds of more than a hundred miles per hour, forcing the evacuation of a million people. It is the same kind of wind that has us pinned in our thin nylon tents. But for us evacuation or heading for higher ground is not an option. Late in the afternoon I ventured outside for a much-needed snow shower, despite the −100° windchills. The rest of the day was spent checking the weather, killing time, sleeping, lying on my sleeping bag in silence, not talking, just waiting. It is like a prison sentence.

Victor's favorite pastime on these "no progress" days is making up rhymes. Each Friday he receives at least two dozen radio messages from friends at the Soviet base of Bellingshausen and the following week he responds to them, in verse. He works on his poetic replies during the day, whether he is skiing on point or lying atop his sleeping bag, and files them in his memory. Every Friday at six-twenty I can hear him in Jean-Louis's tent, shouting out a week's worth of poetry and ozone readings, yelling into the radio receiver as if he were shouting at someone he could see a mile away. I usually try to exit the tent before he begins—he is so loud it makes my ears ring. Whoever is on the other end yells back at a similar level, as if they are engaged in some kind of shouting match.

SEPTEMBER 22, DAY 58

The storm blew all night, and we meet outside at ten o'clock
to consider the day's chances for travel. Victor's morning
weather report has the temperature at a very cold −42°. I did
not see the rest of the team yesterday, so as we stand in a tight
circle and small-talk I ask what they did. Jean-Louis read a
weeks-old newspaper from Paris and "thought about the future." Dahe sewed his mukluks for eight hours. (At one point
he went out for "protocol"—to the bathroom—and got turned
around and almost lost.) Keizo watched Dahe sew. Geoff,
alone in his tent for most of the day, baked and worked on his
embroidery. After ten minutes' time, the consensus is that
even though the visibility is worsening we must try to move
south.

We start to dig out at noon and make ten miles by six
o'clock. We are very concerned about the dogs. While their
spirit is good many of them are severely crusted with a layer of
frozen ice, the worst I've ever seen. We spend a half hour at
day's end chipping some of it away with ice axes. Three of my
dogs—Zap Junior, Panda and Tommy—have cuts on their
chests where the frozen harnesses have rubbed them raw.
With this constant wind there's not much we can do for them;
anything we try will be merely a Band-Aid, hardly a cure. All
we can do is continue to move south as fast as we can, to get
beyond this swath of storms. It was good for the dogs to get
some running in today, to keep their blood circulating. We fed
them each a pound of our own meat tonight, and hopefully
they will get a good night's rest. The fact that our sled loads
are getting lighter should help them preserve some strength.

We all know that the key to our making it across Antarctica
is our ability to keep the dogs strong. Right now they are at
their lowest ebb; another month of these conditions will wear
them down past the point of recovery. They need to eat more
and to have warmer temperatures to thaw their frozen fur. If
we make the Savan cache in three days as we hope, we will be

able to feed them as much as they want. If we can't find the cache, we will have to consider calling in a resupply by air rather than push them another 150 miles to the next cache. I'm afraid such a push would finish off the dogs. I'm also afraid that even if we wanted to call in a plane, it couldn't find us.

SEPTEMBER 23, DAY 59

The sun rose this morning above a cloud bank, illuminating the interior of the tent like a spotlight. We haven't had a clear morning like this since after the Eternity Range blizzard, when the sun rose similarly above Mt. Hope.

The light pervading the tent reminds me of many comfortable camps I have had in the Arctic. These quarters heat up easily if there is no wind; how easy this crossing would be if we had to contend only with the cold. We desperately need a clear, calm travel day. We are behind schedule, the dogs are weakened, and more storms certainly lie ahead. We can't afford to sit on a calm day, though it would help if we could spend it drying out the dogs' harnesses. The best thing we can do for the dogs right now is to keep moving, and get off this peninsula.

SEPTEMBER 25, DAY 61

We sat again yesterday, in the Scott Uplands Blizzard II. Winds gusted to one hundred miles per hour, and inside our tent only two sounds were heard all day: the lonely humming of the guylines and the sizzling sound of snow pelting the tent wall. In the afternoon I took a snow shower and then sat nude on my sleeping bag for a few minutes; it was quite a sensation, knowing that only a fragile membrane separated me from instant death. This is the most isolated I have been in my life, far from everything. Even on long trips into the Arctic I had intermittent contact with people and received marginal news of what was going on in the outside world. When I'm in the Arctic, I always feel at home. Here home seems very, very far away.

This morning Jean-Louis poked his head inside our tent and said, "The weather is not good, the snow is very deep. We will have to travel very slowly."

"How far away is the next cache?" I asked.

"Forty-five miles. We must go soon."

When we got out of the tent, only the top of the handlebars of Keizo's sled were visible above the drifted snow. Our skis, planted in the hardpack, were buried—somewhere. All around us lay evidence of the worst storm I have ever seen, tremendous piles of snow, three to four feet deep, blown by continuous, monstrous winds. It took us two and a half hours to unbury everything, and still it stormed.

The travel surfaces had changed from near perfect two days ago to almost impassable today. And still the wind continued to whip up the soft snow that lay nearest the surface, creating hills and valleys as deep as three feet, making simply walking extremely difficult. Despite the deep snows we were insistent on making progress today, so once unburied we slogged off.

Travel was possible despite the whiteout because the tracks of the preceding sled lasted almost five minutes in the deep snow. But Keizo's dogs—he was traveling in the number three position—kept stopping, which meant he and Jean-Louis would get separated from the pack. The first time it happened Jean-Louis spent a half hour on his hands and knees, literally sniffing out the faint tracks of ski poles or the imprints of dogs' feet, before managing to catch up with the rest of us who had bunched up to wait.

The second time they got separated I stopped to wait for them and then Geoff disappeared ahead of me. Within minutes all tracks, in front of and behind me, disappeared. Stranded and alone, I set up the emergency tent thinking I would probably be forced to spend the night here, even though it was not yet noon. But just as I zipped up the tent door I heard the voices of Victor and Geoff. They had stopped their sled when they realized they were separated from the pack, then placed tent stakes and ski poles every ten feet and come back to find me. The four of us—Dahe trailed behind them—took advantage of the shelter and had a quick lunch before setting out to search for Keizo and Jean-Louis. We strung out more tent stakes and found our teammates just a hundred yards away. They too had set up a tent and were sitting on their sleeping bags having lunch when we found them.

By three o'clock we'd repacked the sleds and were off again. Visibility had improved, but Keizo's dogs were spiritless and refused to pull. Keizo shouted and pushed his dogs, desperately trying to get them to budge, but they would not move. Finally four of us ended up pushing his sled to jump-start the dogs. But they would travel a hundred feet and go on strike again. I felt for Keizo, because I had been in his place many times before.

That struggle made for a very long day, and cost us many miles; we traveled just seven. To me this looked like the beginning of the end. We have to make mileage, we have to find the next cache, we have to get out of these storms; but if we can travel only seven or eight miles a day, the expedition is over. The next cache is thirty-eight miles ahead—two or three good travel days away—and I doubt we'll be able to find it, given the deep snows all around. Keizo's sled was buried overnight, and this cache has been out here for eight months. There is also some confusion over the cache's exact location. All day my mind raced through a dozen options, including flying out the majority of Keizo's weakened dogs and continuing with two sleds and two tent units.

We are getting ourselves into a very serious situation, and I'm not sure the others realize how serious. This weather could continue for weeks, and we have only five full days of dog rations left. Even if we find the Savan cache, what good is the extra dog food going to do us if the dogs are too weak to pull the weight of the heavier sleds? As I try to fall asleep with dozens of variables, options and plans racing through my mind, another storm blows outside the tent walls.

SEPTEMBER 26, DAY 62

There is no way we can travel today due to winds and snow, and we have dubbed this Desperation Camp, for the new blizzard compounds our problems. If the visibility were good, we would have a variety of options. Instead, we are sitting again and the mood is none too cheery.

Prior to a seven-forty-five meeting in our tent, Victor and I went out to reanchor the ground flaps, piling on anything with weight, including dog food boxes and full cans of gas, and then strung out skis and poles between the tents as guideposts for the others. Visibility is back to zero; just a few feet from the tent it disappears in the whiteout. When a blast of wind hits you, you reel backward. The change in temperature overnight is shocking: it climbed forty degrees in twenty-four hours, from $-20°$ to $20°$. That is not a good sign, because it means the storm is going to get wetter.

Our green box is set with a yellow tablecloth and loaded with coffee, tea, milk, sugar, Russian bread made by Victor's mother (we'd brought along seventy pounds of her loaves), and when the others join us we sit three to a side, our knees touching. Jean-Louis was late because he was shoveling snow to reinforce his tent, which was threatening to blow away.

I start the meeting by proposing that the first thing we need to do is arrange to have at least eight of Keizo's dogs flown out, whenever a plane can find us. They can go back to Punta Arenas, rest up, and rejoin us at Patriot Hills in another four to six weeks.

"We got the feeling yesterday as if they had taken a vote

and decided unanimously not to pull," says Jean-Louis, who spent most of the day helping Keizo goad his team. Everyone agrees calling in a plane is the only thing to do.

"It's three hundred-plus miles to Siple," says Geoff, "which is the same distance we've traveled since the beginning of the Weyerhaeuser Glacier, twenty-five days ago. Some of the dogs have deteriorated so much in that period that in the next three hundred miles they are really going to delay us. My vote is to get rid of them." He adds that if a plane can find us he would like to send two of his team out as well.

Jean-Louis then urges us to lighten the sleds as much as possible, by caching anything and everything extra we can. "Minimum, minimum, minimum. We may even need to go to two tents, with three men each. We must keep the spirit of the expedition—our spirit—alive, no matter the sacrifice."

"That's well and good," I point out, "but it's the spirit of the dogs that most concerns me at the moment."

"So let's put together two strong teams of dogs and the men can ski and walk," counters Jean-Louis. "We must think alpine style, very light. Then we just go and go and go and go."

I am in full agreement. "Our biggest problem is weight. Anything that is not absolutely necessary must be left behind —extra climbing rope, extra clothing, clothespins, needles, anything. We can get rid of one of the emergency tents. As for clothing, keep any spare foot- and handgear—they are most important—but if you aren't using your big insulated parka, leave it behind. Change your underwear for the last time, and leave any spares."

It is soon obvious that I wasn't the only one who was up last night plotting. "The heaviest stuff has to go first," agrees Geoff. "If you're carrying four cans of fuel, that's too much. We have plenty of white gas in the caches to come, at Mt. Rex and Siple, so leave one behind."

Dahe and Victor are adamant that their science gear must

not be abandoned. Victor is especially concerned that somebody might suggest he leave behind his ozone machine.

"If Victor returns to Leningrad without that twelve-thou-
sand-ruble ozone machine," I say, "he says they will hang him
by his balls. Victor, what are your balls worth?"

"The same as the ozone machine."

"Which would you prefer to keep?" wonders Geoff.

"Both."

"My feeling," says Jean-Louis, "is that whatever decisions
we make, we must travel light all the way to the end; otherwise
we'll never reach Mirnyy. Nobody will blame us if we don't do
science, but they will blame us if we fail to make it across." No
one disagrees, at least out loud.

"The big question for the next few days is how do we feed
the dogs," I say. "Should we feed them full rations to build up
their strength, or half rations to preserve what little food we
have left? The reality is we could be stuck in this camp for five
days or longer, and run out of food."

"Could it be possible to set up a tent just for the dogs, to
help them keep the ice out of their fur?" Jean-Louis asks.

In my experience anytime you do something "artificial" for
the dogs it only makes matters worse. If we allow them to heat
up inside a tent, that might do them more harm than good
when they go out again. We had tried to cover them with
specially made Gore-Tex jackets, but in the cold and wet the
jackets collected blowing snow, and it melted, encouraging
harness rubs. We decide to leave the dogs outside, at least for
now.

One thing that goes unspoken throughout our consider-
ations is the apparent inevitability that we will have to call in
an airplane, something we said we'd do only in an emergency.
The dogs' condition—they are weak and almost out of food—
makes it a necessity. But when you start talking planes in this
faraway place you have to start juggling and rejuggling weights
in your head. The Twin Otter can carry a maximum load of

2,200 pounds, with a range of one thousand miles. If they are to fly more than a thousand miles, which they'll have to if they are to reach us here, they must carry extra fuel, thus reducing the weight we can send out. If we call for a plane now, we will ask it to bring fifteen boxes of dog food (900 pounds), 150 pounds of human food, and three of the reserve dogs that have been sitting in Punta Arenas (250 pounds), for a total of 1,300 pounds. That leaves space on the plane for the necessary fuel —two drums at 350 pounds each—but we'll be sending out eleven dogs (850 pounds) plus whatever valuable gear we decide to send back. It is this kind of arithmetic that has kept my mind and Geoff's churning day in and day out the past weeks. And every time we think we've considered every variable, something changes and we are forced to start all over. (Planes are hardly new to Antarctica. Eighty years ago the Australian Mawson brought the first aircraft to the continent —a Vickers R.E.P. monoplane— aboard his ship, the *Aurora.*)

In order to pull off these logistical miracles we are relying on the only air charter company servicing Antarctica. My relationship with Adventure Network goes back to March 1986, when I returned from the North Pole and met immediately in Washington, D.C., with Martyn Williams to explain my idea about crossing Antarctica. Since Adventure Network was the only game in town, so to speak, we had no option but to work with them.

Founded in 1985 by Liverpool-born Williams, Canadian climber Pat Morrow and Giles Kershaw, Adventure Network (or Antarctic Airways, as they first billed their small company) was established to fly climbers anxious to reach the tall peaks of the Ellsworth mountain range. The company's first season of business was extremely dangerous, and the owners quickly discovered that running a business on the planet's harshest continent would be an exasperating, if thrilling, challenge.

First, they had to cache hundreds of tons of fuel, supplies and two small planes at their interior base near the Patriot

Hills, in the foothills of the Ellsworths. That entailed dozens of four-thousand-mile round-trip flights from Punta Arenas. Time after time, Kershaw landed a wheeled, four-engine DC-4 loaded with barrels and bladders of explosive gasoline on a narrow strip of rippled blue ice. They put up a semipermanent, weatherproof tented camp, stocked with enough supplies to feed three dozen people for more than a month.

The ink had barely dried on their business cards when, according to one of their first guides, Gordon Wiltsie, disaster struck. The DC-4 limped to Chile from Canada, and when it arrived all four engines needed repair; spare parts languished in customs. Fuel-caching flights were delayed and clients who had paid up to $35,000 to be flown to Antarctica arrived in Punta Arenas, waited, and went home. The $1 million that Williams and his partners had planned to pump into their start-up was nearly exhausted by the time they finally got things straightened out and began regular flights to the seventh continent.

One of their intentions was to break the stranglehold on exploration imposed by the National Science Foundation, which is intent on keeping private expeditions out of Antarctica. Adventure Network's founders believed there was a place for monitored private exploration of the continent, and in five seasons they had proved there was a demand. Our $1.5 million contract with them included laying out our caches the year before, shuttling us to Antarctica, flying supplies and fuel to Patriot Hills, and serving as standby rescue until we reached Vostok.

Unknown to us at the time we made the deal, they were simultaneously negotiating to assist Reinhold Messner, the renowned German mountain climber, who was planning a two-man eighteen-hundred-mile ski trip across a portion of Antarctica from November to February. While our contract stated that Adventure Network could not work with other expeditions while assisting us, they had added small print that said "expeditions from the same country." While the company's business had grown in five years and had attracted the best Arctic and Antarctic pilots, when we learned about their providing aid to Messner we were immediately concerned that they were overcommitted. During their peak season, November to January, they would also be shuttling a full complement of climbing parties and tourists to the peninsula, Patriot Hills and the South Pole. But since our options were extremely limited, we had put our trust in Adventure Network's ability to juggle all of their clients successfully—and safely.

The meeting adjourned and everyone returned to his tent to begin thinning out gear. While I was satisfied that we had a quorum—we had agreed that dogs must be sent out and sleds loads lightened—I wasn't as sure that my teammates truly understood the depths of our dilemma. If we didn't lighten up and attempt to travel as far as we could as fast as we could to the next cache, the dogs would starve and the expedition would be over.

Victor particularly hesitated to throw things out, not fully understanding that every extra pound was a drag on the dogs. For example, I got rid of twenty pounds of gear, including expensive items like a $200 pair of binoculars and a $1,600 tripod. Victor, on the other hand, refused to part with his twenty-pound bag of war-surplus Soviet polar clothes, which he wasn't wearing and which weren't worth $50. But he had a very difficult time throwing things out, and while emotionally I understood why—he'd never had equipment of this quality before—I kept telling him he had to get rid of some of it. He responded that I was overreacting, that the weather was bound to clear, and that we would have easy travel days soon. He did not seem to understand fully why we needed to lighten up and that the cost of the failure of the expedition far outweighed the cost of replacing a parka. (Two weeks later I would spot in his bags a box of colored pencils I had left behind. When I asked him about them, he said he wanted to take them home to his son. While I understood why he still could not understand our more ambivalent feelings toward material things, I assured him that when we got home I would buy Stas a box of colored pencils.)

SEPTEMBER 27, DAY 63

Outside, another heavy snowstorm rages, and my thoughts turn to the Australian explorer who mapped much of East Antarctica, Douglas Mawson. Trapped in similar conditions, he wrote, in 1911, "The winds have a force so terrific as to eclipse anything previously known in the world. We have found the kingdom of blizzards. We have come to an accursed land."

We've been sitting now at Desperation Camp for three days, and the wet, gray days are beginning to take their toll on our moods. We are nearly two weeks behind schedule, have just four days of dog food left and little hope of finding the next cache. Jean-Louis has scheduled two radio contacts for today in order to try to set up a rendezvous with a plane. Our concern is that in these storms a plane may not be able to find us, nor land if it does.

After his first radio chat, Jean-Louis comes to my tent. "Criquet is disappointed that we are calling for a plane," he explains. "I think because he views it only in dollars and cents. But it is impossible for him to understand our predicament, or the conditions. No one could understand."

"Maybe he thinks we're giving up," I say. "But that's not the case. He has to understand that the dogs aren't that bad off yet . . . but that our decision was made to prevent them from burning out completely and ruining our chances of getting across the continent."

SEPTEMBER 28, DAY 64

We are out of the tent at six o'clock, and it takes two and a half hours to dig out, pack our sleds and harness the dogs. The weather is cloudy and misty, as usual, but we have the best visibility in almost a week, five hundred feet. The new snow is a foot deep, which promises a tough day for the dogs.

As we travel, the wind picks up. Jean-Louis attempts to make another radio contact, this time outside the protection of the tent, which is a challenge. My job is to hold the receiver inside my jacket to protect it from the wind while Keizo and Victor brace themselves against "windsqualls worthy of Dante" (Victor's description), becoming human antennae with the radio's dipole wires stretched between them as Jean-Louis struggles to raise somebody in Punta. He is successful, only to discover that the plane is still grounded by bad weather in Chile and is waiting for a lull in the storm before heading toward us.

About three o'clock my dogs start giving out, stopping in their tracks and refusing to budge even as I yell at the top of my lungs. They are tired and hungry, their spirits at low ebb. I nudge them forward at an uneven pace until we make camp, at five-thirty. We've traveled seventeen miles, and are still twenty-one miles from the cache site.

It is now light enough out at three-thirty in the morning to read and write without a headlamp. The sun stays up until eight-thirty. In another month we will have round-the-clock sunshine.

SEPTEMBER 29, DAY 65

Another sleepless night, spent plotting and planning. At five forty-five Victor went to Jean-Louis's tent to listen to his call to Punta Arenas, and when he returned I asked for his opinion on one of the options I'd spent the night considering: the possibility of sending two men back to Punta, to rejoin us at Ellsworth or the South Pole. He looked at me, stunned and then angry. Again he accused me of making rash decisions.

"My decisions aren't hurried, Victor," I explained. "I'm up at night thinking, thinking, thinking, and there is reason right now to be concerned. If we plunge ahead blindly, we are not going to make it. My plan is that if we are stuck here or make little headway in the next week, then we should consider sending two men back, to lighten the load. I have always believed four can travel faster than six, and in this case it may be the only way to salvage the expedition. It is only an option at this point, but I want to run it by the team now to assess their feelings." I asked him what he thought we should do if in fact we were stuck here for many more days.

"We need to go, that's all. But it will be a very bad situation if we have to send people back," he said. It is frustrating for Victor in these tense situations where his lack of English makes it difficult to say what he really means. (My Russian is nonexistent.) I could sense there was a lot more he wanted to say to me, but he simply didn't know how.

"I don't think you really understand the gravity of the situation," I said, though he insisted he does. "I think you'd understand better if you were with the dogs yesterday and saw what was happening. If you were responsible for a team and you had to push your guts out to get them to move I think you'd understand how serious it is."

"But dogs are not cars," he countered, "you don't just put fuel in them and they go. They are like people—one day their spirit is up and they go, the next day they are down and they refuse to pull. They are motivated by spirit."

"My concern right now, Victor," I said, "is the next twenty-four hours. If we cover the twenty-one miles to the next cache fast and the weather clears, all of this worrying and planning will be for naught.

"I can't quit, Victor; that is not an option for me. I have to

make it across. If I don't . . . look at it this way . . . unlike
you, I don't have a job to go back to; the government won't be
there to help me. If we fail here I've risked my name and will
be a million dollars in debt, because sponsors won't be obli-
gated to pay up. As far as I'm concerned I have everything to
lose and nothing to gain if we are forced to quit now. So while
I don't think we will have to exercise the option of sending
men out, we must consider everything."

We gathered in Geoff's tent at seven-thirty and Jean-Louis
reported that the weather is clear at King George, Palmer
Station and Rothera, so Henry has taken off, hoping to find us
sometime tomorrow if the skies stay clear.

I began the meeting. "Even though Henry is on his way,
I'm very concerned about my dogs quitting yesterday, following Keizo's quitting the day before. We must drop an additional hundred pounds this morning. I also think we should
switch to two tents of three men each. And today while we're
traveling we must each be thinking about several alternative
plans I'll outline, plans that will be particularly important if the
plane does not come in and if we can't find the cache." I then
laid out options that included keeping the twenty-four strongest dogs on half rations and cutting back the rations of the
dogs that would go out to the minimum necessary to keep
them alive, and the possibility of sending two men out if the
plane can't find us for a week or so and we end up sitting or
traveling few miles.

"Victor and I talked this morning and he thinks my plans
are too rash. But I've been weighing them very seriously for
the past two weeks, and in some respects since the beginning
of the expedition," I said. "I've had dogs stop on me in conditions not unlike these. I know what's next. With just two and a
half days of dog food left we are facing a situation where we
risk starving the dogs to death if we don't use our heads.

"If we find the cache, then we feed the dogs and keep going. If the plane can't find us, and we wait and wait and wait,

that's when we would have to consider sending men out whenever it does. All I ask this morning is that we start thinking about such a potential. If we've learned anything in the past two months it is that we can't count on anything—especially a plane."

The notion of sending men back struck a chord I had not expected. Rather than cause undue alarm or concern, it seemed to unite everyone. To a man the feeling was that we must continue as a six-man team no matter the consequences. "If a decision is made to send men back, I will quit," said Geoff, knowing that most likely he wouldn't be one to be cut.

Keizo was equally adamant, though he knew that if two men were sent back he, because of his youth, would probably be one of them. "I try never to think about quitting. I never even allow myself to think negative, always positive. Because once you have negative thoughts in your mind, they spread down, down, down through your body and even the dogs will sense it. I am with Geoff—either we all make it, or none."

After the meeting we struggled out of the tent; the snow was now waist-deep.

We left at ten o'clock, and within an hour Geoff's dogs began to drag. Sawyer finally gave up completely, and Geoff was forced to throw the seventy-pound dog on top of his sled.

We took turns leading, since breaking a trail sapped the dogs even more. I took a shift in front around twelve-thirty, but it lasted only thirty-five minutes before my dogs gave in and lay down in their tracks. We tried giving them a rest every half hour, but that didn't seem to help. By two o'clock we had made just four miles. We had our lunch around Jean-Louis's sled in the blowing snow and made the obvious decision that it was worthless trying to go any farther today. We camped seventeen miles from where we think the Savan cache is buried.

We heard by radio that Henry and the Twin Otter flew from Punta to the Rothera base on Adelaide Island, approximately 375 miles from where we're camped, to wait for better weather. But we are still faced with a problem if the plane finds us: while it carries dog food, which we need, there is no way in these deep snows we'll be able to travel with any additional weight on the sleds. In the greatest irony of the trip so far, we are praying for the heavy winds to return, to blow these snow-drifts away.

Antarctica is teaching all of us a great deal about patience. The clock is ticking, days are going by slowly, and we're barely gaining on the area of inaccessibility, Vostok and Mirnyy. We hardly think of those places except as carrots to keep us mov-ing. If we continue to fall behind schedule, we'll never see them.

When I finally fell asleep this night I dropped straight into a vivid, colorful dream. I was in Las Vegas, dropping quarter after quarter into a slot machine and getting nothing, nothing, nothing. I decided to play my last three quarters in one ma-chine. One bell came up, then a second, and a third. Jackpot. I'd won every penny in the casino.

It was the most powerful dream I had during the expedi-tion. My hope was that the "jackpot" was the next cache.

SEPTEMBER 30, DAY 66

Victor and I woke late, at eight o'clock, and he went outside for his snow shower. It was calm, and I could hear Jean-Louis on the radio. When Victor returned he announced it was crys-tal clear, and when I peeked out the tent door I could see the sun and the horizon for the first time in several weeks. Look-ing back over the path we'd traveled blindly made me smile. We'd come over rises and descents and barely felt either. To the south I could see Savan Nunatak, where our cache is surely buried under a dozen feet of snow.

The plane is just three hours away, and since the sky is clear Henry will most likely be able to find us this afternoon, solving our most immediate problem, which is feeding the dogs. He's also bringing in three fresh dogs from Punta, and we have decided to send out fifteen of our most trail-weary beasts, including most of Keizo's team, for a much-deserved rest. We'll be traveling with twenty-four dogs—three teams of eight each —if and when we can move from this camp. Today the snow is still waist-deep, far too deep to travel in.

We heard Henry and his powerful turboprop coming long before we could see him. To land he had to clear his own runway through the deep powder by making a dozen passes and pounding down the snow with the plane's pair of two-foot-wide, eight-foot-long skis. A veteran of such landings, he knew that if he set down without a proper runway, he'd never leave.

When the Twin Otter whined down and Henry jumped out, we greeted him warmly, if hurriedly. He would stay for only forty minutes, so we couldn't afford to waste any time. While the plane is on the ground, one engine runs continuously, spraying the air with a fine mist of kerosene and whipping up wet snow. We downloaded three dogs and dog food, and loaded up the fifteen dogs headed for a warm vacation. But when Henry taxied back to the end of his runway and readied to take off it appeared he'd taken on too much weight. He revved the engines, burning precious gasoline. We thought we might have to run the mile to where he sat and push him off. When he finally raced down the runway a swirl of snow blew down our necks, and our excited dogs strained at the lengths of their chains. He tipped his wings, and was gone. As the plane disappeared, Geoff paid me the only compliment he would share with me in three years. "Incredible," he said. "You don't realize how much luck you have with airplanes. It was the same way in Greenland. Incredible."

I turned to Jean-Louis and we laughed, then fell into an embrace. Minutes later Henry radioed back to say that Savan was nowhere to be seen, so we would skip it and head for the next cache, near Mt. Rex. Savan is the third of the first six caches that we've been unable to find; we had made the right move calling for the plane, since it was obvious we would have never found it. We cried over our good fortune and the relief of having survived the past two weeks. Jean-Louis shrugged. "Don't worry," he said. "We will do this. We will make it."

Tonight we gathered again in Geoff's pyramid, and the mood was much lighter than during our previous conversation in the same confines. We'd been tentbound thirteen days this month, and each day we were falling steadily behind schedule. The talk turned to why we do what we do.

"Reporters ask this all the time," said Jean-Louis, "and I say, 'Because I like it.' I say, 'You never ask the basketball player why he plays. I assume it is because he likes it.' It is like asking someone, 'Why do you like chocolate?' "

"But don't we ask ourselves the same question sometimes?" Geoff said. "In these conditions, don't we each ask ourselves every day, many times, why we do this?"

"Of course," said Jean-Louis.

"And I never have a satisfactory answer."

"Me either, I guess," admitted Jean-Louis.

"Or rather, I have a different answer each day," continued Geoff. "If we'd been asked on that beautiful day we passed Charity Mountain, I'd have said, 'Well, look for yourself.' It's a rhetorical question that has no answer really."

Jean-Louis paused before responding. "It's like small talk, something you would ask your neighbor to open a conversation."

The question I am asked most often is not why, but what do I want to be remembered for. "How do you answer that question, Jean-Louis?" I asked.

"As a grandfather," said the Frenchman. "That is all."

By eleven o'clock we were singing, slightly drunk after downing a bottle of whiskey Henry had left behind. Victor led, singing with little prompting his favorite Russian song, a May Day anthem. Keizo, who has the sweetest voice of us all, took more encouragement. "I'll back you up," promised Jean-

Louis. Soon we were all singing, and our keening was taken up by the dogs. As midnight came and went, we howled together into the frozen Antarctic night.

MILES TRAVELED: 630

MILES TO THE SOUTH POLE: 1,367

OCTOBER

FROZEN BONES

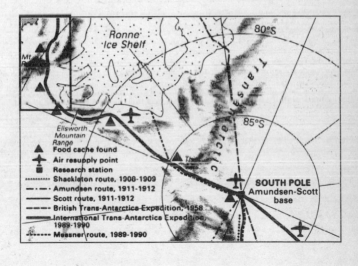

Ronne
Ice Shelf

80°S

Mt.
[illegible]

Ellsworth
Mountain
Range

▲ Food cache found
✈ Air resupply point
🏠 Research station
·········· Shackleton route, 1908-1909
—·—·— Amundsen route, 1911-1912
———— Scott route, 1911-1912
— — — British Trans-Antarctica Expedition, 1958
━━━━ International Trans-Antarctica Expedition, 1989-1990
····· Messner route, 1989-1990

85°S

The [illegible]

SOUTH POLE
Amundsen-Scott
base

The lighthearted mood of last night disappeared with the falling snow we woke to. Nothing had changed after all; the weather we'd had for the past ten days was back.

We'd dubbed this place Camp Patience, a virtue that was being severely tested, since we have been stuck here for three days. There is no physical way we could plow through this snow and carry enough food with us to survive; if we tried to travel we would probably make six or seven miles at best and the dogs would burn out. All we can do is wait for better conditions, fatten and rest the dogs, and try not to get on each other's nerves.

At noon I went outside and found Geoff pacing along his dogs' stakeout line. As we talked in the cold I admitted to him that I was afraid of this area, and its unpredictability. He agreed, saying he'd been in conditions like this only twice before, and then there had been no imperative to move. We *had* to move, and soon. We stood there, crossing and uncrossing our arms to stay warm, and considered our limited options.

"I've run every imaginable option, including heading off east or west of here to escape the storms," said Geoff, "but I think we have to just keep traveling straight on, whether we make four or fourteen miles a day."

"Two days ago I might have agreed," I told him, "but I don't think we *can* move in this stuff. Let's just hang in here a little while longer. The weather could change in our favor overnight. One thing I am sure of: another stretch like the past ten days, and it's over, we'll never make it."

"Antarctica does not treat fools gladly," said Geoff, "and as a result life here can be very, very complicated. All of a sudden it drops its beauty and does everything in its power to destroy you."

These deep-snow conditions have us all worried about what is to come in the area of inaccessibility, if we make it that far. We've been warned, by the French and the Soviets, that it is 750 miles of nothing but soft, deep snow, just like this.

OCTOBER 2, DAY 68

When Jean-Louis raised Punta by radio this morning his message was simple: "The conditions are too bad to describe." Yet after four days stuck at Camp Patience, we decide that unless significantly more snow falls overnight, we will try to move tomorrow with Jean-Louis, Victor and Dahe skiing out front to break a trail for the dogs.

The single advantage of being stuck here is that it has given the dogs a chance to rest. They have put on pounds, their coats are shiny, and they are ready to run. They have been so well fed that the past nights some have been stashing the food they can't eat, sleeping on it to protect it from their neighbors. Unfortunately, they tend to bring out a chunk late at night for a chew, which inevitably starts the others growling jealously. So I now make a round before I go to bed and pick up all extra dog food to avoid any late-night sleep disturbances.

Our plan is to lead with a light sled, carrying just sleeping bags and a few boxes of dog food, followed by Geoff's sled pulled by nine dogs, and then my team with the heaviest load and ten dogs. We decided that even if we make just five or six miles a day for the next several weeks, that might be enough to get us beyond this deep snow.

I remember a similar situation when I was soloing along the north rim of the Arctic Circle in 1983. The snow was waist-deep and I was traveling with nine dogs. It was March and very cold; lows were in the −60°s, highs around −45°. It took me twenty-two days to travel the 230 miles from Ft. Good Hope to the village of Red River. In that situation I relayed my gear and food, which required taking a partial load ahead, dropping it off and returning to retrieve the remainder. The problem with relaying is that you end up covering the same distance three times.

On the seventeenth day I hit the faint remnants of a trapper's trail and tried to follow it by feeling my way along with a ski pole, like a blind man. On either side of the trail were four-foot drifts, and if I had gone off into them I'd never have gotten the sled back on the trail. I thought I was safe, until a monstrous blizzard came in, closing visibility down to zero. On the nineteenth day I ran out of dog food and was forced to feed the dogs what remained of my own stash of cheese, caribou and butter. The lesson I learned there was that I had to keep moving. I was out of food, and stopping to wait for clear weather would have been the end. I managed to make the last fifty miles in three days, but the dogs were near death.

This is different because there is no way we can relay, due to the constant storms. We might get two hundred yards away and never be able to find what we'd left behind. If visibility were to shut down for ten days and our food was behind us, we'd starve. The key is to keep the dogs strong so that as our sleds begin to lighten we can pick up mileage. The worst case is if the dogs lose strength as we lose weight on the sled, then we won't make the miles necessary. This was the whole challenge of our North Pole trip. We started out with very heavy sleds, weighing seventeen hundred pounds fully loaded, and our initial progress was very slow. Our hope was that as the sleds got lighter, the dogs would simultaneously grow stronger and pull us farther every day. Instead, their strength dropped and they burned out more quickly than our sleds lost weight. We were able to relay there only because the visibility stayed good. The breakthrough came when we dropped three hundred pounds off our sleds, in the form of extra sleeping bags, food and valuable gear, but that wasn't until Day 39, seventeen days from the North Pole.

Tonight Victor and I are enjoying our last evening as tentmates. Tomorrow, if weather permits, will be a big change for us all: we will travel, have new combinations of dogs pulling the sleds, and we will be sleeping three men to a tent. We've decided to experiment and split into two groups of three; mushers in one tent, scientists in the other. If successful this will save us carrying the weight of one full tent unit.

In preparation for the transition Victor and I are dismantling the efficient-if-haphazard system we've lived under these first ten weeks. I have taken out of the supper box what is mine, including the sesame seed oil, the hot pepper oil, the lemons and date sugar. Victor takes his mother's bread and French chocolates. It's like a divorce, divvying up all our tently goods. But the change will be good; it's not healthy to stay in the same units for long periods of time under these conditions. Cliques develop, which can be injurious to leadership and the decision-making process, and given our isolation during the day if we were to tent only with one person for four thousand miles we would hardly get to know the other men.

Perhaps the most ritualistic alteration is the changing of the pee bottle. For the past sixty-seven nights Victor and I have shared the same bottle, a one-liter square plastic jug with a two-inch-diameter screw-top lid. Now that we are going to a three-man tent, we're switching to individual bottles. In preparation, tonight we are labeling our new "urinals": Victor's proclaims in bold letters VICTOR'S PISS: KEEP AWAY, FAR AWAY OF FLAME (*sic*). On the top of mine I have drawn a big skull and crossbones and at the bottom written DRINK AT YOUR OWN RISK (and in smaller letters Danger: May Contain Piss). Individual bottles! It's getting quite civilized down here.

As we divide up our goods, we toast one last time with Royal Jelly. Victor admits he believes there might be an aphrodisiac of some kind in this potion after all. "In Greenland I slept very well without dreaming of women. Now that is not possible. . . . Often I see women in my dreams, which is not very useful given the circumstances. I understand that Keizo has been dreaming the same. . . . In some ways it's a nice problem, but last night—after that dinner of hot peppers and meat—all night I dream of women." While I sympathize with Victor, I assure him that I have not been affected in the same way, that the Indian girl on the Land O Lakes butter package doesn't look any better tonight than she did before we arrived in Antarctica.

OCTOBER 3, DAY 69

It's nine o'clock at night and I am crouched in the corner of Geoff's pyramid tent. Keizo and Geoff are tucked next to me in their sleeping bags. The quarters are cramped and barely organized, but we are committed to giving this three-men-to-a-tent routine a shot.

We managed to travel today, slowly, and it was a struggle for the dogs as the powdery snow reached their Science Diet–swollen bellies. My team had overeaten yesterday, and this morning they acted like a bunch of drunks the day after a big bash, pulling strongly but wobbling as if they were hung over. As for us, there was no time for daydreaming. Because of the deep snow we worked for our mileage; the back two sleds continuously slid off the freshly broken trail, so all day long we had to lean hard against the sled—while on skis—to keep it on the trail.

One major mistake made by Adventure Network when they planted the caches is starting to take its toll. We always knew it would be difficult to get good cookstove fuel (white gas) south of the equator, but they assured us it would be no problem, that they would fly premium-grade gas down from Canada. Though we had been explicit in our communication with them about the kind of fuel we needed (top-grade Coleman fuel), they had instead bought inexpensive Chilean fuel. So far we've avoided using the low-grade fuel, because we know it will clog our high-tech stoves and emit nasty black fumes inside our tents. As a result of Adventure Network's mistake, we are lugging along eighteen extra gallons of Coleman fuel that we brought with us from the States. The additional weight adds to the toll on the dogs.

OCTOBER 5, DAY 71

Every time I think our fortune has changed, Antarctica slaps me back to reality. We woke this morning to a stormy, cold day, and as we traveled a forty-mile-per-hour wind pelted us with driving snow; visibility was less than 150 feet. We skied intermittently through big drifts and across deep sastrugi in our first storm since we left Camp Patience. All day the sleds would get partway over the crest of a slick, frozen wave, only to topple over, costing us precious time and forcing the dogs to overexert as they pulled the heavy sleds up and over the sastrugi. The poor visibility also meant we could not send a point man out front, so Jean-Louis, Dahe and Victor skied between the sleds, providing reference points for the dogs. Still, we were separated many times. By camp we had made just six miles in eight hours. Jean-Louis's satellite message: "When is this ever going to stop?"

On days like this I often wonder how many people could put up with a "job" like ours: day after day, pushing and pushing and pushing and shouting at the top of your lungs to encourage the dogs. It is a mammoth physical effort just to keep the sleds inching forward. By the end of every day my body is exhausted, my voice hoarse. And today was a relatively warm one, temperatures climbing all the way to zero. Any pain multiplies as temperatures drop.

We are growing exceedingly worried about a few of the dogs, particularly Tim and Hank, who have lost the fur on the inside of their legs. It is a problem we first experienced in

Greenland and hoped we wouldn't see again. Snow accumulates and freezes in their fur, and in their attempts to clean themselves with their teeth they end up pulling out not only the ice but their fur as well, exposing raw skin to the cold and wet blowing snow. In Greenland the problem cured itself as the days got warmer. But here we can't predict when that will be; warmer days could be one week or two months away.

Our three-men-to-a-tent experiment lasted just two nights. It was far too crowded and no one was resting properly. We had thought three to a tent would bring us closer together, when in fact it was quickly obvious that it might drive us apart instead. We voted today to go back to pairs—Jean-Louis and Victor, Geoff and Keizo, me and Dahe.

We pitched our tent tonight on a hillside, and from my head to my toes is a drop of two feet. Putting it up in heavy winds on the side of a hill was difficult and we broke one of its six poles and punched a hole in the door, which Dahe quickly sewed up. It is going to take a few days for us to reestablish any kind of "tent rhythm"—as I write I am lying on my sleeping bag with a teapot, a cook pot and my big breakfast/dinner cup hanging over my head. Clothing is strung all over the place, and the ceiling sags badly where the pole is broken. Because I sent my stove out when we switched to three-man tents, we are forced to use a stove that Jean-Louis burned kerosene in, and it emits a dirty residue inside the tent. The only good thing about this camp is that we have plenty to eat.

OCTOBER 6, DAY 72

Heavy winds prevented us from leaving until noon, and then we had to dig out from beneath two feet of new snow. By late afternoon the surfaces were perfectly smooth, thanks to the continuous winds. In a period of three days we've gone from deep drifts to rock-hard ice, which is good in that it helps us

rack up miles. But the winds are always a mixed blessing. Today they blew so hard that the powdery snow infiltrated the
zippers on our duffel bags and sleeping bags, coating everything with a frozen mist. In the past such winds have driven
explorers to near insanity. Shackleton wrote about suffering
from *anemomania*, literally *wind madness*. "This disease may be
exhibited in two forms: Either one is morbidly anxious about
the wind direction and gibbers continually about it, or else a
sort of lunacy is produced by listening to the other ame-
nomaniacs. The second form is more trying to hear." So far
we are keeping our complaints to ourselves.

The inside of the dogs' legs are worsening. Ray, Tim and
Hank all have raw patches on the inside of their hind legs, and
the blowing snow aggravates the condition. If the temperatures stay warm (today we had a high of −10°) they should
improve; if it drops back to −30° or −40° we'll have a very
serious problem.

Similarly, the cold, wet conditions are taking a toll on our
bodies. Our lips are sore and cracked and the bridge under our
noses is chafed. We all have frostbitten cheeks, so shaving has
become a torture. Everyone has quarter-inch-deep "cracks"
on his fingers, caused by the daily freezing and thawing, which
eventually splits the flesh. The last is very painful, and Dahe
and Geoff try to protect their hands with Band-Aids or mole-
skin; I just let mine go, because I've never found a satisfactory
cure. The pain goes away after a few days. Perhaps worst of all,
we are each exhausted, our minds and bodies thoroughly worn
from the continuous cold and winds.

Dahe also has a severe problem with the circulation in his
right hand, which we think is caused either by his ski pole
strap cutting into the flow of blood or too tight a grip on the
sled's handlebars. Whatever the cause, every night he must
massage his hand for two hours to get feeling back. I accidentally exacerbated the problem a day or so ago, in one of our
few miscommunications due to language differences. Dahe
firmly believes in Royal Jelly as a medicinal curative/prevent-

ative and religiously drinks one vial each morning and two in the evening. When I found a pint of it on my sled I asked Dahe if he needed it or if I could dump the liquid out to eliminate excess weight. He said yes, which I thought meant he had plenty. In fact, it turns out he had only two days' worth left. When he discovered I'd dumped the last of our Royal Jelly stash he was first angry with me, which he communicated through a kind of silent treatment; then he grew despondent.

OCTOBER 7, DAY 73

The wind was blowing fiercely outside the tent when Jean-Louis poked his head through the door. "I have been looking at Tim's legs," he said. "They do not look very good."

"I know," I told him. "But there isn't much we can do, except pray for warmer weather."

"But sometimes I have a feeling the weather will be bad forever," Jean-Louis muttered, shaking his head and backing out of the tent.

At that point it looked as if we would be forced to sit again. But we met outside at ten o'clock, and after the now routine chore of unburying our sleds and dogs, we were off by noon and traveled twenty-two miles into a strong head wind. It was a strange day; though the snow continued to blow, we could clearly see blue sky and sun through the clouds that besieged us at ground level. When we stopped to make camp Dahe dug one of his periodic five-foot-deep snow pits, to take samples of the ice, and he said he could tell that this was always a windy place.

The terrain we are crossing reminds me of the undulating wheat fields of Saskatchewan, just icier. Stretching ahead of us are hundreds of miles of flat nothingness. No rock outcroppings, no nunataks, no landmarks of any kind. It is a vista seen by just a handful of men before us.

Most people who come to Antarctica these days, whether

government scientists or tourists, confine their travels to the coastlines of the continent or the perimeters of a research base; few see the "real" Antarctica. In part that's for the best, because your survival skills have to be finely tuned in order to survive out here. Over the past few years I've met or heard of a wide variety of people who say they are planning expeditions across various parts of Antarctica. I think of them occasionally when traveling through these whiteouts in –45° weather. As for being "the first" to see some of these vistas, in many respects each day looks to us much like the one before. The storms are sapping our energy and will, and the repetitiveness of our days detracts from some of the majesty of the sights we are seeing and experiences we are sharing. In some ways that is unfortunate, since we most likely will never be here again. But our main concern now must be making progress, not history.

I slept poorly last night, worrying about the dogs and wondering how we could better protect those that continue to chew off their life-preserving fur. I consider putting spare socks on their legs (though Geoff has tried this once and the dogs pulled them off within minutes), or arranging some kind of garter system to keep them on. Tomorrow I plan to harness Ray and Tim at the back of the team, on the leeward side of the sled, to protect them as much as possible from the wind. I also may end up carrying one or the other on the sled.

OCTOBER 9, DAY 75

When I woke this morning, Dahe was recording his journal in Chinese into a tape recorder. It was strange, lying there listening and being able to understand only a few words, like "Siple," "Antarctica," "Geoff," "Victor," "Jean-Louis," "Thiel Mountains," and the multicultural "cold." In my own journal I recorded that we have had forty days of storms in the past fifty-five days.

We were blessed with good weather today, featuring a

crosswind and rock-hard surfaces. But we got off to a late start, due to a minor controversy between Geoff and Jean-Louis about exactly where we are. When they compared bearings this morning there was a twenty-degree discrepancy, the biggest yet in our binavigational system. But no one is too surprised, since we've been traveling almost blind for the past week. After some debate it was decided we are off course by about six miles, which is not too bad since we traveled nearly one hundred miles without being able to see more than five hundred feet. Once the issue was resolved we moved fast, covering fifteen miles before lunch and twelve more afterward. By late in the day my dogs were tiring and came to a stop half a dozen times. Otherwise it was a great day of travel.

We had a curious and bothersome conversation at lunch, though. Out of the blue Jean-Louis asked that we consider again the option of sending two men out to rejoin the team at Patriot Hills or the South Pole, an idea I thought had clearly been rejected when I first mentioned it ten days ago. Apparently he felt our situation was worsening, even though we were making headway. He justified bringing the option up and furthered it by suggesting that if we made it to Vostok—having reached the South Pole and crossed the area of inaccessibility —we could, with our pride intact, hitch a ride with the Soviet tractor-train to Mirnyy. He sounded extremely defeated, and the rest of us were stunned by his negativism. Normally the most optimistic of us, he was at the most defeated I had ever seen him.

I challenged Jean-Louis immediately, saying I thought it premature even to think about not completing the crossing. Although I hesitated to say it out loud, his attitude scared me more than the bad conditions. If he, or anyone, started thinking about quitting early it could be contagious; it might endanger the whole team's spirit, and then of course we wouldn't make it. This had to be a do-or-die effort, with Mirnyy firmly our final destination; otherwise we might as well quit now. Sure, there had been tough days, and there would be more ahead, but we weren't *that* far behind. "We have a lot of time for success," I said. I got the impression from the nodding of the other men's heads that they agreed. But today, for whatever reason, Jean-Louis's spirit had failed him, and I didn't want him harboring such thoughts privately, nor speaking them to the others. It would be key for me to visit in the next few days with the others, to make sure they weren't influenced by his pessimism.

Jean-Louis was allowing the conditions to beat him down. Over the years I've learned to keep such pessimism at bay, in part by allowing blizzards and storms to define my path. It is a lesson I partially learned from studying the travails of our predecessors: Nansen wrote in his journals about conforming the personal will to the Almighty will; modern-day Japanese explorer Naomi Uemerura told me how he often felt like a weak man in the brutal subzero cold, but by adapting to nature's way he was able to reach the North Pole, alone; Admiral Peary recognized the power of the human spirit and its ability to flourish against all odds by conforming to the forces that surrounded him. What these explorers, and their predecessors, had learned from experience was invaluable: human strength lies not in resistance but in giving in. If we are to survive in Antarctica, we must give in to nature, not fight it.

It is obvious that the forces of nature are much stronger than a solitary man (or even six men). Man is not intended to live, or survive, in these conditions. But over the years we have survived, due to our sole advantage over the wilderness, our ability to learn from and adapt to whatever it has in store. The strength this team has is its willingness to take whatever nature hands out. There is a spiritual factor to our success too. Though we have seen bleak times, we must keep our spirits strong and our hope alive. I must admit I have experienced some near hopeless moments here. Yesterday I spent time thinking about what it would be like to just let go of the sled, get lost in the storm, and disappear; any suffering would be over in minutes, and why not, since life seemed to have little

meaning or value when your body was wracked with pain from
the cold. But in such difficult times I have always managed to
revive my spirit when things seemed most desperate. This
morning Jean-Louis showed every sign that his hope was waning, that his spirit was as exhausted as his body. That is what
costs men their lives in these conditions, so it is my challenge
to help him, any way I can, rejuvenate his spirit.

In my tent tonight, writing in my journal by candlelight, I
thought about Robert Scott, and his dying charge that Antarctica was an "awful place." Indeed, Antarctica has shattered the
dreams of many strong men. Scott and his four teammates
died here; Mawson nearly did, and he lost two teammates.
Shackleton tried numerous times to make the South Pole or a
traverse, and failed. Dozens of less successful explorers never
made the history books, their exploits relegated to the dusty
archives of library attics.

Of the early explorers, Roald Amundsen—fully prepared,
aided by a brilliant strategy and a little luck—succeeded best in
Antarctica, by giving in to it, by adapting to its rhythms. He
was the first to reach the South Pole, on December 14, 1911.
Hungry for that first and desperate to best Scott, whom he
knew to be headed for the Pole at the same time, Amundsen
and his men made their first attempt on September 8. But
extremely cold storms (–70° temperatures froze the fluids in
their compasses) drove them back to their base within eight
days. They waited one month, trimmed their team from eight
men to five, and set off again.

Through careful study Amundsen had picked the perfect
route. His team traveled the first four hundred miles at near
sea level, then climbed rapidly to ten thousand feet. He and his
men suffered slightly from the quick climb, but they avoided
having to spend a stretch of days on top of the plateau rocked
by katabatics. Once they reached the plateau they shot across
the flats the remaining four hundred miles to the Pole with
lightning speed, building cairns of snow every two miles as a
guide for their return trip. With good weather on his side,

Amundsen succeeded primarily because he planned methodically and trusted the capabilities of his dogs. He did not panic or give in to the cold. More than any other example, it was Amundsen's success that gave me strength and rejuvenated my spirit in times of doubt.

We understand from a brief conversation with Criquet that a ten-day meeting of the Antarctic Treaty members began in Paris today. Delegates are going to review current Antarctic activity and share information about normal operating procedures at the various scientific bases. In ancillary meetings they will also discuss the future of the treaty that governs this place, as they prepare to review the treaty in 1991. It does not "expire," as many wrongly believe, but may be amended at that review.

Over the past several years a mineral rights agreement has been drawn up that would permit the exploration for minerals in certain areas of Antarctica, only when treaty members unanimously agree that its implementation is reasonable and its environmental impact is acceptable. In the present treaty, signed in 1961, no guidelines exist concerning mineral exploration. Prior to these Paris talks, delegates from France and Australia had already withdrawn their support for the proposed mineral rights measure and requested the treaty nations declare Antarctica a world park. Since a mineral rights resolution (or any resolution to amend the treaty) must be agreed upon unanimously, the withdrawal of support by those two countries means the governing nations are a long way from resolving the issue of whether or not Antarctica is soon to be opened up for commercial exploitation. Though we are a long way from Paris, it has always been our hope that if we make it back from Antarctica, our stories will help educate people about the continent, and encourage its continued protection.

OCTOBER 12, DAY 78

The vagaries of Antarctica's weather pummeled us again. Yesterday we could look back to the north and see low pressure systems building, the kind that carry storms. Ahead of us, south, the skies were clear. Today, we traveled into the teeth of a violent wind and snowstorm and it was brutally cold, the coldest day of the expedition. The temperature was −30°, which would be fine on its own, but we were buffeted every few seconds by gusty twenty-five-mile-per-hour katabatics, blowing right into our faces. By midday it was snowing, and the drift was again penetrating the zippers of our windsuits and parkas. The only things we dared expose were our eyes, and even they ached from the cold and the tension such travel builds. On days like this I often wonder how the dogs survive.

Despite the conditions, we are actually in good shape. In the past week we averaged twenty-one miles per day, including three days of twenty-seven miles. We are stronger for the challenges and obstacles that put us behind schedule, and now we *should* face only better weather. Unfortunately, today's conditions were not promising.

Being slightly behind schedule is actually beneficial. If we were two hundred miles ahead of where we are now we probably would have seen these desperately cold days earlier, and been stuck in them longer. I doubt the dogs, or we, could have survived this kind of cold for very long. Plus we're already seeing just three to four hours of dusklike darkness each day. Within a week or so we will be traveling under twenty-four-hour daylight, which should help warm things up.

This morning we traveled just seven miles before making a rapid ascent to reach the pass that would lead us to Mt. Rex. Coming down the other side, as always, was a wild ride. I marvel at the fact that we're able to control these careening thousand-pound sleds and wild dogs as they sprint up and down hills. Without good dog-driving skills this trip would be impossible. At some point each day we're put in a position where, if inexperienced, our dogs would lead us into inestimable dangers. Two days ago, for example, we crested a nunatak and then plunged immediately down the icy slope of the downside before any of us could get a glimpse of what lay below. In those situations if you don't manage to hang on to just a shred of control over the dogs and your sled, you risk killing the former and flipping the latter.

We found the Mt. Rex cache covered by only four inches of snow and unburied it, encouraged to hurry by the dropping temperature and rising wind (windchills were −80°). Because we hoped to find the cache at Siple 160 miles away within the next week, we loaded only about 130 pounds of human food and 70 pounds of dog food onto each sled. In these cold temperatures we are feeding the dogs extra rations (plus an occasional half block of our own cheese) to keep their energy up, so it was most important that we had plenty of food for them.

Tim's energy continues to wane. Seventy-five percent of the fur on the inside of his legs is gone, exposing raw flesh to these brutal conditions. I keep him harnessed with the other dogs, even though he is too weak to pull. My thinking is that the daily running will keep his circulation going and help keep him warm.

In many respects it was a resoundingly successful day, since Mt. Rex is officially where the Antarctic Peninsula ends. Now we can start focusing our efforts and our thoughts on a new goal—the bottom of the world, the halfway point of the expedition, the South Pole. Hopefully we can be there for Jean-Louis's forty-third birthday, December 9.

OCTOBER 13, DAY 79

As we harness the dogs this morning, I chat briefly with Jean-Louis, who seems to have pulled out of the depression that swept him a few days ago. But this morning's cold (−37°, head winds of thirty-one miles per hour) is enough to depress anyone in his right mind. "You can't walk and think under these conditions or else you will start to ask yourself how we ever got into this mess," Jean-Louis says, smiling grimly. While I sense that he is still somewhat dispirited, his good nature has returned and I'm hopeful he's no longer thinking about sending anyone out.

The physical irritations mount, even though they have become the status quo. Our lips are cracked and painful, a result of the nonstop winds. Each morning, after eight hours' rest, they crack anew. This morning the pain in my bottom lip is so intense the roots of my teeth ache. So far the skin on our faces hasn't been too badly burned, primarily because we haven't seen the sun but a few times and then it has been at our backs. Unfortunately, within the next two weeks, as we head due south to the Pole under a twenty-four-hour sunlit sky, the skin on our faces will inevitably burn and crack. The exception to this is Dahe, whose face was burned and frostbitten within the first weeks and has yet to heal fully. It is so raw we have discouraged him from looking in a mirror.

The cracks on our fingers deepen. Anything we do—tie a knot, put on gloves, pick up ski poles—delivers a cutting pain, as if someone were slicing your fingers with a knife. But perhaps my worst problem right now is a constantly runny nose. As soon as the wind starts up it begins to drip like a leaky faucet. Dealing with it without taking off my three layers of gloves is an unending irritation.

This is a very foreign place, where man was not meant to survive. Today I am so cold I wonder if I have reached the threshold of pain that I can withstand. I've experienced cold like this before, in the Arctic, but only for short spells. Here there is no relief. It makes me consider what it would be like to die in this cold . . . a thought I admit I've had several times these past few days. I know with certainty that freezing to death is not how I want to go, which is a good propellant when windchills threaten to drop you to your knees. I think back as we travel today to the books and journals of our predecessors

here. Often as they neared their goal—whether it was the
South Magnetic Pole, the geographic South Pole, whatever—
they described their effort as a "sprint" or a "dash," and
couldn't wait to turn around and get back to safety. What we
are attempting is no sprint or dash but a polar ultramarathon.
This is simply not a place for warm-blooded creatures. (In
those stories from old, they too recounted the torture of the
cold: Shackleton and his men often warmed their frozen feet
by placing them inside the shirt of one of their tent partners,
against the other's skin. And when their hands turned near stiff
from the cold, one of Shackleton's men wrote, "[I] spied the
vapor rising from the freshly killed seals, stumbled toward
where they lay, and thrust my frozen hands into their blood-
warm bowels.")

Tonight I visited with Jean-Louis and Geoff and we again
pondered what drew us to this kind of life. Geoff was most
agonized. "People often ask me if we enjoy ourselves on a trip
like this. That's a hard question to answer. In a masochistic
way some enjoy banging their head against a brick wall. I see
this travel, though, as a challenge rather than a penance,
though there are many disadvantages. All of your possessions
are at home in a box, you miss your family and your friends, a
favorite picture on the wall, music. This life brings out the
hard side of you, the survival instinct. But it also brings out the
softer side, and makes you realize just how important your
friends and family, that picture on the wall and your favorite
music, are.

"Ultimately, I guess we are just gluttons, gluttons for what
is just beyond our grasp, around the next corner or over the
next hill. Gluttons for adventure."

Jean-Louis was equally circumspect. "I ask myself sometimes 'Why do I choose this life?' Some days I would like to be
the man with a dog, walking along the riverside, very quiet,
maybe singing to himself. But I know that is not for me.

"The biggest challenge here, I think, is spending seven

months within yourself. It is hard to talk in these conditions, we spend a lot of time alone. For me that is harder than any of the physical dangers or cold."

OCTOBER 14, DAY 80

Another vicious storm has us socked in and for the first time in twelve days we cannot move. But it may be for the best, because Dahe has a blistering fever. He got up early and fried his solitary morning pancake and then crawled back into his bag. He's the only one of us who has suffered any kind of sickness here. This is the second such fever Dahe has endured; the first was as we climbed the Weyerhaeuser Glacier. I think it is in part due to his physical makeup—he is thin, with little body fat —and the amount of energy he puts out each day. When he crawls into the tent at night his clothes are saturated with sweat and frost. Considering the conditions we've traveled through the past eleven days, it is not surprising that this day-after-day chill has caught up with him.

These cold storms, identical to the conditions that forced Amundsen to turn around on his first dash for the South Pole, are what I fear most about Antarctica; they are the worst conditions imaginable. We can handle zero visibility. The cold and heavy winds are manageable. But combine them in mid-winter, at this spot on the planet, and we are reduced to sitting, and praying. This cold could take a heavy toll on the dogs, who desperately need to keep running in order to stay warm and spirited. If we're stuck here, if they have to endure several days of this brutal cold without any possibility of warming themselves, it will be difficult to get them going again. Unfortunately, I am still unable to accurately predict this weather, so who knows what we're in for in the coming days.

Generally I am an optimist, but for the first time I allowed myself today to think about what it would be like *not* to finish this expedition. It was not a pleasant day. Shackleton's biographer wrote that "there is no desolation more complete than the polar night." Only those who have experienced it can fully appreciate what it means to be without the sun day after day and week after week. Few men unaccustomed to it can fight off its effects altogether, and it has driven some men mad.

Late in the afternoon I ventured outside to check on Tim, who was tied to the side of the sled out of the wind and had burrowed into a snow cave of his own making. All I could see of him was a tiny hole in the snow, and I reached down inside it to comfort him. Frustrated by the little I could do for him, I unburied him and brought him inside the tent, where he slept without complaint, and without moving, for twelve hours.

OCTOBER 15, DAY 81

Dahe is in the middle of a sardine-and-peanut-butter sandwich for breakfast, which implies he is feeling better.

The cold storms continued, but we made twenty miles today in a hazy visibility of just 150 yards. Late in the day we made one of the expedition's most painful discoveries: Spinner, one of Geoff's dogs, has a frozen penis. It was a relatively boring day and apparently he had something else on his mind. But with windchills nearing −100°, exposed flesh freezes in thirty seconds, so the poor boy has now learned a valuable lesson. Unfortunately for Geoff it means that Spinner will most likely be spending a few nights inside his tent, thawing out. While it may sound funny, and admittedly allowed us a few minutes of sophomoric joking, it is a pitiful sight and very painful for the dog. All we can hope is that he gets over his condition quickly—and that the same thing doesn't happen to any of the six of us.

When we made camp we were 108 miles from Siple, the site of our eighth cache. We should be there, weather permitting, in five days. I speculate that we'll see a better weather cycle about then, in part because we make a hard turn to the south after Siple, which should take us farther from the ocean and its effects on the local weather systems. Right now, though we're officially off the peninsula, we're still within 100 miles of the Bellingshausen Sea, one reason these winds remain so fierce.

It may have seemed a bit on the optimistic side, but I spent several hours tonight visiting Jean Louis and Victor's tent, trying to paste together a mental picture of the stretch from Vostok to Mirnyy, a route that Victor has seen several times by trax and plane. I'm curious about the terrain and weather there, so that I can start thinking about planning our approach across it. Sitting here, having just come off the peninsula, my guess is that we have until March 15 to reach Mirnyy, before winter returns. Once we reach the South Pole the *UAP* will sail for Mirnyy. The ship will take us away from Antarctica, though it sounds as if the 135-foot aluminum-hulled vessel will need the escort of a Soviet icebreaker to get close to and away from the Soviet base. From here all those plans seem very far off, but logistically Mirnyy is just around the corner.

It dawned on me when I visited the others' tents that it would be a very rude shock for outsiders to visit us now, largely because the insides of our nylon homes have taken on some very powerful odors after nearly three months of living, cooking, sleeping and sweating inside them. Jean-Louis and Victor's tent smells like lemke cheese marinated in kerosene. (In fact, you can smell Jean-Louis from a distance even outside, due to the kerosene smell of his clothing.) Fortunately, I am inured to the smell of my own home.

OCTOBER 16, DAY 82

Once again Antarctica is humbling us. It took us two hours to dig out, and conditions have worsened. We made eighteen miles in a blinding, ice-riven fog, and the dogs are suffering. I was so crushed by the cold that just before we stopped for lunch today I nearly cried. Our satellite message at day's end was simply "Frozen bones."

The worst part of these cold days is our stop for lunch; it is a mandatory stop for replenishment, hardly a social event. There is virtually no conversation; everyone concentrates on getting food from the containers inside our bodies. Yesterday I considered proposing that we put a tent up for lunch, and then maybe spending a couple of hours inside thawing out. But I never voiced that thought, because we have to keep moving.

Unpacking my lunch from the sled I made the mistake of pulling off one of my gloves for fifteen seconds, and it stung painfully. I have made every effort to condense all of my chores so that I don't have to take my gloves off for any reason outside, because as soon as they are off snow coats your wrist-lets and soaks your hands. Then when you put your gloves back on, they are cold the rest of the day. We wear glove liners and a mitt over the regular five-fingered glove, but in this extreme cold, layering often isn't enough.

I've even worked out an eating system that allows me to eat lunch without taking my gloves off. The first thing I do is fill my thermos cup with hot water. Then I get out a pemmican bar, rip the wrapper off with my teeth, and plunge it into the cup of hot water to thaw it out. After it soaks I use a Teflon spoon to lift the by-now-soggy bar out of the cup. That course is followed by nuts, which are packed in eight- and sixteen-ounce plastic bottles, and the caps twist off in my gloved hands. I put the nuts into a second cup of hot water to thaw them, not wanting to risk cracking a tooth on a frozen almond. If I have instant soup I pour the mix into a cup of hot water and stir it with the envelope. Even my "dessert"—a chocolate bar—is broken into pieces and dumped into the cup of hot water and eaten by spoon. All to save myself from having to expose my fingers for even a second.

The other necessary evil generally required by midday is

urinating. I have a side zipper on my wind pants and no fly, and once the zipper is down I drop the front of my pants, resulting in a great deal of heat loss. I try to time this effort about forty-five minutes before lunch, to avoid the resulting heat loss just before we sit down in the cold for a half hour. I notice that the others have developed the same habit.

After lunch Jean-Louis tried to make radio contact, always hard outside the shelter of a tent, and especially trying in this kind of cold. Today we all helped, and patiently froze while he attempted to raise Punta. "Romeo Bravo, come in, this is Trans-Antarctica, over. Romeo Bravo, Romeo Bravo, Romeo Bravo, come in, please," Jean-Louis begged. For the first time in our experience, even Victor was impatient, complaining about the cold. When he is cold it means it is really cold. Finally Jean-Louis got through to Criquet, and the faint response, in French, gave us our location of the day before, told us that there was no plane headed soon to Patriot Hills (we hoped if it were it could pick up our two sick dogs, Tim and Spinner) and that the weather ahead promised more of the same.

As we sledded off, Jean-Louis skied alongside me at the back of my sled. We half joked about exactly whose idea it had been to come to Antarctica anyway. "My feeling some mornings is 'Why did we decide to do this? This is crazy.' But now here we are, we have to go, we have no choice," he said. "We have spent three years with this crossing in our heads, and now, sometimes, I feel like I am in prison. A prison of our idea."

That is the biggest difference between Jean-Louis and me. He is always questioning himself and his motives, wondering why he's done what he's done. I rarely question the path I've taken. Though Jean-Louis seldom answers his own curiosities, he is also more willing than I to talk about his experiences in absolutes, like suggesting we are "prisoners of our ideas." I would never formulate, nor certainly articulate, a notion like that, because I don't think it's wholly true.

Too many people attempt to define the parameters of their beliefs, to enforce borders where they cannot exist. In my mind that kind of definition is impossible, and no better demonstrated than while on an expedition. Here we must rely not on a solitary belief system but on our intuition, which encompasses a lifetime's experience and a multitude of beliefs. It is both innate and learned. Those who get into trouble in places like Antarctica are those who allow themselves to fall back on a stringent system, either philosophical or physical. You must be willing to bend; you can't allow yourself to think for one moment that you are a "prisoner" of your "ideas." You can't allow nature, or an undertaking, to imprison you, no matter its rigors. You have to let your thoughts and your spirit help you through each day.

Tim seems to be doing better today. His appetite is strong, and I took him out of the team and trailed him from the back of the sled, out of the wind. He did fine until about three o'clock, when his legs began to give out. But we were in an area of rough terrain and it was impossible to add his weight to the sled, so I had to prod and encourage him to keep going. He made it through the day okay, and will sleep tonight in the sled bag. If we would just get a break in the weather, if the wind would just die down, he would be okay.

I now have three other dogs—Yeager, Hank and Ray—suffering from the same problem of exposed and frozen skin. I've tied them next to the sled for the night, to help shelter them from the wind. The extreme cold and wind compound the problem, preventing their getting a good night's rest. Just like humans, when they are under a lot of stress and sleeping uncomfortably in a wet and cold place, they are unable to revive their energy overnight. The next four or five days will tell how serious their self-inflicted injuries are.

As for poor Spinner, his penis started turning black yesterday. It is a very serious injury, the most serious we've had on the expedition so far. He definitely needs medical attention if and when we can fly him out of here, but that could be three weeks from now. Though we know it must hurt very much, he fools around with the other dogs and shows no expression of pain. Geoff has taken him out of harness and carries him lashed to the sled; as a result, his team has slowed down, though still in the lead position, which tends to slow the whole team down. The key to traveling with an injured dog is to try to keep him walking. It takes a big toll, adding that seventy to ninety extra pounds onto the sled in times like this when dogs and men are already stressed.

From Geoff's journal: "The dogs are seriously run down, and I am constantly worried about them. But the reality is there isn't much we can do. I build snow walls to protect them, only to come out the next morning to find them sleeping atop them. Keeping just one dog in the tent occupies a lot of space, though I have Spinner in the tent now, wrapped in a $500 DuPont coat, and it is a great burden for Keizo and me. But I am concerned every morning when I leave my tent that I will find a dead dog outside the door."

OCTOBER 17, DAY 83

When we broke camp this morning we were about eighty-five miles from Siple, four days' travel time if conditions remain as good as they were today. The weather finally gave us a break— a high of −30° with very little wind and perfect surface conditions. We traveled beneath daylong cloud cover, but visibility was good; we could see shadows and contrasts for the first time in many days. As we set up camp, after making twenty-three miles, the clouds cleared and the view south was spectacular. The pastels of August are long gone; ahead of us now is just big sky and big country, painted entirely in shades of blue and white.

Once again we stopped to try to make radio contact mid-

day, desperate to set up a rendezvous with the Twin Otter we
know is headed for Patriot Hills as soon as the weather coop-
erates. All we want is for the plane to touch down and pick up
our most ailing dogs, Tim and Spinner, then fly on. But when
Jean-Louis got through to Punta he was informed the plane
was still grounded at the British base of Rothera on Adelaide
Island, four hundred miles away, unable to take off because of
continued bad weather.

The blue sky filled me with optimism for the first time in
nearly six weeks; it has been that long since we saw clear skies.
All three teams literally stopped in place at one point and we
marveled at the beauty above. Hopefully it's an indication of
fair weather ahead; this rhythm, traveling twenty to twenty-
four miles a day, feels good, and we would like to keep it up.

Tonight as we set up camp—Dahe tending to the dogs, I
shoveling snow onto the ground flaps—I thought about the
irony of a forty-five-year-old man doing this as a "job." Most
men my age at this time of the day have just pulled off the
freeway, turned into the driveway and are readying for a cocktail, dinner and TV. Maybe they've been to the health club,
perhaps they're going out later to a community meeting or
planning on reading to their kids. And here I am, in unreal
cold, shoveling snow around the base of my little nylon shelter
that hopefully will protect me through the night. It is not
unlike many nights I've spent during the last thirty years, so
I'm not surprised by my situation. In fact, going back to my
childhood, none of what has befallen me in my life surprises
me. When I was young and people asked me what I wanted to
do when I grew up, I said that I wanted to be a pioneer, and I
think I've stayed true to that desire.

OCTOBER 20, DAY 86

Today as we closed in on Siple I clung to the back of my sled
and tried to keep my mind busy. I thought about how many

gallons of white gas we will need to reach Vostok and exactly how many boxes of dog and human food and air resupplies we will need to cross the area of inaccessibility. All day I ran numbers and weights through my mental calculator, adding and subtracting, over and over and over. I calculated that if we were to travel twenty miles every day, that would account for one half percent of the journey's total distance. Employing that math, by lunchtime each day we would cover one quarter percent of the traverse, then after lunch another quarter percent. I find my mind dropping into some pretty deep chasms for stimulation as one long day of skiing follows another.

We hope to find Siple by late in the day. We had been warned that the buildings of the base, closed for good in 1986, are completely covered and that we would be lucky to spot the antennae that still stand near its center. Such a sighting demands clear visibility, and when we left camp this morning it was cloudy and foggy. Finding Siple may prove doubly hard since for the past two days we've not been able to make radio contact; thus we don't know our exact longitude and latitude and have been traveling blind because of the featureless terrain for the last sixty miles, with no reference or land features to guide us. The only way we've been able to stay on any kind of direct course since Mt. Rex has been by a combination of Geoff's keeping very close track of our overall direction by compass and map and Jean-Louis's going back over past Argos reports.

Fortunately, as the afternoon progressed the cloud cover lifted and by five o'clock patches of blue sky shone above. We quit traveling at six, having already put in a good twenty-four miles, but still had not spotted Siple. That wasn't a good sign, since the skies were clear; there was a possibility that we were way off target. We decided to camp for the night, hoping we could make radio contact, establish our exact location, and then locate the cache first thing in the morning. But even as we began to set up camp, the ever persistent Jean-Louis balanced precariously on top of Geoff's sled and peered through binoculars, scanning the horizon for a hint of Siple's antennae. Back and forth. Back and forth. And sure enough, with the dogs already staked out and tents about to be set up, he spotted an antenna. We each took a peek to confirm what he saw. It was difficult to tell just how far away they were; we guessed three to five miles. By six-thirty we were packed up and moving.

As we closed in on the antennae (the base turned out to be 7.5 miles from where we'd spotted it) the skies cleared even more, revealing not only our cache spot but another glimpse of the true beauty of Antarctica's interior. It was crystal cold, −45°, but the air felt charged with something new, a fresh, clean pressure system that seemed to carry the promise of clearer, calmer days ahead.

Prior to its closing, Siple was one of the United States's four year-round Antarctic bases, and the most remote. But despite the station's importance for the study of the magnetosphere (the area in space affected by Earth's magnetic field), supply problems had made the base impractical, and costly, to maintain. To fly supplies and men from McMurdo, aboard LC-130R Hercules ski transports, required the giant planes to carry so much fuel that their payloads were severely limited. Since Siple's closing there has been talk of building a Soviet-U.S. base in the same region, one that could be supplied from the Soviet base of Russkaya Station on the Sulzberger Coast, six hundred miles west of McMurdo. But so far that is just talk.

Of all our caches, this site proved the most intriguing, simply because there were signs of man. The research done at Siple involved measuring radio waves, and long antennae snaked along the ground for miles. As we approached we could barely make out the main building under a sizable hump of snow, and then we stumbled across a smaller, partially exposed building, with a hatch visible above the snow.

It took us about five minutes to shovel away the snow, open the hatch, and climb down into the pitch-black. I went first, the ladder breaking in my hands as I descended, filled with the hope that below lay some history. It felt as if we were climbing down into one of Scott's long-buried huts. Instead, when I switched on my headlamp, I saw mirrors, a sink and stalls. We'd come down into one of Siple's bathrooms. We explored the twenty-five-by-twenty-five-foot cave and found a small kitchen, boasting electric and oil stoves, some frozen jelly and copies of *Playboy* and *Penthouse* from 1986.

As it turned out, we were fortunate that Jean-Louis spotted Siple when he did, because we were unable to make radio contact. Due to our late arrival we didn't fall into our sleeping bags until one o'clock in the morning and though exhausted I had a hard time falling asleep; it had been a good travel day and we had reached one of the expedition's first big landmarks. From here we will travel nearly due south to the Pole and each day distance ourselves from the sea, which should mean less unpredictable weather. As we close in on the Ellsworth Mountains we should see clearer, calmer days.

OCTOBER 22, DAY 88

So much for escaping the "unpredictable" weather. After last night's clear skies, which were a help in digging the cache out from beneath twelve feet of snow, another storm is percolating this morning. Winds are thirty miles per hour from the north, temperature is −20°, visibility 150 feet. While I voted to travel since the wind is at our backs, the consensus was that we should sit a day and wait out this storm. We deserved a rest, since we'd taken only one day off in the past seventeen.

Inside our tents it was a miserable, wet day. But the worst blow of the expedition came when I ventured out to feed the dogs at eleven o'clock. Tim was dead.

I had known he was in bad shape these past two weeks, and we had tried desperately to get a plane in to take him out. Yesterday it was sunny, and he seemed to rebound a little, his black fur absorbing the sun's heat as he lay on a rubber mat we'd found in the abandoned building. Rather than put him in the sled bag last night, I had left him lying on that warm black mat. We had twenty-four-hour sun, and it was clear and calm when we went to bed. No one expected the blizzard that blew up overnight, but it had killed him. At some point he must have left the mat, which was quickly covered with snow, and he had nowhere warm to lie down. He had been dead three or four hours when I found him, and it was a pitiful sight. He was such a tough dog, one of the strongest I've ever known, and he died a harsh, undignified death. Looking at him I knew I never wanted to die in the cold.

Tim was one of my favorite, most experienced dogs; he'd been to the North Pole and was one of our lead dogs across Greenland. Recalling his lineage brings back a swell of memories. His mother, Snowshoe, was a wolf, and his father was Goliath, a brother of Hank and Yeager's.

In the summer of 1985 I borrowed Snowshoe for breeding from my old friend Lloyd Gilbertson, who lived on Lake Superior, sixty miles from Ely, Minnesota, my home. I drove over in my gold 1970 Cadillac. It was the first car I'd owned in fourteen years, and its condition was indicative of the style of my existence in those days. The heater refused to turn off and the gas tank had a leak, sizable enough that it required I drive as fast as I could between Lloyd's and the Homestead so that a tankful of gas wouldn't leak out on the road.

With Snowshoe sleeping peacefully in the backseat and only the driver's window half cracked, despite the 90° heat and constantly running heater, I was headed along Highway 1 when somehow the dog managed to shoot over my head and out the window. I saw her in the rearview mirror as she hit the ground, rolled and headed into the deep woods. This was big trouble, because she was one of Lloyd's best dogs.

I screeched to a halt and looked for her for several hours, without any luck. I ran ads in the local paper and over the radio, beseeching someone to bring me Snowshoe if they had found her. After a week of worrying, both Lloyd and I had nearly given up hope that Snowshoe would be found. Then one day I spotted a canoe coming across the lake below my cabin, and in it stood Snowshoe. The paddler was a wolf trapper who worked for the forestry department; he'd found her in one of his traps four miles from where she'd escaped.

I nursed Snowshoe back to health, keeping her near my cabin and soaking her injured leg three times a day. That fall I bred her with Goliath, who was one-quarter wolf, and Tim was one of the four in the litter. Half wolf by breed, he was shy but stoked by a wild streak, which I quickly identified and admired. To encourage his socialization, when he was three months old I lent him for two months to a student at Ashland College, where he was carried from class to class. That experience cured him for good of his instinctual distrust of people, yet he remained a one-master dog and was always protective of his team, his sled and me. Strong and black-coated, he outpulled dogs much larger than his seventy pounds and he could be ferocious in a fight, whether it was with one dog or ten.

Perhaps Tim's moment in the sun came at the North Pole; he was one of twenty dogs to make the complete journey. A camera crew and reporter from "Good Morning America" had flown to the Pole to interview the team shortly after we arrived, and while they worked they left a microphone dressed by a fur windshield lying on the snow. While I talked to the reporter, Tim ate the microphone, cover and all.

I went tent to tent and reported the news of Tim's death and everyone was saddened. Victor nearly cried, Geoff was stunned into silence (and as a result would carry Spinner on his sled for the next two hundred miles). Jean-Louis was convinced it was an omen, and not a particularly good one.

Tim's death adds another sour note to the expedition; there seems to be no end to the hardship. By day's end the wind has shifted to the south and is blowing directly into our faces at twenty miles per hour. But we must travel tomorrow; we have to get out of here, distance ourselves from this place. Siple has lost its charm, its specialness; for me it will always carry the memory of losing Tim. His death has affected me more than I would have expected. I feel today that it will take a superhuman effort to keep this expedition going.

OCTOBER 23, DAY 89

For me, today was the worst of the expedition. We woke to tent walls blanketed by cold, dripping frost; turning up the heat just made it wetter. As we traveled I pulled my face mask up and my hat down so that just a sliver was exposed for my right eye to peek out. My sunglasses were in a pocket under my windsuit, but the zipper of my parka was frozen shut and I couldn't get to them. It was so cold I could barely get my hands out of my gloves to make even minor adjustments to my clothing. Keizo had only one word for this kind of day: "*Semite*," he muttered when he emerged from his tent, which means "touching the ice."

I carried Tim's body on the front of my sled and dropped him off a mile beyond Siple. I tried not to think about him as I sledded away, my mind blank and spiritless. His death hasn't diminished my hopes for the success of the trip, but my desire was jolted when I found him. Life seems to have less meaning in times like these, though I know that with time, some clear weather, and a change of scenery my spirit will bounce back. At least it wasn't one of my teammates we were leaving behind.

By five-thirty the wind picked up, and by six o'clock the windchills were at the limit of what a warm-blooded creature can stand. Any exposed skin on our faces—cheeks, nose, chin —froze. Some of us had previous frostbite on our faces that had been healing but now, painfully, froze again. I'd never experienced cold like this. We had expected good weather to come after we topped the Weyerhaeuser Glacier, but it hadn't. Then we expected it to clear up after 73° latitude, then 74°, but it did not. Now it was the worst.

Tonight perhaps even more than ever our biggest concern

is for the dogs. In my mind I couldn't erase the image of dogs
dropping like flies in this cold. Ray is now in the worst shape,
and Hank isn't much better, the skin on the inside of their legs
raw and exposed. As we huddle inside our tents, the winds are
blowing a steady fifty miles per hour and the temperature is
–43°. Cruel, brutal conditions. We have had no radio contact
for four days, so there is no hope of getting a plane in to take
the injured dogs out. The only thing we can do is keep traveling.

Before we came south I was asked often how this trip would
compare to our 1986 run to the North Pole. In many ways
they can't be compared. The North Pole was intensely difficult, cold, concentrated. The difficulty of this expedition is its
length. Here I keep repeating to myself "Next week we'll get a
break," but next week just brings more of the same, and worse.
I've never felt this low on any expedition. No one's talking
about quitting, at least out loud, but sometimes you can't help
but consider it. The dogs are nearing the limit of suffering
they can withstand. Even our "home" is conspiring against us.
Two of its poles are broken, so it sags in the back; inside it is
wet and crowded. Pools of water collect on the roof, and then
leak and drip on top of us and everything inside. We are tired,
wet, cold, miserable.

From Keizo's journal: "We talked tonight about Robert
Scott, comparing these conditions to what he traveled through
in his last days. They are very similar, though we are in colder
weather. I remember one of Scott's team members, a very
strong man, a small guy, but tough [Edward Wilson]. He carried two sleeping bags with him that trip. The one he slept in
was very wet and frozen, and he saved the other, fresh, for
emergency. Near the end he gave his clean, dry sleeping bag to
his teammate Oates, who was very weak and near death. I
think often about him giving his sleeping bag to the weaker
man. That was especially hard for me to believe, now having
seen these conditions. I don't know if I were in the same situa-

tion—with a fresh sleeping bag—if I could give it up. In these conditions a dry sleeping bag may mean your life. These are the kinds of thoughts you have late at night, in a wet, cold tent, trying desperately to fall asleep."

OCTOBER 24, DAY 90

Overnight the sleds froze solid beneath hard-packed snow, and this morning we dug them out in a –100° windchill. Our tents are half covered and the weather is a repeat of yesterday, but even colder. Fortunately as we traveled, Antarctica smiled upon us. Visibility improved and by lunch the winds had dropped from twenty-five miles per hour to ten, and the temperature warmed to –40°. Unbelievably, by six o'clock the wind had stopped completely. It was eerie, like a dream, as if we had taken a wrong turn and ascended to some kind of heaven. I took my parka hood down, and for the first time in two weeks could actually look around and see the entirety of the landscape we were traveling across. It was so comfortable that I almost didn't want to go inside the tent. I took my wind clothing off outside and brushed the ice from it, then removed my pile jacket, which was also coated with snow, and brushed it. The dogs, warmed by the heat of the sun, rolled luxuriously on the snow. Tim would have loved this day.

The Ellsworths are our next big milestone, and we will follow the range its full 250-mile length, which will bring us to about 80 1/2° latitude. From there it is a straight 700 miles to the South Pole. This range is the most dominant land feature in Antarctica, and its peaks the highest, starring Mt. Vinson, or Vinson Massif, at 16,066 feet. For us they are another gateway to a trio of anticipations: the Antarctic Plateau, better weather, and the one-third mark. For the next few days they will spread out in front of us, and then behind. At the end of the range is Patriot Hills, where we will stop for two days' rest.

Once again Antarctica has proven quite a paradox. A killer

one day, dreamscape the next. When I finally did crawl inside the tent, I was overwhelmed by thoughts of spring. But we must be careful not to get lulled into a false sense of security, since we are still in a storm zone. Dahc dug his five-foot-deep snow pit this evening and showed us that historically this is an area of very high accumulation and strong wind. The odds favor more cold, violent weather ahead. For the fifth day in a row, we were unable to make radio contact. We are three hundred miles behind schedule, and not sure exactly where we are.

OCTOBER 26, DAY 92

We now have round-the-clock sunlight, which should help improve visibility. In fact, this morning we can see the northern reaches of the Ellsworth Mountains, fifty miles to the south. It's been weeks since we've had that kind of clarity.

Unfortunately, I wrenched my back severely yesterday, which is going to make traveling difficult for me, if not impossible. It happened sometime yesterday afternoon when visibility was still low and we were cutting at awkward angles across hard-packed, icy sastrugi. Dozens of times my ski tips rammed into the far face of a drift, and I barely kept my balance. Another half-dozen times I was not so lucky and fell, one ski flying up in the air, the other beneath the sled's runner.

The pain didn't surface until I was shoveling snow around the tent last night, when it shot through the lower left side of my back, well below kidney level. I couldn't straighten or maneuver and could just barely stay on my feet long enough to crawl into the tent. Brushing off was a mammoth task and undressing nearly impossible. All I could think was that if this was a serious injury, my trip was over. It's bad enough that the weather continues to conspire against us, but traveling with this kind of injury would be inconceivable.

I managed to sleep, on my back, and during the night a storm blew up and I crossed my fingers that we would have a day off so I could spend it recuperating. But Victor's morning weather report indicated that it was clearing above, so we would travel. I didn't know if I could even get out of the tent, and I tossed around options in my head. I could ride on the sled, but the pounding of the sled over the hard snow would be even more painful than trying to ski. Skiing is out of the question, far too painful. Over nearly fifteen thousand miles of dogsledding, I've never hurt myself this badly. Thankfully it didn't feel as if I'd damaged my spine. The idea of flying out crossed my mind, but I prayed that wouldn't be necessary.

Though I'd kept the injury to myself the night before, I had to tell the others this morning, and so we delayed our start. Jean-Louis—Dr. Etienne—came into my tent to see if he could recommend any medicinal help, armed with his usual remedy for everything, an oversize bottle of aspirin. Somehow it helped just to talk with him, and relax.

We are all very comfortable being far away from the rest of the world; that kind of isolation doesn't bother us. But we have been extremely isolated these past weeks, even from one another. That is a problem. If we can talk every day, we can draw strength from the others in moments of weakness or doubt, but even that hasn't been possible of late. So this morning it was good to talk alone with Jean-Louis about the difficulties we'd survived so far.

We share a special bond, primarily because we have endured together the pressures and responsibilities of organizing the expedition. We were responsible for raising the money, coordinating the logistics, acting as liaisons with the various governments and contractors, dealing with the press and ultimately accepting the failure and disappointment of everyone if we don't make it. We put on the show and ultimately accept responsibility for everything. The stress of those pressures alone could result in or encourage injury.

I finally decided I should try to travel, by walking rather than skiing alongside my sled. We left camp at ten and despite my limping made twenty miles. Before I went to sleep Dahe gave me some Chinese medicine for my back, a six-inch-square gauze patch laden with natural healing agents. When he peeled the plastic away from one side, it revealed a black sticky potion of herbs, snake skin and crushed bones (Dahe explained). He warmed it in his hands and then over the flame of the stove before slapping it on my aching back for five minutes. It seemed to help right away and I slept comfortably.

From Jean-Louis's journal: "Will is fragile and generous. He can convince people to work together, and he has the appetite to commit to long, hard jobs. But we are very different in that he keeps everything inside. This morning he asked if I could visit him in his tent, he said he had hurt his back. I of course said yes, but I realized soon that the problem was not his back. He was devastated by what had happened to Tim. So we spent one hour together, talking and sometimes crying. It was good, and affirmed our friendship and our desire to continue.

"Our talk reconfirmed though that Will is the most determined of us all. I think he would survive the longest of any of us, he of all of us would be the man to survive, to walk the last step across Antarctica."

OCTOBER 29, DAY 95

The gods of Antarctica continue to smile on us. Yesterday the temperatures soared to 10°; today it was calm and −5°. The sun had considerable heat to it by the time we left our tents this morning, and by ten o'clock we had our wind parkas off, traveling in just pile jackets and stretch fleece. It was the first time in the expedition I felt the warmth of the sun through my clothing; it was like the first day of spring after a long winter, a reprieve for us from the nightmare of the previous days.

The Ellsworth Mountains now surround us. It is a range similar in appearance to the Brooks Range in Alaska, which I'd crossed in 1983 with Bob Mantell; continuous peaks featuring two- to three-thousand-foot rock faces connected by rolling hills. It is a strange and magical view, and for the first time since we arrived in Antarctica these mountains do not appear threatening. Until now, though I could see the beauty of the mountains we had passed and crossed, I was so distrustful of the weather they hid that I didn't enjoy looking at them. Today for the first time I allowed myself to drink in some of the seventh continent's truest beauties.

The only distraction on an otherwise perfect day was that we were skiing across four-foot-deep sastrugi, frozen waves of ice that swallow dogs, sleds and men as we climb to their peaks, then drop to their valleys. They are the biggest I've ever seen, and we slipped, slid and rolled through them all day. It is hard work because you are constantly pushing the sleds uphill and then balancing them on top so that they don't slide sideways, which could easily snap their runners.

Our cache at Fisher Nunatak is twelve miles from where we camped last night, and it should be easy to find. The mountain the cache site is named for sits isolated ahead of us, a beautiful pyramid-shaped peak thrust proudly into the blue. To reach the cache we must sled completely around the base of the mountain and into a four-hundred-foot-deep pit on its southern exposure, a cavity hollowed out by the wind.

It turned out we were lucky to find the cache; only two and a half feet of its nine-foot marker were visible above the snow, and surrounding it were ten-foot drifts. Once again Adventure Network had picked a poor location, an area of obvious accumulation. It would have been very easy to have lost this cache, and then, despite the beauty around us, we'd have been in big trouble.

We located the cache at twelve-thirty, and as we dug it out from underneath the hard-packed snow we stripped to our long underwear tops in the sunny near-zero calm. Taking full advantage of the balmy conditions we stretched our sleeping bags out across the sleds and draped our clothing across ski poles and handlebars, turning the scene into the appearance of Antarctica's first-ever rummage sale.

The three hours we were at the cache site were the first in a hundred days that we were able to totally drop our guard and relax. The dogs stretched out like fur rugs on the snow, rolling and napping in the sun. Even hounds like Hank, Yeager and Panda, who are always on edge, ready to growl and snap at their neighbor at the slightest provocation, mellowed here and crashed in the sun on their backs, their legs splayed as if someone had pumped them full of anesthesia. This is exactly what they needed; a rest, some warmth and a good feed.

As we unpacked the cache some heavy East-West trading was conducted, as it always was on such occasions if temperatures allowed. Sardines have turned into one of the expedition's major currencies. Victor, Dahe and Jean-Louis favor them and the rest of us trade ours for brown sugar, toilet paper and fruit and nut bars. I try to trade for as much soup mix as I can get my hands on, since I use it in just about everything as a spice. The others covet my granola and organic bread, so bartering is fast and furious.

The only minor problem of the rest stop involved Dahe's sleeping bag. He stretched it across Geoff's sled to dry, and when our backs were turned Hank peed all over it, then lay on it. That is so typical of Hank; he can be such a jerk. As soon as Dahe told me what happened, I knew it was Hank. Dahe was understandably angry and shouted at Hank in a language we could not literally understand but emotionally followed word for word.

Having now shared a tent with Dahe for almost four weeks, our understanding of each other is improving each day. I try to let him do most of the talking, listening to tales of his previous scientific forays, his life in China, and his dreams of what the future there holds for him. His hope is to continue to do field research until he is fifty (another eight years), then go back to the Lanzhou Institute in his hometown for good, to teach Quaternary geology, a study of the most recent ice age. He has led a fascinating life: his scientific work has allowed him to travel all over the world, including two stints in Antarctica; it also led to him and his wife (who is a physician) being branded "intellectuals" and banished to the rice paddies during the Cultural Revolution of the early 1970s.

Despite our initial concerns Dahe has become a competent skier ("the best in China," he jokes) and can handle a dog team when necessary. Still, in crevassed areas or blowing conditions Geoff yells at Dahe (as he would an errant dog) to stay tethered to his sled. Our concern for him increases during whiteouts, because his Coke-bottle-thick glasses are easily fogged. In many ways even he admits he is a stereotypical "scientist."

Like Victor, Dahe was chosen for the expedition by his government. When we set off for our training mission across Greenland we intended for our sixth team member to be Martyn Williams, one of Adventure Network's cofounders. But he missed the Greenland training mission, and afterward we mutually agreed he should devote his energies to his business. Also, upon our return from Greenland, Jean-Louis found waiting a response to a letter he'd sent to Beijing in January 1988 inquiring about the possibility of our including a Chinese teammate on the expedition.

Jean-Louis went to Beijing and was told by the Chinese government that while they could give us no monetary support, we could use their base on King George as a staging ground and they would be happy to provide us with an experienced teammate. We were ecstatic about their offer for many reasons, but particularly because one quarter of the world's population is Chinese. If we hoped that Trans-Antarctica would help introduce people to Antarctica, then gaining access to China's huge population by including a Chinese team member was incredible good fortune.

Dahe was not the first "candidate" presented. The first was an engineer who'd spent two years at China's Great Wall Station on King George Island; the second a thirty-three-year-old maritime physics expert who had also been based at Great

Wall. But those "nominations" were reversed soon after we learned of them, because, according to the Chinese national committee, both men became "sick." On December 20, 1988, a telex arrived from Beijing informing us that in fact our teammate would instead be Professor Qin Dahe, a forty-two-year-old glaciologist who had been to Antarctica twice, first with an Australian team based at their Casey Station in 1985–86, then as base manager of the Great Wall Station in 1987–88. Our suspicion, later confirmed by Dahe, was that the committee was torn between sending a "strong boy" (an athlete) and a scientist. They finally decided upon Dahe.

His full title at home at the Lanzhou Institute of Glaciology and Geocryology is vice-chief of the Division of Applied Physics in Snow and Ice, vice-chief of the Division of Polar Glaciology. Married and the father of a son, Dahe was born into an "intellectual" family; his father is a veterinarian. In 1972 Dahe and his wife were sent to the rice paddies, where they worked side by side with the peasants for a year and a half. The peasants were amazed at Dahe's strength, as well as the number of bowls of rice he could down each night.

Dahe told us at length, in broken but improving English, of how he came to be "nominated" to join Trans-Antarctica. In April 1988 he was working at Great Wall when a friend called from China and mentioned that the government was looking for a candidate to join a "dogsled" expedition. "I felt even though I could not ski that I was the only Chinese qualified," Dahe insisted. "I had learned English working with the Australians, so in November I wrote to Jean-Louis, detailing my qualifications. First, I was a glaciologist, an iceman. Second, I already had experience on the interior of Antarctica. Third, I was used to conducting my scientific work at high elevations, having spent many months climbing and digging in the Himalayas. My last reason was that my health was good, I am strong. The only thing against me was I could not ski.

"Many people in China wanted this position, and I was

number two or three. Fortunately I was chosen. That the others were sick was very bad for them, very good for me."

The only opposition to Dahe's participation came from his wife. They had met in elementary school, married young, and he had already been gone for many years of their marriage pursuing his studies of ice and rock around the globe. While she understood how important his career was to him (and what a stepping-stone being a member of a successful expedition could be), it was hard for her at home alone raising their son, who was in the midst of preparing for college exams, perhaps a young Chinese man's greatest test. "In the past ten years we have been separated many times," Dahe admitted to me one night before coming to Antarctica. "So when she heard that I was interested in this expedition she said no, it was not permitted. But I talked to her and explained why I must go. I sent friends to talk to her. Yet even when a letter from the national committee arrived at our house saying I had been selected, she said no."

She went as far as to call the committee and ask that Dahe's selection be rescinded, but her plea fell on deaf ears. Dahe came home from Antarctica, spent ten days with her and their son, then came to the Homestead. He returned for a visit shortly before we left for Antarctica, and while he was there, tragically, his wife was in a serious car accident and broke her back. Dahe was in torment and considered quitting the expedition in order to stay home to help his wife recuperate. Just weeks before we were to depart, assured that his wife would be able to walk again, he decided to join us. "In important times she always stands by me," explained Dahe, "she understands. If I were my wife, I'm not sure I would. . . ."

But Dahe's membership on the team was threatened right up to the time we departed, for another reason. There was some concern among us about including a Chinese on the team in the wake of the Tiananmen Square massacres. Jean-Louis wanted to issue a statement, signed by Dahe, critical of the crackdown in Beijing. From China, Dahe informed us he could never sign any such letter and that if he did he would not be allowed to leave his homeland. It was a very uncomfortable situation and when we tried to debate with Dahe over our concerns, he would smile and imply there was no way we could understand the complexities of the situation in Beijing. Ultimately the decision was made to keep him on the team, as an example of international cooperation and the importance of democratic decision making in all walks of life.

His face masked in concern, Jean-Louis came to our tent after finally making radio contact with Punta Arenas for the first time in nine days. His conversation with Criquet had been spent mostly talking about the concerns of the Soviets, who were readying to serve as our suppliers and guardians once we passed the South Pole. Apparently, Arkady Sosnikov, the head of the Soviet Arctic and Antarctic Research Institute, was very concerned about our tardy progress and had informed Cathy deMoll, our business manager, that if we weren't at Vostok by January 10 he would insist that we ride the eight hundred miles from Vostok to Mirnyy aboard a Soviet tractor-train. The Soviets apparently felt that since we were going to be under their watch during that stretch, they didn't want us to get into trouble in East Antarctica and were going to demand we take the "safest" way to Mirnyy.

Jean-Louis and I were miffed, and surmised that Arkady was mistakenly equating our traveling abilities over the next three months with the preceding three, which we knew was an unfair comparison. We knew that with clearer skies and less snow we would start averaging twenty-five miles a day, and we estimated arriving at Vostok around January 25, plenty of time to be at Mirnyy by March 1.

But Arkady's concern brought up the issue of exactly what role the Soviets' trax would play once we reached Vostok. As we understood it, their intention was to rumble ahead of us by fifty to two hundred miles as they returned along their regular route from Vostok to Mirnyy, caching our supplies along the way. As far as I was concerned that was the only help they needed to provide us; they were essentially replacing the Twin Otters, which were able to supply us and serve as rescue backup only until Vostok. I told Jean-Louis that under no circumstance would I be willing to ride the trax, but that if severe weather threatened the dogs' lives, I might agree to send them out via trax. My rationale was simple. We had been risking our lives out here these past three months, rationing our food and equipment, pinching our whole lives down to the barest essentials, moving ahead. Now some Russian bureaucrat in Moscow was trying to dictate our schedule for us. As far as I was concerned, if we rode the trax the expedition was a failure.

Jean-Louis had also fleshed out in his conversation with Criquet another concern on the outside. Apparently the Frenchmen in Punta Arenas were worried that once we got word of the Soviets' January 10 deadline, we might decide to change our route and head from the South Pole to the U.S. base of McMurdo, skipping the area of inaccessibility, Vostok and Mirnyy altogether. But there was no way we would consider McMurdo—we had never even talked about it—it was a scenario dreamed up by our helpers. First, we had had a lot of help and cooperation from the Soviets. If we went to McMurdo, that would cut their role in the expedition down to little more than a supply deliverer, which would hardly be fair. Second, if we went to McMurdo we would have to deal with the NSF-administered base there, and we knew they would not give us much cooperation. We certainly did not want to have to ask them for help getting off the continent. Last, we had been saying for three years that we were going to make the longest possible traverse, and it was far too late to go back on that pledge.

Long after Jean-Louis had returned to his tent, I pondered the concerns of our friends back home. They must not realize that one of the reasons our mileage has been slow these first three months is the storms and low visibility. Once past Vostok the wind will be at our backs all the way to the Indian Ocean.

As for the cold weather we expect near Vostok, it can't be much worse than what we've just come through. I'm still confident we can make Mirnyy, our way. There is no way, if we reach Vostok, that I'm going off this continent under any power but my own two feet.

OCTOBER 31, DAY 97

We made twenty-three miles under clear skies today and camped at the base of Mt. Vinson, Antarctica's tallest mountain. We are starting to average twenty miles per day, and if we stretch our days, by sledding ten rather than eight hours, we should begin to make up the miles we've fallen behind.

MILES TRAVELED: 1,142

MILES TO THE SOUTH POLE: 855

Three sleds, pulled by thirty-six specially bred polar huskies, transported our international team of six across Antarctica.
Will Steger

On December 11, 1989, our Trans-Antarctica team became the first since 1912 to dogsled to the South Pole, covering nearly two thousand miles in 138 days. *From left:* Qin Dahe (People's Republic of China), Keizo Funatsu (Japan), me, Jean-Louis Etienne (France), Victor Boyarsky (Soviet Union), Geoff Somers (Great Britain). *Gordon Wiltsie*

Handmade of pine and ash, and modeled after the sleds of the turn-of-the-century explorers, our sleds needed to be sturdy enough to carry a thousand pounds of gear, yet flexible enough to glide over the rolling waves of ice that confronted us at nearly every step. *Will Steger*

Our team—men and dogs—were forced to travel no matter the conditions. Temperatures dropped to −60°, winds raced over one hundred miles per hour. At night, the men huddled in nylon tents; the dogs allowed themselves to be buried by whipping snow (they stayed warm as long as they didn't move until the next morning). *Will Steger*

Along the first leg of the trip, down the eight-hundred-mile-long Antarctic Peninsula, hidden crevasses were a constant danger. Many times dogs harnessed to the sleds broke through a thin crust of snow and fell into the dark holes, which could drop one hundred feet or more. Rescuing them was a challenge, but ultimately no dogs were lost to crevasses. *Will Steger*

Though crowded and damp, tent life offered a relief from the hardship of the day. Here Victor, the team's meteorologist, adds to his records. *Gordon Wiltsie*

Communication with the outside world was difficult and infrequent. Jean-Louis was responsible for attempts at raising radio contact at various Antarctic bases or the team's base camp at Punta Arenas, Chile. *Rick Ridgeway*

Several scientific studies were conducted during the crossing. Here, glaciologist Dahe conducts a sampling of the ice in the area of inaccessibility, aided by his teammates. The samples—which he collected every thirty miles—provide a history of pollution in Antarctica's atmosphere. *Will Steger*

Past the South Pole, in the vast area of inaccessibility known for its distance from all coasts and its lack of landmarks, the team built six-foot-tall snow cairns every two miles. In case rescue was necessary, a plane could find the team by following the shadows cast by the cairns. *Will Steger*

Each morning, no matter the cold or wind, Victor braced himself for the day with a quick but thorough "bath" in the snow. *Per Breiehagen*

Often, we felt as if we were traveling across another planet. Many days were spent in whiteouts, with visibility less than fifty feet. Sleds were separated by curtains of blowing snow and it could take hours for one of us to find the sled team ahead of him—even though it was only one hundred feet away. *Keizo Funatsu*

To keep our fragile homes from blowing away during storms, one chore each night was to heap snow on the tents' ground flaps. In raging storms, snow would blow from the shovel before it could be strategically placed. *Will Steger*

Lunch was often the cruelest part of the day, given the cold and wet conditions. Everything—nuts, chocolate, granola bars— had to be thawed in thermos cups of hot water to prevent teeth from cracking on the frozen food. *Will Steger*

"Sometimes it is like Antarctica has no soul, . . . is not a place for man," said Jean-Louis one day in the middle of our journey. "But other times, when you have a very nice sky like today, . . . I feel like I am in a big, wondrous temple." *Will Steger*

The Soviets at their base of Mirnyy fashioned a grand welcome for the team when we finished our 3,741-mile crossing on March 3, 1990. Trans-Antarctica's successes were many; it was the first time the continent had been crossed on foot and it served as a blueprint for international cooperation. *Per Breiehagen*

Jean-Louis and I turned our dreams—about adventure and cooperation, about preservation and the environment—into realities. *Per Breiehagen*

One of our goals from the beginning was to emerge from Antarctica as a team, as friends. At the end I looked around at my five teammates and realized we'd been successful. *Will Steger*

NOVEMBER

QUITTING IS
NOT AN OPTION

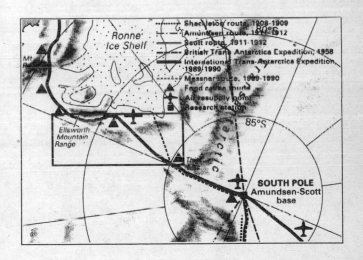

NOVEMBER 1, DAY 98

For the past two days we've been paralleling the tallest mountains in Antarctica; thirteen- to fourteen-thousand-foot brutes with walls of rock and ice scaling their surface. Today we had a splendid view of a handful of the Ellsworths' most majestic peaks—Vinson, Tyree, Anderson, Hubley, Dawson. We were fortunate to snare the view when we did, because as we traveled on we descended into a thick bank of fog and dropped more than a thousand feet during the day cloaked in a wet blanket of haze.

As we descended, a thick layer of hoarfrost covered the ground, making travel slow and treacherous. Our sleds were braked the length of the eight-mile descent. Just before lunch Victor, on point as usual, made a very steep descent without signaling to Keizo, who was right behind him, of what was to come. As a result, Keizo and his sled raced down the five-hundred-foot slope and both flipped at the bottom. Bags were scattered, dogs were howling, Keizo was angry, and the previously split runner on his sled was broken again. Thankfully, due to experience we've gotten adept at such repairs, and we lashed the runner back into working order and were off in less than an hour.

We made camp after twenty-one miles and, since we have just three days' worth of white gas left, made a quick dinner and crawled into our sleeping bags to preserve our dwindling supply. It had been a mistake to leave two thirds of our gas cache, ten gallons, behind at Fisher. We thought at the time that the film crew was going to drop in on us before we arrived at Patriot Hills, bringing more. But they are still stuck in

Punta Arenas awaiting Adventure Network's repair of their troubled DC-6; as a result we are low on gas, without promise of more until we reach Patriot Hills.

In conditions like these gas is as critical as food, integral to our heat and water supply. Each night we cut eight-inch-square blocks of snow to boil for our evening meal, breakfast and the next day's thermoses. We bring a nylon bag filled with two dozen snow blocks into the tent before zipping up for the night and then wedge them one at a time into the nine-inch opening of the ever present aluminum teapot that dominates the center of our tent. Every day we spend four hours melting snow and ice, which makes me long for the faucets we so take for granted back home. As well as time, though, this process demands fuel. One quart of white gas is needed to produce three gallons of water; on average we make at least two gallons a night and another one and a half gallons in the morning. The temperature inside our tents ranges from 0° to 40°, from the tent floor to its ceiling, but the melting procedure robs heat, with its focus on melting not heating. Every night we look forward to the melting process's ending so that the stove can devote full attention to warming us. Even then it is never too warm inside; a spilled drop of water on the tent floor usually freezes on contact.

The worst part of gas rationing is that it affects our drying process. As a result of the shortage we are crawling into slightly damp clothes in the morning, which makes for colder days, more fitful sleeps and all-around miserableness. To help stave off the dampness, we have a new member in our tent, an MSR stove we are using to burn the bad gas that Adventure Network planted in the caches. Geoff has been lugging along three gallons of it for just such an emergency, and now Dahe and I are using the Coleman stove and white gas for cooking and the MSR and black gas for heat. Though the black fumes the MSR spews are nasty, the heat the little stove provides is welcome.

NOVEMBER 2, DAY 99

We were delayed slightly this morning while we debated our route. We are aiming for a narrow pass that will take us twenty miles to the southwest, and there was a disagreement between Geoff and Jean-Louis on which of two paths ahead would be our quickest course. Once on our way (Geoff and his sextant prevailed) we traveled fast over smooth surfaces, in −20° temperature and winds in our faces at ten miles per hour. By ten o'clock the skies had cleared a bit and the unequivocal route to the corridor we sought lay straight ahead. The soft lighting made for spectacular traveling: a five-hundred-foot curtain of ice rose to our left, and the base of Mt. Vinson spread to our right. Once through this pass, we would start heading directly south, toward Patriot Hills.

I spent most of the day at the rear of the pack, skiing alongside my sled by myself, my usual position. Even in the best conditions traveling by dogsled is quite an isolated life; here that isolation is compounded by the international makeup of the team. It is hard enough traveling and communicating in cold weather if you speak the same language as your partners. Here, with Victor, Dahe and Keizo still struggling with English, it is often hard to have much of a conversation. Often body language and grunts of approval are our best forms of communicating. At lunch we are split into two groups of three, and lately I have been spending mine with Geoff and Dahe, the quieter group. In the tent at night, conversation between Dahe and me is spare, made even more difficult by the drape of clothing hung to dry between us. When we do talk I must speak very slowly and directly; as a result often we find it easier to be silent.

So I was glad when Geoff dropped back and rode with my sled for a few hours this afternoon. It was the first in many days that either of us had been able to talk back and forth in clear, unadulterated English. Still, conversations on the back of a jouncing sled are always truncated. At least with Geoff we can mumble and still grasp each other's intent. It is a relief especially to be able to share a joke, which because of the multicultural background of the team can be difficult. Little puns spun back home without thinking are often misinterpreted in this setting. Slang and colloquialisms often require definition. Subtle humor is a lost cause. The six of us laugh together often, but more likely over the day's actions, not words.

Our nine-hour-a-day travel pace is perfect right now, for both dogs and men. We are getting plenty of rest, resulting in maximum energy and efficiency, which is the only way we are able to keep up this day-after-day-after-day cadence. If we were to travel just one more hour a day, both we and the dogs would tire more quickly and be forced to rest more often, ultimately delaying our progress to a degree where we probably wouldn't make it to Mirnyy. Establishing a steady rhythm is essential.

I thought a lot today about pacing, prompted by thoughts of Reinhold Messner, the Austrian-born mountain climber who will soon begin his attempt to ski and man-haul across an eighteen-hundred-mile section of Antarctica. While he is perhaps the world's best climber, accustomed to storming a mountain, often without carrying spare oxygen, I am curious how he will adjust to having to pace himself over what will be a one-hundred-plus-day march. Because this kind of travel demands a steady rhythm, he faces the possibility of burning himself out. I wonder if he knows his own limits. I'm sure he's in excellent shape, but from what we hear—since Adventure Network has yet to drop him at his starting point—he's already behind schedule.

If anyone can accomplish the man-haul, Messner (and partner Arved Fuchs, a veteran German polar explorer) probably can. The first man to successfully climb all of the world's fourteen tallest peaks, each taller than twenty-six thousand feet, he is held in high esteem by mountaineers around the globe. At forty-five, my age too, he has led quite an adventuresome life.

He lives in a castle outside Juval, Italy; has lost two of his brothers in mountain climbing accidents, as well as eight of his toes to frostbite; and has documented his travails in two dozen books. He has more high-altitude experience than any climber alive. But by tackling the flat plains of Antarctica he has entered a new realm. His plan to ski from the edge of the Ronne/Filchner Ice Shelf to McMurdo in 120 days will take all the stamina he and Fuchs can muster. It will also demand a great deal of luck.

While I have heard a lot about Messner, we have never met. That opportunity will come, though, since we hear he will be at Patriot Hills during our two-day stopover. What I have heard about him has not been positive, especially that he views our both being in Antarctica this season as a competition to be the "first" to cross the continent. But in my mind competing in Antarctica is an extreme act of self-indulgence. It is a place born for cooperation. That's why I am anxious to meet Messner, so that I can explore his motivations for myself. I'm also anxious for him to meet the six of us too, so that he can understand better what we're here for. But there is another, more selfish reason I'm curious about Messner. Face it, few men even attempt such travel, or lead the lives we both do. I would like to think that for those who have chosen this life there could be some fraternity. Unfortunately, by past experience, I know that may be too great an expectation.

We heard tonight that the DC-6 headed for Patriot Hills—carrying the French film crew, some of our rested dogs and our supplies, as well as Messner and Fuchs—left Punta Arenas yesterday. Unfortunately for those aboard, the plane flew for eight hours but was forced to turn back midway across the Drake Passage due to strong storms. The delay is developing into a serious dilemma, especially for Messner, who is falling further and further behind schedule.

Fortunately for us, if the plane does not make it to Patriot Hills we will still have enough supplies to enable us to head for

the South Pole, since we have a cache waiting for us at Patriot
and another 350 miles beyond, near the Thiel Mountains.

NOVEMBER 4, DAY 101

Due to a lack of wind and excellent surfaces we made twenty-
five miles today. The dogs were at their most enthusiastic
since we pulled out of Siple; each day, in fact, they seem to get
stronger, more spirited. Most are gaining weight, and their
coats are full and shiny. Only Ray is still bothered by having
chewed out the fur on the inside of his legs. One of the youn-
gest dogs we brought, Ray has good instincts but fewer miles
under his harness than the rest. Two and a half years old, he is
from the same litter as Thule. I plan to let him run easy all the
way to the South Pole, in hopes he'll make a full recovery
before we get into the area of inaccessibility.

While the dogs are benefiting from being on one and a half
rations, we men are rapidly running out of almost everything.
All of our sugar is gone, as is the granola, pasta, rice and soup.
Tonight my dinner will be just bread and peanut butter.
Thankfully we should make Patriot Hills in two days' time, so
we're not overly concerned by the lack of food; we're just
hungry.

Despite our days getting slightly easier, it is still too early to
let down our guard. Yesterday I badly frostbit my cheeks. With
the wind in our face and temperatures in the –20°s, even a
five- or six-mile-per-hour breeze can wreak devastation on exposed flesh. The dilemma is that in those conditions it is just
warm enough so that when you ski you slightly overheat and
unzip and pull your parka back to compensate. The result is
that any exposed flesh freezes; yesterday it was the skin between my face mask and goggles that suffered. In the next few
days that frozen skin will inevitably scab, then thaw, then
freeze again, turning from white to black to pink to red as it
"heals." If it gets to a stage where it's bleeding from the expo-

sure, anything you press to it for relief freezes fast (as happened to Paul Schurke on the North Pole trip, when his face mask literally froze to his raw skin). There's no way to win. The method I opted for this morning—tucking my face mask up under the edge of my goggles to cut down on exposure—fogged my goggles, and for most of the day I could barely see.

On such days lack of visibility rivals the cold as our biggest difficulty. Our goggles are constantly fogged and, worse, the black gas we're burning leaves a smoky, greasy coating of film on the lenses. (The same sooty residue also coats the inside of our noses.) The only cure is to wash them off with hot water and soap, a painstaking procedure.

The saga of the DC-6 stuck in Punta continues. We are becoming increasingly suspicious about Adventure Network's claim that bad weather is delaying the plane's departure; we are convinced it is mechanical problems that are keeping the big, old plane grounded. The purchase of the DC-6 in recent months surprised us. We assumed they would be using the same reliable DC-4 they used last season. But according to Criquet, who has seen the DC-6 up close in Punta Arenas, it is in questionable shape. He is very dubious that it can make the dozen round-trips necessary to fly the aviation fuel we need for the second half of the trip from Punta to Patriot Hills, where it can then be shuttled by Twin Otter to the South Pole. We must have that airplane fuel at the South Pole if we are to continue past it, because we will be supplied twice by Twin Otter as we cross the area of inaccessibility. (Only in the last few years have light planes, their fuel tanks enlarged, been able to fly into, land at, and return from the area of inaccessibility. But any such visits are still extremely dangerous—and expensive.) We have pledged since we began talking about this route that we would have the Twin Otter standing by at the Pole in case of emergency while we trudge toward Vostok. Without fuel at the Pole neither resupply nor rescue can be done. Adding to the problem, the Chilean Air Force, which was to be our backup fuel supplier, now says they cannot help us, due to some mechanical problem of their own. In our minds, what this whole logistical travail boils down to is that Adventure Network is dropping the ball; straightening out these logistical tangles is one reason we are anxious to get to Patriot Hills.

To make it to Patriot in two days we must average 23 miles a day; yesterday we traveled 24.7. The only physical trip wire standing in our way is a climb over the Heritage Mountains, and we have yet to resolve exactly what route we will take. If due to low visibility we are forced instead to go around the Heritages, it will take us several days longer than we had hoped. Already short on fuel and food, that would be problematic. We are praying for clear skies and looking forward to whatever adventure the climb brings.

Victor has now officially relieved Jean-Louis of the responsibility of collecting, thawing and sampling the weekly "piss jug." Jean-Louis's patience had apparently run out after too many spilled samples, and he has offered a "reward" to Victor for assuming the task. If Victor handles the chore through the end of the trip, Jean-Louis has promised to buy him a car. Since Victor has never owned one and does not even have a driver's license, it is a great incentive. Now, when he comes around to remind us to pee in the bottle and picks up the sample, we joke that this week he has earned the steering wheel, next it will be the two front tires. By March he will have earned a whole car.

NOVEMBER 5, DAY 102

We woke to screaming winds and a total whiteout, the worst conditions we had seen in the past twelve days, but we had to travel. With winds of thirty miles per hour in our faces and blowing snow penetrating our clothing, we were separated many times during a morning of frustratingly slow progress.

As we packed up after lunch the wind began to die down,

and by two o'clock it was calm. With visibility improved, we began to climb; ahead we could see only the black shoulders of a series of ridges. Cresting the first rise, a steep, icy descent lay below, and we quickly decided it was far too treacherous to try. Instead we turned around and began to travel at a right angle from the foot of the mountains, to distance ourselves from them. Our hope was that if we got away from the mountains, we would be better able to distinguish our options for crossing them. But by five-thirty, though we had succeeded in distancing ourselves from the foothills, we had hardly outskied our predicament. Instead we found ourselves in the midst of a giant crevasse field, pocked with seventy-foot-deep fissures surrounded by icy, sloping terrain.

Low on fuel and food, we were in no position to wait until morning so we agreed to keep traveling, still at right angles to our route, now in an attempt to escape these crevasse fields. But the farther we traveled, the deeper the crevasses became. At six o'clock a heavy fog began to roll in and we were forced to make camp. By darkness our tents glowed beneath a blanket of fog.

We had barely enough fuel to cook dinner. Our concern was that while we knew a pass existed somewhere in the vicinity, if this fog hung in we probably wouldn't find it. And even if we did, it might not be passable. Our situation was made worse by the fact that it was achingly cold again. When we made camp it was −25° with winds of ten to fifteen miles per hour slanting across our faces. But we were not going to give in to this storm. Unlike on the peninsula, where these conditions might have lasted for several days, we were convinced here they would be short-lived.

But the return of the cold was taking its toll on everyone. Tonight after dinner Dahe chanted, "No more blizzards, no more blizzards, no more blizzards." We are all tired of storms, tired of the cold, and I find myself identifying more and more with what Tim must have felt in his last days. I'm afraid our tolerance, and patience, with Antarctica is currently very thin.

* * *

As if the day weren't struggle enough, our radio check with Punta brought more bad news. Apparently due to all the delays Adventure Network does not have enough fuel cached at Patriot Hills to service both us and Messner. This is a dilemma none of us could have predicted. Both expeditions put down cold hard cash many months ago with the understanding that Adventure Network would deliver on time certain services. It seems now they are unable to live up to their contract and are endangering the ability of either expedition to continue. To compound the problem further, no one is certain exactly who "owns" the thirty-two fifty-five-gallon drums of fuel that are at Patriot. We assume they are ours; Messner claims it is the fuel necessary to fly him to his start and provide him with two resupplies before the South Pole. If this confusion isn't straightened out within the next few days, both expeditions may be finished, Messner's before it has even begun.

The DC-6, which was supposed to be Adventure Network's major resupply carrier, has yet to take off from Punta on even its first trip to Antarctica. Yesterday cyclonic winds, some of the worst Atlantic weather conditions ever seen by the pilots, forced the plane to turn back for a second time.

NOVEMBER 6, DAY 103

By the time we set off, the skies were clear, encouraging since we were forced to negotiate our way past dozens of deep crevasses. The winds had calmed to ten miles per hour and the dogs were well rested and full of energy. Unfortunately, the rest of our luck did not match the clarity of the skies.

Just before noon Keizo fell into a crevasse. The three sleds were running close together and continually bogging down in deep snow. At one point Dahe began to take off his skis to help push, but Geoff shouted at him scoldingly, "Get on your skis, get on your skis. Crevasses." These were the deepest we'd seen on the trip, and it wasn't safe for anyone to walk anywhere. But Keizo's sled was very difficult to push when stuck in the soft drift, in part because he had cut the handlebars off it some weeks ago. Up front his dogs were spinning paws on slippery blue ice and could gain no traction. Without thinking, Keizo unstrapped his skis in the exact area where Geoff had warned off Dahe. He slipped into a crevasse before anyone could shout a warning. Luckily he was able to grab hold of the one-inch orange nylon climbing strap that hung from his sled and pull himself out.

After lunch we headed up Horseshoe Pass, which had made itself clearly evident under crystal blue skies. Its rim was literally shaped like a horseshoe, its sides jutting a thousand feet vertically, at a forty-five-degree angle. The challenge, though, was not so much the climb; it was, once on top, to find a safe route down the steep descent on the other side, into Horseshoe Valley.

Victor and Jean-Louis headed up the mountainside first, to scout, and from behind we could see their figures silhouetted in the bright sunlight. Near the top of the pass they turned back toward us and raised their poles above their heads and crossed them—our agreed-upon "okay to proceed" signal—and we began to work the three teams up the hill.

We rose very gradually over the saddle between two mountains. The surfaces were extremely slick, and as we neared the top of the rim the wind picked up. Once on top, below us stretched what appeared to be a steep but short descent of five hundred feet. But the view was deceiving; we were actually peering down at the top of yet another mountain, not the floor of the valley. What looked like a relatively simple drop of five hundred feet was instead a steep fourteen-hundred-foot drop-off. Being high on the shoulder of this ridge was definitely the wrong place to be.

My skis skittered as I sidestepped down a few feet to check out what lay below, while the others waited above for my report. Wisely, Geoff and Keizo were already affixing brakes to

their sleds. I climbed back up and it was decided that we
should look elsewhere for a safer way down. For the rest of the
afternoon we searched the five-mile-long rim of the mountain
for such a route. But every option afforded the same view;
steep drops to the floor below. Eventually Victor and Jean-
Louis skied far to the western edge of the rim to see if it
offered an escape.

Frustrated by the seeming dead end and refusing to accept
the possibility we might have to go back down from where we
had come and travel around the mountain range, Geoff, Keizo
and I carefully tacked the three sleds down the side of the
glacier, succeeding only in working ourselves into a corner
where the only escape was straight down. From there the drop
was six hundred feet at an angle of sixty-five degrees, and
though it looked dangerous I decided I could take my sled
safely down the incline. It was intermittently icy and snowy
and I suspected that if I could brake my sled enough, using
four harnesses, two on each runner, I could make it.

I "hupped" the dogs and turned my sled straight down the
hill. The steepness frightened them at first, and they valiantly
spread their legs as far apart as they could and dug their nails
into the ice. As we descended through a mix of deep snow and
blue ice I hung from the back of the sled, alternately helping to
push it over giant drifts, then hanging on for dear life as we
slid down the next ice-riven mountainside.

When we finally bottomed out onto flat terrain, we traveled
another quarter mile before I was able to holler the dogs to a
stop. I turned, and back up the steep slope I could barely make
out the others, including Jean-Louis and Victor, who had returned thinking we would have to go the long way around.
When they spotted me at the bottom, they realized they had
an option. As they began the descent, from where I stood they
looked like tiny dots dropping off the edge of a monstrous
cliff. Quickly I could make out the dogs, then a rooster tail of
powder spraying behind them as they neared the flats. Geoff
banged to the bottom first and allowed his dogs to continue to

race over the valley, with Dahe hanging on tight. Keizo, Jean-Louis and Victor clung to the third sled.

Keizo drew his team to a halt at the bottom of the hill 500 feet from me, and Jean-Louis jumped off the sled and started stalking deliberately in my direction, without pausing to put on his skis in the heavily crevassed area. From a distance he appeared mad. Instead, he walked straight up to me, threw his arms around me and gave me a smack on the cheek. "You're real good, I don't believe what you did," he said, laughing. He had been convinced that the slope we'd just run was too steep, too dangerous to negotiate, and that we were going to have to go several days out of our way to reach Patriot Hills. Quite honestly, I didn't see it as that big a challenge. This was where my years of dogsledding in the Arctic proved valuable to the team.

We traveled several miles away from the foot of the mountain in increasing winds, and made camp. It was a grand, adventurous day, featuring some of the most beautiful scenery we'd seen, and we were all invigorated by it. Everyone agreed this was the kind of adventure we had come south for and that we wouldn't mind a little more.

NOVEMBER 7, DAY 104

After setting out this morning we looked back at the descent we'd made yesterday and due to blowing conditions could barely pick out the path we had descended. What we could see was heart-stopping: to the left of the path we'd taken was a cliff that dropped well over one thousand feet, straight down to the valley floor. It hadn't sunk in until then that our descent could have been a disaster rather than high adventure. I, or any of us, could have easily misstepped, and led us over the edge of the cliff. If a dog team had panicked they likely would have skidded over that precipice, to sure death.

We traveled 29 miles today—making our total 1,227—and

reached Patriot Hills at eight o'clock. It was a welcome sight, a friendly lamplit haven set in the foothills of the Ellsworth Mountains. The camp itself is comprised of five small portable canvas Quonset huts, each with cots and Thermopane windows. Two of the tents are joined to make a kitchen/dining room, complete with heaters and a gas cook range, a radio center and a long dining table. Once inside, we quickly forgot the dangers that lay just beyond the tent doors. It felt like home.

Four Adventure Network employees awaited us, and we had our first "fresh" meal—of chicken and potatoes—in nearly four months, seated in chairs and at a table. During the course of unpacking and winding down, we each took a peek in a mirror hanging from the tent wall, and our raw, frozen cheeks and noses were grim reminders of the struggle we'd seen so far. Energized by the warmth, good food and new faces, we sat and talked until early morning. Sleep finally came at 4:00 a.m.

NOVEMBER 8, DAY 105

Two hours later the DC-6—loaded with twelve of the fifteen dogs we'd sent out earlier, the French film crew, a pair of Saudi scientists who had been conducting experiments from aboard the *UAP*, seven journalists, John Stetson and Messner and Fuchs and their three tons of gear—landed, and we were back on our feet to welcome them.

The plane came to a stop at the end of the runway, a half mile from camp. It was a very windy morning, and the props continued to spin as we neared the plane, sending a wash of kerosene spewing into the air. The door to the plane opened, and a fifteen-foot aluminum ladder was dropped down. The surface beneath the door was extremely slick and dangerous, and we had to pound in two ice pitons to secure the ladder and then all fifteen people aboard had to crawl backward, hand over hand, down the ladder. The dogs were passed down by hand, and in all the excitement those already on the ground roamed free. In our hurry we had forgotten that Thule, tied in front of one of the nearby tents, was in heat.

Kuka, one of Keizo's dogs, raced in her direction. When Keizo realized what was about to happen he took off after the dog, screaming madly in Japanese, slipping and sliding and losing ground every step. If it weren't for the potential seriousness of what we could see unfolding, it would have been a hilarious sight. By the time he reached the two dogs, it was too late; they were locked in bliss. While we won't know the damage, if any, for another sixty days, Geoff was none too pleased that his lead dog was now at risk of being a mother.

We spent our sixty hours at Patriot Hills reading mail, doing interviews, repairing worn-out equipment, sleeping little, and most important, wrangling with the managers of Adventure Network back in Punta Arenas, trying to ascertain exactly how they planned to live up to their contract and deliver our fuel to the South Pole. Jean-Louis and I traded off time on the radio with Messner, who was in an equally precarious position, uncertain though he had come this far if it would be possible, or safe, for him to actually venture out into the interior without promise of caches being delivered, or rescue planes available. Hugh Culver, Adventure Network's general manager, had just flown to Punta from Vancouver and deservedly received the brunt of all our frustrations.

Our biggest immediate concern was the obvious fact that the DC-6 they had bought (with the money we'd paid them in advance) was proving to be useless. It was in bad repair and did not have the necessary range to make the Punta-Patriot Hills run. When it arrived the other morning, the pilots had been lost for an hour, unable to find the landing strip, and when they set the big plane down it had just fumes in its tanks. When it left three hours later headed back for Punta Arenas, refueled from stores it had carried onboard, the plane made it only as far as King George Island, where it was now stuck, out of gas and with a broken landing gear. ABC's Bob Beattie had gone back with the plane and reported that sparks were flying around its interior during the flight and smoke billowed from its engines. We were adamant that the plane not be used for our delivery of fuel or to carry our visitors back to Punta Arenas.

I was first on the radio: "Our concern, Hugh, is the success of this expedition. It appears that Reinhold may not go ahead with his attempt; apparently he'll make that decision later today. But as you well know, Trans-Antarctica does not have the option of quitting at this stage. Therefore we need to know now your alternate plans for fulfilling your obligations to us. Last year you made seventeen or eighteen trips with a DC-4 leased from Kenn Borek Air in Canada. We would like you to immediately get that plane back in service."

"I copy, Will. I've been talking to Borek about that." Culver was being exceedingly polite at this stage.

"We are leaving here tomorrow and we have supplies and fuel to reach the South Pole," I said. "But once at the Pole there is not enough fuel here now to allow us to safely continue. That is our present situation, and you have twenty days to solve the dilemma."

"I understand that, Will."

Jean-Louis, impatiently pacing at my side, wanted to get his two cents in too, and delivered Culver our ultimatums.

"Our major concern, Hugh, and your first priority, since the DC-6 does not appear capable of flying anything in but its own fuel [it had failed to bring us supplies we desperately needed, like long underwear and new goggles], is that you should arrange another plane immediately to come here and bring out the people. They do not want to spend the summer here.

"I do not want to listen to an answer like 'We will see tomorrow.' Tomorrow is already too late. The question is what do you plan for the safety and the resupply of both expeditions." Jean-Louis was very angry. "Look back at the past

twenty days. Nothing has happened. Nobody trusts you anymore. It is impossible to trust your airplane. My question is
'What do you plan to do now?' I don't want to hear any more
about the DC-6. It is too dangerous. No more DC-6, Hugh.
What do you plan to do now?" Because of the logistical wrestling, what we hoped would be a well-deserved rest turned into
a series of round-the-clock negotiations. It was obvious we
would have to leave Patriot Hills in order to get a good night's
rest.

NOVEMBER 10, DAY 107

We left Patriot Hills at twelve-thirty with twenty-four dogs,
ten of them freshly rested. It is like a rodeo whenever we start
like this—surrounded by a crowd of people, cameras whirring.
The dogs were wild, ready to run straight for the crowd, and I
struggled to keep my team in place without shouting and well-
intentioned threats. Even then they almost got away without
me. I barely grabbed the back of the sled's upright as they took
off after Keizo and Geoff, a feat similar to catching a football
by your fingertips in the end zone. Though I was on my skis I
managed to make a leap for the handlebars, caught them with
the index and middle fingers of my left hand, and pulled myself
upright as we went careening and bouncing over the slick surface, heading south. Though we passed no road sign as we
pulled away, we all knew the mileage to go by heart: South
Pole, 750 miles.

Unfortunately, sometime during the day I again wracked
my back severely, most likely by simply hanging on to the sled
as we traveled over two-foot-deep sastrugi. It was in similar
terrain that I had pulled it out the first time, but this injury was
different. The first time I bent down and couldn't stand back
up, but I could lie on one side and the pain would go away.
Now, lying in my sleeping bag, there was no way to relieve the
pain. I took some aspirin and applied another of Dahe's heat

patches, to no avail. I didn't get to sleep until four o'clock, and coming on the heels of three virtually sleepless nights at Patriot Hills, my mind and body were jangled.

Traveling is going to be difficult for the days to come with this injury haunting me. I can't hang on to the sled; I will have to walk and jog alongside. Riding on the sled is out of the question. After the most recent resupply it is so loaded (with twenty-one days of food) there's no way I can add my weight on top. What I really need is a day off.

NOVEMBER 11, DAY 108

I tried to ski once today, but it was very slippery and painful. Ironically, I wasn't the only one on foot; extremely icy conditions and twenty-seven-mile-per-hour wind in our faces made walking the most prudent way to progress.

From here to the Pole it's going to be grin and bear it, face the wind and keep marching, which we've become very good at, though the conditions should not be as bad as we faced on the peninsula. Many of the challenges we wrestle with for the middle third of the trip will be psychological. Have we planned right for the area of inaccessibility? Do we have enough food? Will Adventure Network ultimately let us down? If they do, how will we get fuel to the Pole? When we reach the Pole, how will we be received?

Abetting those mental concerns were some fresh physical discontents. While we had picked up plenty of white gas and food at Patriot Hills, we pulled out of there lacking a few necessities, things that for one reason or another did not come in on the DC-6. We had no new socks or underwear, no sunglasses or goggles to replace ours, which are badly beaten and cracked. We had no fresh meat, which our aching muscles desperately longed for. While it is a luxury to have a new batch of soup mixes, I think we would have all rather preferred a fresh set of long underwear.

NOVEMBER 12, DAY 109

I went over at nine-thirty tonight for the radio check and spent an hour talking with Jean-Louis and Victor. The dilemma we now face is that there has still been no decision made on how we will get fuel to the South Pole. Outside, Criquet and Cathy are working nonstop to find a solution, convinced there is no way that Adventure Network will be able to live up to their promises. It is obvious the DC-6 is incapable of making the necessary trips, and they are already too far behind schedule to find a new plane and make all the round-trip flights necessary from Punta, where our fuel sits on a dock. Cathy is investigating everything from chartering our own plane to convincing one of the governments that operates a base in Antarctica to lend, sell or donate us fuel.

Shortly after we left Patriot Hills, Messner decided to proceed, even though he would not be able to make a full traverse due to the delays he'd already suffered. He and Fuchs are to be dropped off near the edge of the Ronne Ice Shelf tomorrow. Their final destination is the American base of McMurdo, and they plan to travel via the South Pole, an ambitious if not historic attempt (from the Pole to McMurdo their route will mirror Robert Scott's).

For me, meeting Messner was the highlight of our stay at Patriot Hills. Despite the press he's gotten, which often paints him as egotistical and self-consumed, he seemed to be a good man; intelligent, sensitive, with a warm heart, someone I could possibly see traveling with on a future expedition. What impressed me most was that he could laugh at himself. While I'm not convinced he understands how difficult his trip will be, he is physically much stronger than Jean-Louis or I. I could never do what he is attempting and have absolutely no interest in man-hauling. For his part, Messner told Jean-Louis and me that he was glad to be doing a "horizontal" expedition and that because there would be no "getting to the top" involved in this trip it would be a good lesson. When we parted, I told him that I hoped he would succeed. After meeting the six of us, I think he wished the same for Trans-Antarctica.

NOVEMBER 14, DAY 111

Visibility dropped drastically around eleven o'clock this morning as the winds picked up. A heavy snow fell and the temperature dropped to −26°; it felt as if we'd been transported back to the peninsula, except now the sastrugi were much worse. We took solace knowing that storms in this early summer season would probably not last more than twenty-four hours. On the peninsula it seemed they could last forever.

Surprisingly, by lunch break we had covered 11.6 miles, not bad considering the wind racing against us. Lunch itself was miserable, however. We've taken to calling these breaks "powdered lunch," because everything—clothes, food, the insides of our mouths—is coated with snow.

After lunch things got worse, with visibility dropping to one hundred feet. Thankfully we've gotten pretty accomplished at traveling in whiteouts and blizzards. Victor tried staying in the point position, but the rough surfaces and low visibility made that impossible, so Geoff and his dogs took the lead. During the course of the afternoon his and Keizo's sled tipped several times. Still, by day's end we had made twenty-four miles.

In part based on the mileage we covered today, we have made a commitment to try to average twenty-four miles daily. We are twenty-seven days from the South Pole, and if we can maintain that average we could arrive there on December 10. (Two years ago we guessed we'd arrive at the Pole on December 12.) Though we're still uncertain if we will be able to travel beyond the Pole, given that there is no fuel awaiting us, we still need to try to maintain our schedule.

Today Jean-Louis and I discussed an option in case we don't have any fuel waiting at the Pole. If we could get one Twin

Otter to the South Pole from Patriot Hills, crammed with the bare essentials—twenty-two hundred pounds of dog food, man food and extra equipment—we could take the risk of crossing the 750-mile area of inaccessibility without resupply or rescue options. If we could make it to 83° latitude, we could then try to arrange with Vostok for their trax to come out and meet us with supplies. While it was a risky plan, at least it would keep us going. The greatest danger would be if someone was injured, because there would be no way of getting help.

NOVEMBER 15, DAY 112

We woke to the same storm we traveled through yesterday, and the day before that, some of the worst whiteouts we've seen, stirred up by thirty-mile-per-hour winds. The weather, in fact, has been horrendous since we left Patriot Hills. Hopefully we'll be able to keep our mileage up despite the wind and poor visibility.

While we have learned to deal with the elements pretty well, a general exhaustion seems to be affecting everyone. I can never seem to get enough sleep, and I'm still tired when I wake in the morning. As a result, I drag during the day and am exhausted by camp time. Our exhaustion is encouraged by the fact that during the day in these storms we rarely relax. It is difficult to see, you are always straining and tense. I continue to run alongside the sled all day long because it's easier than skiing, which makes me even more tired. I stumble often, am always on guard, and use my upper body more than usual. Even the constant resistance of the wind against our bodies wears us down. I'm already desperately looking forward to our next day off, which isn't for another two weeks. All I need, I tell myself over and over, is an entire day spent in my sleeping bag. But now is when we have to make up the days we lost on the peninsula, we have to keep plunging ahead, we have to keep moving.

NOVEMBER 17, DAY 114

We're maintaining an average of twenty-four miles per day, thus covering one degree every three days. Though the temperatures have warmed, visibility is still nil. The worst result of this combination is that the contrast that illuminates snowdrifts is all but eliminated, making Victor's job of leading especially difficult, and he stumbles and falls dozens of times during the course of each day. Still he's out there on point without complaint, leading us in a remarkably straight line, regardless of the conditions. Often he is forced to travel without his parka ruff and face mask in order to see just ten feet ahead of his ski tips; though conditioned by the almost four months we've been on the ice, his face is still badly frostbitten.

Despite the past four-day stretch of whiteout conditions and strong winds, the dogs continue to surprise us with their strength, freshness and playfulness. I have never had a team quite like this; I'm convinced if I let them have their head they could run forty miles a day. My team has been traveling at the back of the pack, and if I stop and let the other two teams run ahead for five minutes, we catch up within ten. There is obviously power to spare, which is good because they will need that strength when we come off the western plateau and head toward the sea at Mirnyy. For now I'm going to try to preserve a little of that rambunctiousness. Some of their strength can be credited to their extra rations. I have been feeding them one and a half portions a day since we left Patriot Hills, and the result is they are full of spunk. The temperatures are mild, the sleds are getting lighter, and they are sleeping well. All bodes well until the next tough physical phase, once we've passed Vostok.

Last night we finally made contact by radio with Messner and Fuchs. They are traveling an average of twelve miles a day, pulling heavily loaded, two-hundred-pound sleds over ice-slickened sastrugi. Their course has them headed off to the southeast, almost as if they are trying to avoid traveling into the wind (which is impossible), and they have met a lot of sastrugi right away, which has been discouraging. I have a hunch this is the first time Messner has traveled in this type of whiteout across flat, almost plateaulike country. From experience I know that in these conditions your first instinct is to favor a windless direction, rather than face it head on. I'm sure they're surprised by the journey's difficulty even if Fuchs is navigating, though he gained more experience earlier this year on a team with the British adventurer Robert Swan that successfully man-hauled to the North Pole. That is totally different. Heading north you don't have the open spaces you do here; you travel more from ice ridge to ice ridge. This is new to them, and I'm sure they're still getting used to their traveling systems. I can only imagine how sore their bodies must be. Every step of the way for them is painstaking; for them there is no jumping on the back of the sled for even a few minutes of relief.

Currently we're not exactly "gliding" along smoothly ourselves. Today we met the most unusual snowdrifts of the trip: one foot of snow covering a hard-packed surface beneath. The sleds plow through the drift with little difficulty, but only because the dogs are feeling so spirited. We're surprised by this terrain, because our research led us to believe we would find this area clear, windy, and hard packed. Instead it was overcast with blowing snow, snowdrifts and soft snow on the surface.

We are also surprised that this storm is hanging on. I expect every morning to wake to a bright blue sky; instead, visibility is nearly zero. In these conditions all perceptions are dulled, the days flow into each other, and travel is like a dream. The clouds make our mood slightly lazy and flat.

We crossed 82° latitude today, which means within nine days we should find the cache near the Thiel Mountains and then reward ourselves with a much-needed day off. We are very worn and on my many rest stops during the day, as I waited for others to catch up, I lay down in the snow out of the wind, and slept, hard. I did that probably twenty times today,

just for a minute or two. Once I lay down, reality blended
quickly with fantasy, resulting in hurried, jumbled sixty-second
dreams. I would bolt awake after a minute or two and glance
around to remind myself where I was, searching the horizon
for the others. I did this all day long. If fog or a sudden windstorm had come up I could have easily lost sight of my teammates. It was a very strange day, and the only thing I could
think to blame my mood on was the stretch of long, cloudy
days.

NOVEMBER 18, DAY 115

Today began the same as the last five: zero contrast, high wind,
temperature −3°. Traveling was tough due to the endless sastrugi. Victor stumbled dozens of times in the nine miles we
covered before lunch. Worse, it was impossible to see the in-
cised, wind-cut snowdrifts because of the lack of contrast.
Geoff led, and his sled tipped five or six times, dumping gear
and slowing our progress. It is extremely difficult in these conditions for the lead sled, because there is absolutely no depth
of field. On a follow sled at least you can usually see the dogs'
footprints and the trace of the previous sled's runners. But
despite the endless struggles, Geoff remains ever stoic, never
complaining.

When it finally cleared late in the afternoon the terrible
terrain we'd been crossing revealed itself; an unending frozen
ocean of jagged, waved ice stretched ahead. The sunlight made
the sastrugi appear far prettier than we had imagined them as
we struggled over them blindly, cursing them each step. At
least when it is clear it is easier to travel over, because you can
see what's ahead and avoid the larger drifts, instead of slam-
ming into them. Our mileage of 20.5 was a low for the week.
(From Geoff's journal: "This sastrugi is snow, carved and
sculptured by constant wind, into great uncoordinated waves
and flutings, every shape and size, from a few inches high to

four, five or six feet tall. The snow making these is iron hard, icy and unrelenting. The sled, like a small boat on a rough sea, rises and falls over these waves—up and down, left then right. Some of our most frustrating days have been spent traveling across sastrugi in complete whiteouts. Then, even when standing atop them, we could not see them, let alone anticipate their effect on sleds or ourselves, which was to send the sled lurching over unseen objects of unknown shape and size, often capsizing and on one occasion pinning me underneath. Another time I tried to stop the sled falling toward me; it lurched and fell over the other way, flinging me head over heels to the opposite side where I landed in an ignominious heap. A day of sastrugi would leave us totally shattered, and it was all one could do to make camp, melt water, cook supper and crawl into bed.")

I have been traveling in the middle position recently, and this afternoon Victor skied with me. It was good having company, someone to talk to, even in garbled snatches of Pidgin English. For the past week I've traveled alone and sat for lunch with only Dahe. The last two or three minutes of lunch break I'll go over and small-talk with the others, but other than that any conversation I've had in the past week has been confined to the tent, and then it is just more small talk over supper with Dahe. In some ways it feels as if I've been soloing all week long beneath these cloudy skies.

One impact of the isolation is that my thoughts are beginning to resemble our trail food: boring, repetitive, stale. At the beginning of the trip there seemed to be endless variation to our days, plenty of new sights to enjoy and plans to make. But now, 115 days into the expedition, the view has become somewhat mundane, my mind is exhausted from the simple lack of outside stimulation, and the food has grown tasteless. Even escaping into my mind has become difficult. Sometimes I feel as if I am fasting—socially, physically, and mentally. The best I can do is remind myself that this is a cleansing process, the ultimate cobweb clearer. Just like the skies here, clouds come and go, and so do moods.

NOVEMBER 19, DAY 116

Keizo's thirty-third birthday party was celebrated with a very non-Japanese dinner of Norwegian salmon and Bordeaux wine (sent to Jean-Louis at Patriot Hills by friends) and turned into yet another grave logistical hashing. The subject was the continuing Adventure Network saga. As we ate, Jean-Louis reported that the ship that left to cross the Drake Passage two days ago—carrying fuel to resupply the DC-6, which is still stuck at King George Island—was forced to turn back, due to winds of one hundred knots at Cape Horn. Apparently, their next plan is to fly a Twin Otter from Punta to KGI, loaded with fuel for the DC-6. We also learned that one of our last options, bringing down a DC-4 from Canada, has been ruled out because the plane needs maintenance in Calgary.

The fuel crisis gets more serious each day we step closer to the South Pole, and before heading off to bed I suggested that Victor write a telegram to Arthur Chilingarov, our primary benefactor in Moscow's bureaucracy (delivered, of course, by radio to Punta Arenas, then on to Moscow), informing him of the seriousness of our situation. It seemed like a last-gasp effort, especially stuck here in the middle of the ice as we were, but if the Soviets could fly an Ilyushin-76 to the Pole with eighty barrels of fuel we could pull this thing off yet. Asking the Soviets for help, I said, explaining to them that without their help the expedition will come to an end, was our last best shot.

Getting fuel to the Pole was not our only concern, though: we were still responsible for the thirteen journalists and staffers stuck at Patriot Hills. They had been there now for twelve days, and Adventure Network still had no firm plan for evacuating them. As a result of all these nagging complications, I was barely sleeping.

NOVEMBER 20, DAY 117

Jean-Louis rode with me for a while this afternoon, and we kicked around yet more alternatives, one of which we dubbed our "Doomsday Plan." It involved retreating from the South Pole shortly after reaching it. The very last thing we wanted to be forced to do was ask the NSF for help or rescue. "Doomsday" included leaving a cache of our own making at 87° latitude in the Thiels, skiing to the Pole, and then making our way back to Patriot Hills, via the Thiel range. This would allow us to make it as far as the South Pole, and then possibly come back next year to complete the South Pole–Mirnyy leg. If we were able to get back to Patriot Hills under our own power, even if we were flown out from there, the trip would not be a total loss. Though difficult to even talk about, this was a time when we had to remind ourselves that our real mission here was drawing attention to Antarctica, not necessarily being "first." In many ways, as long as we came home safely the expedition would be a success no matter how many mileposts we passed.

Completing the traverse, however, was still our goal. It was important not just to us but to the staff and volunteers who had helped us over the past three years and the millions who had heard about and were following our crossing. Dahe cited the efforts of the Chinese at Great Wall Station on KGI as the perfect example of how others had truly invested in our expedition. He was at the base last year when our fuel came in by ship. Over the summer the snow covering the fuel barrels melted, then froze, and then the barrels were buried again by new snow. The entire base spent seven full days chipping our barrels of fuel free from the ice. That all of this hard work should go without the reward of seeing us complete the traverse was unbearable for us to consider for long.

Two days ago during one of my many waits for the others I sat on the leeward side of my sled in relative calm, facing the sun and feeling its heat on my face. Snow crystals whipped by in the twenty-five-mile-per-hour wind and I looked out over the gathering snowdrifts we had yet to travel over. All of this snow and ice is constantly on the move; shifting, never melting, lasting for centuries. The snow I was sitting on would eventually turn into the ice that is Antarctica.

I pondered the role this shifting, piling drift will play in the years to come. If in fact the Earth continues to warm, as many predict it will due to mankind's overuse of atmosphere-altering chemicals, this snow will be a key element in Earth's future. What I saw as I hid from the blowing snow behind my sled were flakes made up of tiny molecules, the base of an all-important ecological chain. At that moment I saw them not as a hindrance, not as something to be swept out of our clothes and off tent walls, but as intrinsic elements of the world system, important players in the planet's—and man's—future. In a way, the snowflakes I was watching were the foundation of the future here, a foundation that must be protected and preserved.

Tonight we had a long radio conversation with Criquet; it appears Cathy has worked out a possible solution to our fuel crisis. Without prompting from us here on the ice, the Soviets have agreed to airdrop approximately sixty barrels of fuel at the South Pole.

NOVEMBER 21, DAY 118

We are nearing the Thiel Mountains, and as we climb in altitude we are reentering difficult crevasse areas. Today we found ourselves confronted by a giant "ice fall" rising 240 feet above us, formed by a section of glacier moving faster than the rest. To get around it we were forced to travel far to the west; but behind the ice fall we found a crevasse zone that stretched for miles. We needed to find a tongue, a river of ice, that would lead us to the top of the ice fall. While a distraction at the moment, we drank in the beauty of these obstructions, since they were some of the last land features we were going to see for some months.

Despite the delays caused by the difficult terrain, we covered twenty-three miles, four in the last hour. At camp time it cleared above, and the temperature rose. I went outside in just my underwear and gazed at the horizon.

Tonight I met with Geoff and Jean-Louis and we made our final decisions on the amount of dog food, man food, fuel and equipment that we will need at the South Pole and for resupply in the area of inaccessibility. Crossing the area of inaccessibility is a very serious undertaking, and we are just now starting to allow ourselves to think about what it will entail. Though the Soviets' offer to deliver fuel to the Pole is a godsend, in a way it only allows us to move ahead to our next set of worries.

NOVEMBER 22, DAY 119

Morale is good and superb weather continues. Today was clear and 0°, with very little wind. We're above 84° latitude and should reach the Thiel Mountain cache four days from now, at 85° 04′.

I ran alongside the sled for the first three hours this morning, until the surface smoothed out, then jumped on my skis and stayed on them for the next twenty-four miles. It was a fast day, and we played sled-tag throughout. Victor was in front, trailed by my sled, then Geoff, and Keizo. My dogs would catch up to Victor every half hour, with the other two sleds fast on my heels, then we would all slow up and drop back, and race again. It was a pleasant way to spend the day, something to distract our minds from the increasing monotony that four consecutive months of such travel invariably breeds.

On days like this life in Antarctica seems easy; they are what I crave about such travel. You are inspired by the exhilaration of the dogs and feel truly alive. It's like being a young boy all over. You forget about the cold times, the wind, the storms, the wet snow, the long days wasted inside tents. I just hope the weather stays good for another two months; we don't expect cold storm conditions again until nearing Vostok, and by then we'll be ready for them. Until then my thoughts are buoyed by the good weather. Today I started organizing my next expedition in my head and designed a small cabin.

Dahe and I are getting along quite well as tentmates, the only bone of contention being that he is a "brusher" and I am not; before entering the tent he carefully brushes as much snow and ice from his clothing and mukluks as possible; I generally allow the accumulation to melt down once inside. Like Jean-Louis and Geoff, Dahe is more a perfectionist than I am, especially when it comes to simple things like tent organization. I have to admit I often fall far short of organizational perfection, and my only excuse is that *I* know where everything is. I organize things in heaps, which may look unorganized in Dahe's or Geoff's eyes, but to me it makes perfect, if not visual, sense.

The only other impediment to comfort inside our tent is Dahe's size—he's six feet three. Because of his lankiness he simply takes up more room, and I find myself and my things pushed into one third of the tent. To keep peace I am not complaining, because I have found that the worst thing you can do is crowd Dahe: it makes him very ornery. Being the perfectionist he is, he knows immediately if I try to grab a few inches more space than I've allowed myself in previous nights. He knows exactly where the strings line up above his head, and if I move over just an inch and a half when we set up camp, he knows immediately and takes back his space by not-so-casually pushing things aside. Everything in a Dahe tent has to be kept in exactly the same place all the time. Nothing can be out of order. Pots must be spotlessly cleaned, and an errant grain of rice found in a cooking pot can lead to that night's dinner being thrown out and started anew. I wonder if this comes from his having lived his whole life in small places. His apartment in Lanzhou, where he lives with his wife and son, is only one room and a shared sleeping space. The toilet is a hole in the floor of a tiny bathroom.

NOVEMBER 24, DAY 121

Surface conditions were perfect for the second day in a row, the hard-packed snow was gently undulating and had a smooth veneer. We had a ten- to fifteen-mile-per-hour wind against us, daylong sunshine and a high of −5°. The only natural phenomenon hindering us these days are the katabatics that gust twenty to thirty miles per hour and "attack" us from out of nowhere, randomly all day. While conditions are vastly better than they were one month ago, the winds blow constantly in our faces, requiring us to travel with our heads bowed, like bicycle racers. The constant winds and resulting blowing snow mean we rarely stop to rest or even heed the call of nature, for fear of losing sight of the other sleds.

One of the reasons our mileage is picking up is that our sleds are so light. Each sled is carrying just one box of dog food apiece, and in the last three days we've made 27.5, 27.6 and now 28.5 miles, which is helping us make up for the days lost on the peninsula. We hope to find the next cache, the only one between Patriot Hills and the South Pole, a day earlier than planned and then take a day off.

At midmorning we topped a slight rise, and the Thiel Mountains rose up ahead of us. Within ten minutes the entire

range dominated the horizon. It was so breathtaking, so perfect, it was as if we'd stumbled onto a Hollywood back lot;
since we're still thirty miles away from the mountains there
was a Disneyland-like quality to its beauty. We will spend as
many hours as possible as we travel past the Thiels gazing at its
peaks, knowing they will be the last topographic feature we
will see until the mountains near Mirnyy, more than eighteen
hundred miles from here.

Our satellite message tonight was "Nice Thule sleep by
Geoff's tent." While it may confuse Argos, the message's
explanation is simple. At Patriot Hills, Geoff had acquired a
harmonica, which he had taken to practicing for ten minutes
every night. As would be expected from Geoff, he practiced
with precision, at the same time every night, for the exact same
period of time. At first Thule would whine and cry when he
played, disturbed by the high pitch, and she was so distressed it
affected her usually strong pulling power. Now Geoff plays his
harmonica blanketed under his sleeping bag and Thule is
much happier. So is Keizo, Geoff's tentmate.

Good news, finally, from Punta Arenas: the journalists, film
crew, and the pair of Saudi scientists arrived there this morning aboard the repaired-but-still-questionable DC-6. They
had been stranded at Patriot Hills for seventeen days.

NOVEMBER 25, DAY 122

So much for idyllic travel days. The wind whipped today between twenty-five and thirty miles per hour, and temperatures
averaged –10°, resulting in windchills of –60° and worse.
When we left camp we could see a monstrous blowing drift in
the air near the base of the mountains, which indicated that
strong winds lay ahead. Geoff assured us the cache was buried
near a patch of blue ice, generally an indication of strong
winds and lots of sun. What we saw ahead of us was most likely

a combination of both a local phenomenon and the katabatics that would inevitably grow stronger as we approached the plateau that rose above where we stood.

In the morning my goggles fogged and then iced, and I couldn't see a thing. I tripped often on the slick surfaces, and the poor visibility gave me a giant headache. For most of the day I hung on with both hands to the uprights of the sled's handlebars, running in back of it as if I were pushing a shopping cart. Holding on meant that if I stumbled I could still catch myself before falling. As we traveled, the afternoon turned bitterly cold and despite my running, my feet were chilled until long after we crawled into the tent.

In spite of the difficult conditions we still made twenty-six miles. Victor continues to do an amazing job in the point position. He is so strong he is able to keep pace *ahead* of the dogs and sleds all day long, rarely asking for a break. I am amazed he is able to stay on his feet as well as he does, since it is hard enough just walking on these slick surfaces against the wind. He is without a doubt the strongest polar man I have ever met.

We remain isolated by tent units, and the time the six of us spend together is very limited. We gather for a few minutes in the morning after all the sleds are packed, talk and hear the news from Jean-Louis. At lunch there's only a few minutes to talk because we're usually split into two groups of three. In the evening when we're making camp I usually run over to Jean-Louis's tent to give him a radio message or two to pass along, and I chat with him and Victor for a few minutes. I see Keizo and Geoff for just a few minutes each day. Most of our contact is nonverbal, and a hug or pat on the back often carries more power than "How are you doing?"

NOVEMBER 26, DAY 123

The Thiel range is dramatic-looking, featuring miles of white-and-blue ice falls and exposed rock ridges, set against a backdrop of the bluest Antarctic sky we've yet seen. The range stretches across the horizon like a dam; because of its relative proximity to the South Pole and exposed rock croppings, it is a popular spot for scientists from around the globe to visit. The vivid blueness is attributable to both the extreme cold and the fact that these skies are the first we've seen influenced by the atmosphere that hovers above the Antarctic Plateau, which sits atop the Thiels and stretches east to Mirnyy.

We found the cache late in the afternoon and camped near the base of the mountains. One of the few pleasures for me of these cache finds is the abundance of powdered milk buried inside; these days I consider it the best food we have since we've had no meat for weeks and I can't bring myself to eat pemmican anymore. Cheese and nuts are my only source of complete protein, and I know part of my restlessness these past weeks is related to our recent bad diet. After a continual grind of almost thirty straight days without proper nutrition we have all lost weight and our muscles never properly relax, thus can't replenish themselves. Hopefully at the South Pole we will get a shipment of beef from Chile and start rebuilding our worn muscles. Until then, Canada Boy powdered milk is the best nutrient we have in stock.

Something else we haven't had much of recently is radio contact. Personally, I think the blackout is good preparation for the area of inaccessibility, where our radio will be nearly worthless. Jean-Louis disagrees, preferring to have some kind of daily contact with the outside world. But the lack of radio contact is emblematic of the limits of what technology can do for us, this far from civilization. On one hand we thought we were going to be heavily if not overly supported during the crossing, but that hasn't been the case. We have been unable to find three caches, broken valuable sleds and equipment, failed to get planes when we needed them, and endured weeks of radio silence. As a result we've traveled far heavier than I could have predicted and we've been wearing essentially the same clothes since Day 1. (I've been wearing the same fleece underwear now for more than 120 days.) Though we have plenty of equipment, most of it is stuck in Punta Arenas.

In some ways I'm glad we've been as undersupported as we've been. We're leading a simpler life than some might have expected, which makes the expedition a lot richer in experience because of the ensuing adventure and the unknown. There is really only one necessity we can't do without: dog food, which thankfully we have plenty of.

There were several times during our three years of preparations when we simply didn't have the money to proceed and the expedition looked as if it might be over before it began. So far the closest call we've had came as we prepared to leave for our training run in Greenland, early in 1988. One week before we were to depart we had only half of the necessary $120,000 to cover the trip's cost. Ironically, the media in the Twin Cities was then painting Trans-Antarctica as a fat and sassy venture, which made our last-minute pleas for cash doubly hard since people were led to believe we had *plenty* of money.

Just a few days prior to flying to Greenland we wrangled $20,000 from W.L. Gore & Associates and three individual donations of $10,000 to cover our deficit. But in my experience expeditions and money are like oil and water, and they will remain that way, I assume, until every step has been taken, every mountain seen, every new vista discovered. In other words, forever.

Money hassles are hardly a challenge singular to our expedition, though. Shackleton called financing expeditions his "primary headache." When he set sail aboard the *Endurance*, his biographer wrote, "Shackleton was immensely relieved. The long years of preparation were over . . . the begging, the hypocrisy, the finagling, all were finished." Both Amundsen and Scott struggled to raise money up to the last minute before departing for their Antarctic trips. They sold the rights to their stories to newspapers and publishers, they lectured, they begged for and borrowed money from friends, rich uncles, sponsors and governments. Roland Huntford, in his book about the two great explorers' race for the South Pole, detailed Amundsen's attitude toward money: "[He] had long ceased worrying about balanced budgets. His aim was to get his ship on the sea and out of reach of his creditors. If he won the race to the South Pole, all would be forgiven. Failure would be his only crime." The same is true of Trans-Antarctica.

NOVEMBER 28, DAY 125

We broke camp at the usual time in strong winds and headed straight toward the escarpment of the Thiel range. Towering walls of ice rose like a dam before us, their tops interrupted every twenty miles by a towering mountain peak. We were headed for King Peak, the tallest of them, which should take four or five days to climb. We started this morning at five thousand feet, and when we top the Antarctic Plateau we'll be at nine thousand. With our fully loaded sleds it will not be an easy climb.

As we approached the pass that would lead us to the plateau the wind increased to a steady thirty miles per hour against us. The closer we got, the harder—and more slick—the surfaces became, and they were soon coated with blue ice. Snow could not possibly collect here because it was far too windy. As we began our climb, at a thirty-degree angle, the wind roared in our ears. It was as if we were standing under a waterfall, but instead of water pouring down on us, here it was wind. It fell very fast over the edge, picking up speed as it dropped, hitting the surface below with turbulent, hurricane-like force.

When we topped the escarpment we were at seven thousand feet, the winds dipped to twenty miles per hour, and we stopped for a comfortable lunch, protected behind a sled. Afterward, traveling due south once again, the winds quieted further and from the plateau we had a spectacular view of the top of the Thiel range. Off either side, at the bottom of the sheer walls, stretched two-mile-wide spans of blue ice, sheered flat by the nonstop winds that raced down the mountainsides, gaining strength as they dropped. Columns of snow washed from the side of the mountains the length of the range and spun off into the distance. Ahead, to the south, large clouds of blowing white drift hung in the air, hovering close to the ground. It was a nightmarish vision of what we would be traveling through the next few days.

The plateau was blanketed with choppy sastrugi, which wasn't as hard on the sleds as it had been in recent days since the chop was close together. Still, it made skiing very difficult. We camped ten miles from the point where we crested the plateau, having covered more than twenty-three miles, a fantastic travel day considering the heavy sleds, the ascent and sastrugi.

Between here and the South Pole we will climb another two thousand feet, and our elevation has already begun to exhibit its side effects. When I was running alongside the sled today I got short-winded a number of times and had to pause to catch my breath, which hadn't happened once in the previous two thousand miles. So far the dogs are not showing any effects, which is critical because we'll be traveling at between nine thousand and ten thousand feet for the next two thousand miles. In the last three months we've gone from three thousand feet to seven thousand feet and back down again, which has conditioned them; as we start the climb to nine thousand feet, I don't think we'll see them falter.

NOVEMBER 29, DAY 126

During the course of a day marked by very large, razor-sharp sastrugi we climbed another fifteen hundred feet and then crossed over the shoulder of a rugged nunatak and descended its length, which was scarred by undulating terrain. We repeated that maneuver all day long, with a nonstop wind blowing twenty miles per hour in our faces. The area reminded me of a sluiceway on a river, filled with whitecaps. We paralleled an escarpment and in a few areas the rock was exposed through the glaciated ice falls, but for the most part we were surrounded by ice and snow.

At the top of the tallest rise we ran into a pair of well-bridged crevasses, similar to many we had crossed previously without incident. Victor and I arrived first, and I decided the route would be to cross the two crevasses and then head downhill. But when the other two sleds popped to the top of the hill, Geoff warned that since this was a heavily crevassed area we should turn around and cross at a lower elevation, which would involve an extra two and a half hours of hard travel. My opinion was that there were only these two crevasses, not a field, and I volunteered that Victor and I would drop down three hundred feet to check out the descent's safety. We braked my sled carefully, and waved good-bye.

All appeared smooth ahead, and when Victor skied to the edge of the crevasse to check out the hill below I turned to wave the others to follow. But they were already vanishing in retreat, retracing their steps. I was miffed. Sometimes Geoff gets these notions in his head in which he has to do things his way, but this didn't make sense; the descent had proved quite simple.

Victor and I continued our drop, which took just ten more minutes, and stopped within one hundred feet of the bottom of the hill to wait for the others. I was very anxious—this was the first time during the whole trip that we'd been separated from them by such a distance. I was concerned that we would wait and wait and they would not appear, and we would be separated for the rest of the day without any means of contact.

While we waited we sat in the lee of the sled and had a cup of tea. It was very warm, and the scene stretched out to the south looked like the desert of the American Southwest, complete with snow-capped mesas and rolling plains. After a half-hour wait the other two sleds rounded the curve of the mountainside, heading straight for us. They had followed our path after all. When they arrived, Jean-Louis stormed toward Victor, yelling, "Use your head, please, use your head."

Jean-Louis was upset with Victor not for making the descent but rather because we'd ended up in this precarious situation to begin with due to Victor's leading us off course all day. Jean-Louis had tried to correct him several times earlier, but his logic apparently fell on deaf ears. As a result we were off course fifteen degrees.

When Jean-Louis finished his brief tirade, Victor countered, and they argued back and forth for a few minutes until the debate lost steam. It ended with Victor's throwing his arm around the diminutive Frenchman, and Jean-Louis's responding with a smile. While Victor can be hardheaded to the point of frustration, in the end he is ruled by an enormously warm heart that inevitably erases any hard feelings.

It took us only an hour to regain the correct bearing, and after camping for lunch on the shoulder of the last nunatak we would see until the end of the trip, we continued through an afternoon of roller-coaster sastrugi riding. The sastrugi were extremely slick, so the sleds would ride up to their crest then skitter and crash down the other side. The front runner would take the full brunt at a forty-five-degree angle as it slammed into the opposite side, bringing the sled to an almost complete stop. All afternoon sleds tipped, and we rode out the day praying nothing would crack or split.

When we camped, we'd made twenty-three miles. Ahead we could see miles and miles of sastrugi similar to those we'd been crossing all afternoon, promising at least two more days of difficult sledding. Once past this field the topography should smooth out fast, and we should coast into the Pole in less than two weeks. The dogs remain strong, and we are in fine rhythm.

NOVEMBER 30, DAY 127

Sunspots continue to play havoc with our radio signal. Last night we could pick up only the Soviet base of Bellingshausen, but they couldn't hear us. From what we overheard, Bellingshausen couldn't make contact with Punta Arenas, even with their transmitter's 1,000-watt capacity, so the atmospheric conditions were affecting the whole continent.

I have to admit I am somewhat surprised by the excitement that is building among the ranks as we close in on the South Pole. It is the general consensus that we should try to pick up our tempo, in order to arrive at the Pole as quickly as we can. I have been lobbying hard against such a move, arguing that we must keep our same pace and not rush, so that we might preserve any sense of rhythm we've built up. We said we'd arrive on December 12, and I don't see any advantage to hurrying. Ironically, Amundsen was faced with the same problem: his men desperately tried to speed up the closer they got to the Pole. But I'm convinced that it is very important for us to maintain the same pace we've been traveling, for the sake of both dogs and men. As conditions improve there is a natural tendency to want to go faster and travel longer days. But saving an extra day at this point means nothing; saving the dogs means everything. My suggestion is that rather than pick up the pace, we slow down, take an extra hour off each day, relax before the buzz saw of activity we're sure to encounter at the Pole. Keizo's dogs are wearing down and have been running third each of the last several days. Let's let them rest, I say, and regain their strength. Let's slow down. So far my suggestion has not had any takers.

MILES TRAVELED: 1,729.5

MILES TO THE SOUTH POLE: 267.5

DECEMBER

WHAT HAD WE LEARNED?
CONFIDENCE

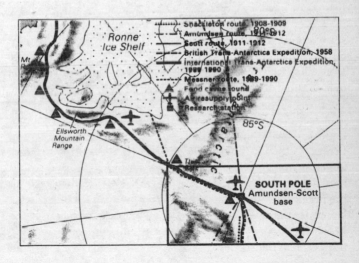

DECEMBER 1, DAY 128

When I unzipped the tent door this morning it felt as if I were throwing open the windows back home on that first fresh day of spring. Instead of a bite and a sting, the breeze carried a stimulating, vibrant tenderness.

On the ice the surface was nearly level and we rose slightly, three hundred to four hundred feet, as we traveled south. The dogs pulled easily despite a heavy load, their paws punching through four inches of crust. I'm carrying six boxes, or 372 pounds, of dog food, roughly 200 pounds heavier than any load we'll carry on the rest of the trip. The extra is in the event the plane carrying our resupply doesn't reach the Pole. Despite the awkward load the day passed uneventfully, and we covered twenty-eight miles.

Tonight, more radio silence. Jean-Louis couldn't even raise static; it was as if the radio wasn't even turned on. Fortunately Geoff has his sextant, because as we draw near to the Pole knowing our longitude will be extremely important and with this radio blackout the Argos system is worthless.

The really difficult navigation will begin when we cross the 88° latitude line and are within one hundred miles of the Pole. Once we're that close even the slightest mistake in our bearing could send us many miles off course. Near the Pole the lines of longitude come closer and closer together; right now—we're just past 86°—they are about twenty miles apart. At 89° they are separated by just three or four miles. If we misread our watches, the sun, or the sextant, we will certainly follow the wrong bearing. Hitting the South Pole head-on, though, is much easier than hitting the North Pole, due to the constantly drifting ice of the Arctic Ocean over which you must travel to get there. Fortunately for us, the Amundsen-Scott base anchors this Pole, and we should be able to see it from twenty miles out. That's a navigational advantage neither of its name-sakes had.

It was such a pleasant day we cooked dinner with both doors unzipped, and the temperature inside the tent remained a balmy 50° at eye level. Having fresh air inside is a luxury. The only thing that threatens to disrupt this pleasantness for the next fifty days or so is something we also faced traversing Greenland, a challenge we are dreading almost as much as crevasses and high winds. Monotony. Passing the time of day. Boredom. For the next two months we will live totally in the world of the future or the past, because each day of travel will be nearly identical to the one before and the next. We will count the days, the miles, the degrees, the steps yet to travel— and then count them again. What we face these next two months is a little like a jail sentence. We'll put in our time, and hopefully get out on the other side.

When we left the United States last July we were each "al-lowed" four pounds of personal gear. The limit was imposed to save the dogs from pulling any more weight than was abso-lutely necessary. As conditions improve, we're starting to spend more time with the various gadgets and time killers we each brought.

Jean-Louis packed the most books, including *Meditation in Action*, two small picture books of birds, a biography of a Nobel prize winner he'd appeared with on a TV talk show in Paris, a novel by a writer from his hometown in the south of France. He also brought tapes of bird and nature sounds and music, including Dire Straits, J. J. Cale, Veronique Sanson and the soundtrack to *Gigi*.

Geoff's personal bag was the lightest: a Frisbee (for tossing at the South Pole), a book on knots (and a piece of string), a book on origami and an embroidery (a time-killing expedition trick he'd practiced many times before). Victor's bag was perhaps the heaviest, crammed full of outmoded Soviet clothing like fur socks, fur jacket, heavy felt boots. While he appreciated all the new gear we'd brought along, he'd been based in Antarctica four times and felt better bringing some of his old standby clothes. He also packed a photo of his wife and son. The only other sentimentality he packed was a wood carving of a bird, given him by a new friend from Duluth.

Dahe also had pictures of his wife and son, some Chinese books and a small stock of foods and spices from his homeland to accentuate the starchy, bland diet we'd packed: dry soup, sea sauce, bean sauce, jasmine oil, egg noodles. Similarly, Keizo packed special rice, ramen, soy sauces, seaweed and Japanese spices. A Japanese folk song book was his only extravagance, and he'd brought a loon whistle, a present really for the dogs, to remind them of their home in Minnesota.

I had packed mostly tools for drawing, including a six-inch ruler, a protractor, colored pencils, erasers, a pencil sharpener and a small tape recorder. The only book I carry is Gretel Ehrlich's *The Solace of Open Spaces*.

DECEMBER 4, DAY 131

When we made camp last night we were at 87° 14′, according to Argos, which is back in service due to a good, clear radio signal. Today, after traveling twenty-five miles, we estimate we're at 87° 35′. Sometime tomorrow morning we should cross south of 88°. The miles, and the degrees, just keep ticking by.

Today was spent battling head winds, which was not easily done on foot or ski, and I ended up running alongside the sled most of the afternoon, taking up the rear position. The running helped keep me warm on a day when both Geoff and Dahe complained of being cold.

There is a shared sentiment in camp that the most welcome

change upon arriving at the South Pole will be our diet. Dahe's breakfasts are getting stranger by the day. First he boils up granola bars in water—they are too hard on his teeth otherwise—and mixes in a little oatmeal, to create a kind of "trail soup." He chases that concoction with biscuits slathered with peanut butter, a can of sardines and a Shaklee chocolate "Energy Bar." As for me, I've switched to a compulsory eating program and am forcing myself to swallow one package—eight ounces—of cheese every night on my noodles or rice. That makes dinner one of the most unpleasant parts of the day; I often wish we could somehow get by without eating.

With the clear radio signal last night we were also able to contact Messner. He was within two days of his first cache site but uncertain whether Adventure Network planned to meet him there. He asked if we could contact Patriot Hills and ascertain if and when he should expect a resupply; apparently the radio he's carrying is very small and, given the difficult atmospheric conditions, he's been unable to raise anyone there for days. We advised him we would try and then contact him again tomorrow night. He was at roughly 85° latitude and hopes to be at the South Pole by December 20. He has been covering about one degree every five days, and at that rate I don't see how he'll get there until at least the twenty-eighth, which threatens his ability to get to McMurdo before conditions make overland traveling impossible, sometime near the end of February. He knows he must pick up speed, but the conditions for man-hauling have hardly been good; he reports that deep sastrugi and soft snow continue to slow them down.

DECEMBER 5, DAY 132

It was formally announced today that the Soviet Antarctic Expedition has agreed to provide twelve tons of fuel to the expedition at the South Pole. While they had seriously considered air-dropping it, that plan was scrapped as too dangerous and costly. Instead, the Soviets made a deal for fuel already in Antarctica and will pay back the debt out of their supply at King George Island. After many sleepless nights—here on the ice, in St. Paul, Paris, Moscow and Punta Arenas—our biggest logistical problem appears now to be behind us. The only flaw is that the Soviets' help cost the expedition considerable money; hopefully we will be reimbursed by Adventure Network, whom we had paid up front for the fuel.

We learned of the Soviet announcement during a long radio check tonight with John Stetson, who is still at Patriot Hills. As soon as he gave us the good news, the preciousness of the remaining barrels sitting at Patriot Hills dissipated. Immediately Stetson oversaw the loading of twenty-four hundred pounds of supplies—from meat to underwear—aboard a Twin Otter heading for the Pole. That planeload contains all the supplies we will need to cross the area of inaccessibility. The same plane will also drop off Messner and Fuchs's resupply. They are at 85° 11′, very close to King Peak in the Thiels, and have just one day of food left.

I am constantly amazed at our luck in pulling this expedition off. The stakes keep getting bigger, more complex, more expensive, yet we keep rolling along . . . though many times we are hanging on by our fingertips. That we have managed to continue is attributable to more than luck, really; it's a credit to our years of organization and planning. We first met with the Soviets in 1987, for example, and at that time they offered to deliver our fuel to the South Pole. (We naïvely turned them down, putting our faith in Adventure Network.) The spirit of our undertaking is contagious; everyone is pulling for us, wants us to succeed and is willing to help whenever possible. Because of that spirit I had a blind faith that somehow there would be fuel waiting at the South Pole and tried not to let the potential for failure bog down my thoughts. In many ways the continuation of the expedition is out of our hands. All we can do here is put in the miles . . . and keep our fingers crossed.

DECEMBER 6, DAY 133

We cracked 88° latitude yesterday, and the temperature dropped to −15°. When we left this morning we had the wind in our faces, and I found that when I did just the slightest exercise, like bend over to cinch up my mukluks, I lost my wind. That state of breathlessness has haunted us for the past week and is becoming more pronounced daily, as we climb higher and higher. Our altimeter read 9,300 feet yesterday, which meant we had climbed 1,000 feet in two days. The return of the colder temperatures the past few days is also an indication we have finally reached the top of the plateau, as is the heat of the sunshine, which increases daily.

At nine o'clock Jean-Louis was on the radio and for the first time had been contacted by someone at the South Pole. Victor yelled for me in the clear night air, and I hurried to their tent.

"How you doin' there, Trans-Antarctica, is this Will Steger? Over."

"Yeah, this is Will. Good to talk to you. We'll see you in five or six days."

"I'd like to try and fill you in on the policy change that has happened in the past week, since you were not going to be greeted at the Pole originally." Because of the NSF's hands-off policy toward all private expeditions we did not expect any greeting. That they had aided us in securing aviation fuel, though, implied at least they wouldn't be hostile.

"Okay," I said, "what has happened? We have not heard anything."

"Okay, I have to make a statement before I go any further, because I'm already in danger of losing my job by talking to you. This is an unofficial contact. My name is Chris. I'm the winter-over communications technician and I am in a ham-radio shack outside the base's dome. Originally you and your film crew were going to be put across the runway and the people at the station were not going to be allowed to talk to you, except briefly. But apparently the Soviets have asked the NSF to greet your Soviet 'diplomat,' so now they're going to give you a slightly better welcome. Just a week ago the NSF wanted nothing to do with you."

"Roger, Chris. Thank you for the information, and we're glad that we'll get some greeting there. We're looking forward to seeing you all."

"We're looking forward to seeing you too. We appreciate what you're doing to bring public awareness to Antarctica. We would like to ask you to take the time to give us a brief talk when you arrive, to tell us what's been happening and how things have been going. I know you probably have a very busy schedule, but we would appreciate it sometime while you're here."

"Yes, Chris," I said, "we will be there for three days and we would like to do that."

"Though the NSF doesn't want me talking to you, I've been monitoring your frequency and watching out for you the best I can. While you are not going to be allowed to do much here, we still look forward to seeing you."

"Okay, Chris. I want to check watches with you. Stand by. Our time here is Chilean time, and it is nine p.m., December sixth. We will arrive our time either on December eleventh, between six and eight p.m., or around eleven or twelve on December twelfth."

"Okay, that is understood. We are on New Zealand time, and it is eleven fifty-four in the morning on December seventh."

"Okay, you're operating a day ahead of us, so we will most likely arrive early morning on your twelfth. What is your temperature there?"

"Minus twenty-seven."

"Same here. Maybe we better not talk anymore, tonight. But could we make another contact when we get closer? We'll try you on December tenth, our time."

* * *

I have run into this kind of welcome before, where the troops are anxious to meet us but the "policy" of the base won't allow it. In Greenland we passed a Distant Early Warning (DEW) Line station, as did Mantell and I in 1983 in northern Alaska. At both, the official policy was No Visitors. What we hoped and tried to avoid in both those situations, and what we needed to avoid at all costs at the South Pole, was to provide any reason for a rift to develop between the staff and the base management. We were just passing through; they had to live together, in isolated conditions, for many days to come. At the South Pole we would go along with whatever policy headquarters had passed down. As for our reception, since we weren't expecting much, anything would be appreciated.

Our history with the National Science Foundation, which administers all U.S. programs in Antarctica, goes back to September 1987, when Cathy deMoll, Jean-Louis, Adventure Network's Martyn Williams and I went to Washington to lay out our plan for them, to hear for ourselves what they thought of our expedition. We knew from the experience of others that the NSF's stated policy is not to help or even recognize private ventures in Antarctica, in part going back to the Mt. Erebus plane crash in November 1979.

Regularly scheduled tourist flights over the continent had been run by Qantas and Air New Zealand since 1977, but when the ANZ DC-10 crashed into the side of Mt. Erebus, killing all 257 aboard, they ended quickly. The plane had no provisions for emergency survival on ice; there was no mechanism for rescue or evacuation; and had it not crashed in the vicinity of the American and New Zealand bases, the wreckage might never have been located. The search for scapegoats, according to Antarctic historian Stephen Pyne, "extended to the U.S. Navy, as families of planes' crew members pressed lawsuits amounting to $17 million on the contention that the airfield maintained by the Navy on the ice shelf at McMurdo had been negligent in failing to warn the New Zealand pilot adequately about weather conditions and about his flight path in the lower levels of Mt. Erebus."

That incident—particularly the lawsuits that followed—cemented within the National Science Foundation a reluctance to have anything to do with private missions in Antarctica. But we hoped that with our high level of polar experience, the backing of several other governments with Antarctic bases, and our overriding intent to help educate people about the seventh continent, we might persuade the people at the NSF to at least become a viaduct for information for us, even if they could neither support nor recognize our expedition.

We were very frank about our plans, even though Martyn was hesitant to give them too many specifics. He was concerned they would "warn" other governments not to give us support. The attitude of the NSF administrators was simply "We don't want you there," and they repeated to us that their main objection was that if we got in trouble and called for their assistance, it would be expensive and take away from their scientific mission. (Though we didn't know it until some months later, after our initial meeting the NSF sent a telex to the Soviets, implying that it was not in "Antarctica's best interest" to help us.) Convincing the NSF of our expertise and legitimate concern for Antarctica was to be one of the biggest challenges of our years of preparation.

Our appeal to both the NSF and the State Department, which represents the U.S. in all Antarctic Treaty meetings, was simply that Antarctica is changing. It is getting easier to get to, thus attracting more and more tourists and expeditions each year. In coming years, we suggested, they were going to have to develop a way to deal with people traveling to Antarctica, other than just simply saying no. We suggested they pick an expedition like ours, review our plans, point out any pitfalls, and work with us on the dos and don'ts, so that our expedition might be a precedent for future ventures. Before we crossed Greenland, for example, we worked with the Danish government that governs there, to organize a safe and successful traverse. We were required to fill out dozens of applications that detailed why we were going and to prove that we had the necessary equipment, expertise, insurance and rescue plans. They held the right to approve or disapprove our application, and approved it without qualification. Our experience there was a resounding success, and most importantly, it was safe. When we went to the NSF we knew rescue would be the biggest sticking point. They were concerned that if we got into trouble we would call on a U.S. base to bail us out. We assured them that we planned to set aside $400,000 in our budget for rescue, to avoid having to rely on any government's assistance. The NSF said our "escrow" made no difference to them. (In fact, we didn't escrow money, but instead took out an insurance policy to cover any rescue costs.)

During our three years of planning, the NSF took a spectator's role, though we were always aware they were watching. One of our biggest worries was that at the last minute they might make it difficult for us to fly the dogs to Antarctica. Although nobody governs Antarctica, except for the treaty, each country is responsible for its own citizens who travel there. Because the dogs were coming from the U.S. we had to comply with NSF guidelines for importing dogs to the continent. We'd been advised that such applications were routinely rubber-stamped, but we were convinced ours would endure more scrutiny.

Sure enough, no rubber stamp for Trans-Antarctica. Instead, the NSF enlisted a panel of experts to read every word of our application. When they could find no fault in it, we got approval, but that wasn't until May 1989, less than two months before we were scheduled to depart.

DECEMBER 7, DAY 134

I often wonder what the dogs think about during the day. Lately mine are behaving just as we are: slightly bored, not excited about pulling, just putting in the miles. They look forward to the noon break, because they get to sleep. Toward the end of the day when the sleds up front stop or turn to the side, or if one of the skiers stops or bends over to take off his skis, the dogs go into a sprint, because they know it's quitting time.

At lunch today we talked about the formalities of arriving at the South Pole: Should we arrive on their time or ours? Would they invite us in for a hot meal? Would we get a hot shower? Would we be allowed in one of the base's three bars? Apparently, due to the Soviets' intervention, the South Pole base is receiving us officially as the "Soviet Antarctic Expedition." Our understanding is we will be invited in for a quick tour of the base. Victor, the Soviet "diplomat" traveling with us, will be our designated "leader."

We also talked about what different concerns Amundsen and Scott must have had when they arrived at 90° south. Amundsen got there first, on December 14, 1911, fifty-six days after he left the Ross Ice Shelf. He, four companions and sixteen dogs stayed for four days, boxing the Pole with three sets of readings so there would be no dispute where they had been (though it was later proved they never quite stood at the geographic Pole but came within two hundred yards of it). They put up a tent, marked "South Pole" on all their equipment, and had a feast. When Scott arrived, on January 17, 1912, the tent and a black bunting flag fixed to a spare sledge runner were his first indications he'd lost the race to the Pole. In the tent Scott's men found a miscellaneous assortment of mitts and socks, a sextant, thermometer, a letter to him from Amundsen and another, to be forwarded by him to Norway's King Haakon. A stone tablet, signed by Amundsen and his men, proclaimed only "Welcome to 90."

It wasn't until October 31, 1956, that another man set foot on the ice at the bottom of the world (though Admiral Richard Byrd flew over the Pole on November 29, 1929). Rear Admiral George Dufek landed that day in a DC-3 to officially open the

U.S. research program in Antarctica, as part of the International Geophysical Year. The first tourists arrived there on January 21, 1988, by commercial aircraft, at $34,900 per ticket; and on January 17, 1989, the first tourists to travel overland on skis, traveling seven hundred miles from Patriot Hills and accompanied by snowmobiles and Adventure Network's Martyn Williams, arrived, paying $80,000 each for the privilege. Trans-Antarctica would be the first to arrive at the South Pole by dogsled since Scott, and the nearly two thousand miles we'd crossed to get there was twice what either he or Amundsen had traveled round-trip.

DECEMBER 9, DAY 136

Another 24.5-mile day, which leaves us just 45 miles from the Pole. We traveled with a cross wind, the first we have had in almost two months, and the temperature was a fairly mild −10°, though the morning was highlighted by blowing, snowy conditions, unusual this close to the Pole. Otherwise the surface conditions were soft and flat.

Between ten o'clock and one o'clock we experienced a series of very large, very loud "snowquakes," a phenomenon we had begun to witness with regularity. It is something I have experienced in the Arctic, when traveling across wind-drifted, snow-covered lakes or open fields. But like many things in Antarctica these are the biggest I have ever seen. Snowquakes are caused when snow that has built up in a layer several inches thick, covering an area from room-size to bigger than a football field, collapses from its own weight, dropping a few inches all at once. Today's were the loudest I've heard, resembling the rumble of distant thunder as it "crashed" around us. They can be very frightening, though totally harmless. During the first one this morning I half expected to be shot into midair and sent tumbling down a mammoth crevasse. The next shook the whole sled as I hung tightly to the handlebars. After the first two we were on guard for more. But it is the dogs who start walking gingerly once the quakes begin; when they come, all three teams scatter, attempting to run away from the loud noise. During the first today Thule veered hard to the right, and during another she turned in fright and ran straight back into her team for protection.

The quakes marked the beginning of a day that featured a display of Antarctica's most unusual and breathtaking natural phenomenon. Late in the afternoon we saw the most fantastic display of sun halos I've ever seen, apparently in honor of Jean-Louis's forty-third birthday. The entire sky was filled with ice crystals; "diamond dust," the scientists call it. There were double halos and even a rare triple arc opposite the sun, caused by the sunlight refracting on the ice crystals. It was as if somebody were setting up an entrance for the Messiah; it was one of those fleeting moments when all six of us stopped dead to absorb Antarctica's radiance.

As we near the bottom of the Earth the sun is becoming more intense each day. I was in Jean-Louis's tent for the radio check in the early evening, and we unzipped the doors to let in the sun's rays. It was as if we'd clicked on a very bright 250-watt light bulb. The sun did seem to have regenerative powers, and in fact on Douglas Mawson's 1912 expedition —the time he lost both a sled and two teammates to crevasses and the conditions—he used the sun for just that purpose. He was in East Antarctica, at a slightly lower elevation than this, and during the day he would lie naked in the leeward side of his sled, on a piece of canvas, and soak in the rays of the sun for several hours. He insisted the sunlight renewed his strength, as powerful as if it were food or a vitamin.

As Jean-Louis and I sat, waiting to make contact with Patriot Hills, he talked about the day. "Sometimes it is like Antarctica has no soul," he said, "like it is another planet, not a place for man. But other times, when you have a very nice sky like today, when you realize you really are on Earth, I feel like

I am in a big, wondrous temple. Today when we saw triple halos I thanked the sky out loud."

His birthday party turned into the usual logistical meeting but was a very warm, friendly affair. We talked about the area of inaccessibility resupplies, rehearsed the statement we planned to read at the South Pole, discussed the watch time that we would keep after the South Pole and the general schedule of events for our three days off. The magnetic spirit of the South Pole is drawing us now, and everyone has mellowed. Though the Pole is still a few days away, the past mornings have begun with a fresh feeling, a sense that this was not to be just another day of the same old grind but one that brought us closer to the Pole. It actually felt, for the first time since we'd arrived in Antarctica, as if there was an ending nearby, though we are well aware we're only halfway home.

Our arrival at the Pole does represent an ending of sorts. Prior to just ten days ago it seemed as if there would never be an end to this trip. My mind couldn't even consider the concept of "ending." But reaching the South Pole is as if we're walking through a gateway to the other side of Antarctica. Already I can feel the effect on my mind of passing that mark; I feel more positive, reinvigorated. It's funny how, after this arduous physical ordeal, it is our minds that need a break more than our bodies.

While I have tried to hold off getting too excited about our arrival, I have to admit that there is a magic about the poles, a feeling engendered in us of being very young and excited. Now Jean-Louis and I—and only a few other men in history— have traveled overland to both, and the fascination continues. I think the others feel the same way, and as always Victor's excitement is the most intense. He told me today arriving at the South Pole will be "like visiting Disneyland, Las Vegas and Mars simultaneously."

Dahe was excited too, for both himself and his research. He hopes while we are at the Pole to meet fellow scientists and try to establish contact so that someday he might come back and study there. "I have many pictures in my head of Antarctica already," he said, "but I know my favorite moment will be arriving at the South Pole. That will be very special, maybe because not everyone who tries can reach it. When I was a boy I wanted to go everywhere on the Earth. So far, for a Chinese, I have been many places. But I never thought I would ski across Antarctica."

DECEMBER 10, DAY 137

"Come in, South Pole, come in, South Pole, this is Trans-Antarctica, Trans-Antarctica, do you copy? Over," I said.

"Hello, Trans-Antarctica. Who am I talking to?"

"Chris, this is Will. We are now twenty-two miles from your base coming up on eighty-nine degrees. We should be there between five and seven o'clock tomorrow evening."

"Okay. This is all unofficial, but right now we have minus twenty-five degrees, clear visibility, and blowing ice crystals."

"That is similar to what we have right here. Can you tell us if our airplane, the Twin Otter with the film crew, landed there today?"

"That's confirmed. They came in today and were given a tent and told to stay on the other side of the runway, because they are not part of the official 'Soviet Antarctic Expedition.' "

"That's good, Chris. Can you pass word to them somehow that we will be in between five and seven? We're having a difficult time reaching them on the radio."

"I will pass it on, even though I'm not supposed to be talking to you. But I know the base manager here is interested in exactly when you're coming in."

"Okay, Chris. We're in good shape here. . . . See you tomorrow. By the way, the Soviet diplomat wanted me to remind you that he was very thirsty for vodka."

"Okay. How many bottles would you like me to pick up?"

"He says two to start."

"Is there anything else you would like? If not, have a good night, pleasant dreams, South Pole clear."

"Okay, Trans-Antarctica clear. Over."

DECEMBER 11, DAY 138

We broke camp at the usual time, in fairly good weather: −20°, wind whipping across us at fifteen miles per hour. We traveled our now standard three miles an hour and until midday the visibility was very poor, with low clouds and fog hugging the surface.

Around noon the heavy skies lifted and we spotted a large Hercules LC-130 aircraft on the horizon ahead, making a low angled approach to what we assumed must be the Amundsen-Scott base. We couldn't hear the plane, yet we knew we were close to where it was landing. When we stopped for lunch we could just barely make out an antenna on the horizon.

As we traveled after lunch we were surprised at how fast the base appeared. By two-thirty we could see its well-known dome under which most of the base's activity takes place, as well as plowing equipment, snowbanks and the end of the runway. By three o'clock we could make out the tent they'd set up for us on the far side of the runway and then a semicircle of flags flapping in the distance and what appeared to be a big row of red gasoline drums sitting beneath them.

The red barrels turned out to be the base personnel—sixty of the ninety currently stationed there—bunched around the ceremonial barber's pole that marks the geographic Pole. They were waiting for us with handmade signs and cheers. The dogs ran as a bunch rather than in a straight line when they saw the people, and as we drew near we could hear their clapping and I could read a sign that said HELLO FROM MINNE-SOTA! It was almost as if my dogs could make it out too, because they veered off ten degrees and crashed right into the crowd that held it, tails wagging. We wrestled the dogs to a halt, took off our skis, and were swallowed by the crowd of well-wishers.

It was a joy meeting the people, shaking hands, and especially for me, talking to fellow Americans. Several were from Minnesota; the base commander was from Grand Marais, one woman was from Ely, another from MacGregor. It was a real homecoming, and as excited as we were to see them, they seemed even more so to greet us. Many later told us our arrival was the high point of their stay in Antarctica.

We gathered around the barber's pole for pictures, then were told we were going to be allowed in the base for coffee and a question-and-answer period, for a maximum stay of three hours. We couldn't simply head inside, though; we first had to stake out the dogs, unpack our sleds, and get situated. An hour later we were snowmobiled down the ramp that led into the dome, into the heart of the Amundsen-Scott base.

The base commander and several of his underlings gave us a very quick tour of the station—the communication room, the weather-tracking facility, the lounge area (it felt very strange to be on a carpet in a warm room). We then signed a number of certificates for them and kind of stood around, unsure of what was to come next. They made a big deal over, and we joked about, the Soviet diplomat in our midst. Then we went down to the galley, where they offered us a cup of coffee (nothing more, despite the fact that hot food was being prepared, and on our clocks it was already past dinnertime).

We were then led to the gymnasium, a small building off one of the dome's major corridors. An announcement had been made over the public-address system, and seventy of the base's employees had crammed into the gym. We walked into cheers and clapping.

We answered questions for about an hour, many addressed to Victor and Dahe. Perhaps the best question asked was, What had we learned during the first half of the trip that would help us on the second?

Jean-Louis replied with one word. "Confidence."

* * *

Since we had entered the dome a small brunette woman in her mid-forties had trailed us but was not introduced at first. It turned out she was Carol Roberts, an NSF representative who had flown in from McMurdo on the Hercules we saw landing, to monitor our arrival. Her orders were to read us the NSF's official position discouraging private expeditions in Antarctica, then tag along and take notes on what we said and did, and report what the base commander and others said to us.

As the Q & A wound down I asked, in front of everyone, if we could discuss the rules we were expected to abide by during our stay. Roberts, obviously nervous, stood and read a five-minute statement that reiterated the NSF's policy of non-recognition of private expeditions. We were to stay on the opposite side of the runway from the base at all times, she explained. There would be no "fraternization" with base personnel. She was in a very uncomfortable position. When we were first introduced she seemed quite hard, even militaristic. But as she followed us around she softened up a little; I could see she was in a tight spot.

I sensed everyone with authority felt on the spot, including the base manager. I think they wanted to give us a bigger welcome, but felt constrained by the orders from headquarters, back in Washington. After Roberts read her statement— and since it was obvious we wouldn't be offered the things we craved most, like hot showers and a hot meal—we prepared to leave the dome and return to our tents.

I felt more than a little ashamed and embarrassed for my country. Throughout the planning and duration of the expedition, we had nothing but support from the other bases we'd come into contact with. But here, because of government policies, our welcome was formal, strictly by the books. Dahe was particularly confused by the welcome; it made Americans look inflexible, and uncaring, when by comparison we had had warm welcomes at Chinese, Chilean and Soviet bases. Why were the Americans mad at us, he asked me. I attempted to explain the policy to him, but he couldn't grasp it; he said that while he could understand the policy, he couldn't understand the lack of basic hospitality. Unfortunately, it was the people at the base who suffered the brunt of the policy standoff, because we sensed they wanted to spend more time with us, asking questions, visiting, hearing about what we'd seen and learned since we left Seals Nunatak.

As we filed out of the gymnasium, Jean-Louis approached the NSF representative and said that he felt sorry for her and that she had "a very difficult job." He tried to express that we understood she was in a bind, the messenger delivering bad tidings. When he said, "We understand," she began to cry. Simultaneously, we were being mobbed by members of the audience, who were falling over themselves in apology for the NSF policy, saying things like "Please understand it is their policy, not ours," "If you need anything, please let us know." We were so glad to be there, none of this confusion stemmed our excitement.

At that time we assumed Roberts was going to be on hand for the length of our stay. It was unsettling that the NSF felt they needed to "watch over" us, and I hoped I could visit with her and discuss how in the future the NSF could alter their policy to allow well-organized, safe expeditions to travel in Antarctica. But to our surprise, within hours she flew back to McMurdo aboard the same Hercules that had brought her. That made me feel better about the NSF. They had done what they felt they had to do: read us their policy—and then left.

Before we slept Geoff made a point of going for a walk around the globe. Choosing a ten-foot radius around the South Pole, he crossed every line of longitude and passed from Monday into Tuesday and back into Monday. Tomorrow, he says, he's going to take Thule for a walk "around the world."

DECEMBER 14, DAY 141

We had been set up in a very comfortable camp three quarters of a mile from the dome, on the far side of the runway. We slept in our own tents, but a pair of larger ones had been erected for our use, one of which we used as a dining room; in the other we separated and repaired equipment. The weather was mild and the three rest days were spent writing letters, working on equipment, and passing time with the film crew and two Adventure Network pilots. We also met with the two Saudi scientists from the University of Jidda, Dr. Ibrahim Abdulhamid Alam and Dr. Mustafa Omar Moammar, who had flown in from Patriot Hills, the first Saudi Arabians to visit the South Pole. They would be continuing their oceanographic research onboard the *UAP* as it circumnavigated the continent, on its way to Mirnyy.

I tried to learn as much about the base's operation as I could. It was a place that had fascinated me since I was a young boy. We quickly surmised that the arrival of a Hercules was a major event, in part because it usually brings mail. Sometimes up to three planes a day will land, and on our last day at the Pole one arrived filled with congressmen, an admiral, several other military officers and a cargo of South Pole souvenirs, which would be sold at the base's commissary. The big plane idled on the runway for four hours as its passengers went inside the dome. It was the strangest visit: apparently these "leaders" came all the way to the South Pole and proceeded to spend an inordinate amount of their time in the commissary, buying the very T-shirts and trinkets that had flown in with them. (I understand the commissary does a thriving $60,000-a-year business in such souvenirs.) I would have thought these visitors would be interested in how the base runs, how they melt water for ninety people, how they keep the snow cleared, those kinds of things. Apparently not.

The most unique aspect of the base is the 165-foot-wide, 55-foot-tall geodesic dome, half buried by snow. Most of the living space at the South Pole—including the dining room, poolroom, library and bars—is housed beneath the dome, in three oversize orange meat lockers, mounted on stilts. They have no windows, since their only view would be of the gloomy half light of the dome's interior; they do have hot water, flush toilets, showers and a small sauna. American scientists have been at the South Pole since 1957; the dome was built in 1975. It's an ingenious design and ultimately practical. The problem with any land base in Antarctica, whether on the plateau or the peninsula, is that snow very quickly covers any building, requiring base personnel to spend an inordinate amount of time keeping walkways and roofs clear. That would have been very difficult at the South Pole, due to its six months of blackness and –100° wintertime temperatures. By putting a dome over the buildings they eliminated the never-ending hassle of snow plowing and constantly monitoring snow-covered buildings. Also, at the other stations there is always the danger of getting lost when going from building to building in a storm; they've eliminated that problem here.

A pervasive gray feeling dominates the inside of the dome. Heavy machinery buzzes around, including garbage trucks and huge d-50 bulldozers. The air is exceedingly dry; inside the buildings humidifiers run constantly. I can see how people could grow very stale here, especially if they were to stay a full year. We were told that the staleness can turn its residents into what are called "dome slugs," workers who don't step outside for days, or weeks.

We are here during the base's peak summer season; from mid-November through mid-February as many as ninety people work here. That drops to twenty during the eight months of winter—March through October—when the station is cut off from the outside world except for daily radio communication. The scientific studies done at the Pole are diverse and invaluable: they monitor seismic activity around the world; listen in on the nearly inaudible murmurs of the planet; and track satellites in polar orbit.

As I studied the dome from a distance, sitting under a bright sun outside our tent, I was struck by how much has changed here since Amundsen arrived, seventy-eight years ago today. But then I turned my back on the dome and studied the flat horizon that stretched beyond for hundreds of miles, its surface virtually unbroken, and realized that no, in many ways the place has changed not at all.

DECEMBER 15, DAY 142

Before we left the Pole we posed for more pictures around the barber's pole, beneath the semicircle of twelve flags representing the original signatories of the Antarctic Treaty. Forty people saw us off at 5:00 a.m. I had brought a flag with Peace written on it specifically for these pictures, hoping it would make for a powerful international statement, and when we raised it among the six of us the gathered crowd responded with applause and some tears. That was the most magical moment of our stay at the South Pole. Quickly, due to the cold, we packed the flag away and with little fanfare sledded off. After five miles the base disappeared behind us, masked from sight by the undulating terrain.

We had now entered the biggest, most remote expanse of flatlands anywhere on earth. The area of inaccessibility, an ice sheet half the size of the United States, never changes. It earned its name for its equidistance from all coasts; the logistical difficulty and expense of getting here, combined with extremely low temperatures, have made the region unattractive to most of Antarctica's visitors.

The route we're taking, eight hundred miles from the South Pole to Vostok, has been crossed only once before, in 1959, by a Soviet scientific expedition using special forty-ton tractors, or "trax." It has never been crossed by foot. Before we came south we were warned repeatedly, particularly by Soviet and French polar "experts," that we would find deep snow all across this stretch; they were convinced it would stop us. The Soviets insisted that on the 1959 trip they dropped a barrel of fuel into the snow and it disappeared deep into the soft powder. I was suspicious when I first heard that story; it sounded like a tall tale exaggerated over the years by Soviet polar men.

No matter what snow conditions we were to find, once we were a third of the way into the area of inaccessibility we would be difficult to rescue. Weeks would likely go by without radio contact. Once again we were testing the boundaries of technology, perhaps beyond a safe limit.

Despite any nagging concerns we might have had individually, as we skied away from the Pole we felt confident as a team. We had plenty of fuel at the South Pole, and an Adventure Network Twin Otter would remain there until we neared Vostok in case of emergency. At Vostok the Soviets anxiously await our arrival, in roughly thirty days. Having crossed 1,450 miles in Greenland without resupply, this expanse doesn't worry us as much as it might others. We made that run purposely to prove to ourselves that we could do it. Here our sleds are lighter because we're carrying fewer supplies, and we are confident that within a month the area will no longer be regarded as so inaccessible.

DECEMBER 18, DAY 145

As we expected, radio contact has immediately proved impossible, for a number of reasons. Solar interference typical of January has come early this year, due to intense sunspot activity. Furthermore, we're carrying only a 20-watt radio for the sake of weight, and both of our base camps, at Patriot Hills and Punta Arenas, are getting farther and farther away. The next semireliable radio contact we can expect won't be until we near Vostok and can start talking to their radio men.

We have developed a new daily routine to help break up

our days, an exercise we all welcome. Every forty minutes, roughly every two miles, the lead sled stops and builds a snow cairn about five feet high out of ice-and-snow blocks shoveled and ice-picked from the frozen ground. The intent is to snake a line of cairns behind us, the shadows of which can be followed by the two resupply planes we are expecting. The planes will fly either in the early morning or late afternoon so that the cairns will cast a shadow at right angles easily followed. Without dependable radio contact, the cairns are our only link to safety.

We have already established a routine for building the cairns: Victor skis out front, Geoff and Dahe are on the first sled, Keizo's is second with Jean-Louis, and I am last, by myself. Keizo's sled stops first, and Jean-Louis grabs a shovel and digs two-foot-square snow blocks, which Keizo stacks. By the time they have finished building, my team has caught up with them. The whole procedure takes less than five minutes. By the time we are moving again, Geoff is five minutes ahead of us, and forty minutes later he and Dahe will stop and build a cairn. Their stopping allows us to catch up, and then Jean-Louis and Keizo build another cairn forty minutes later. So far it hasn't affected our momentum in the least; today we traveled nearly twenty-five miles in just-below-zero temperature, with ten-mile-per-hour winds. Rather than slow us down, the "snowmen" we are building provide some relief from the sameness of the landscape and help quicken the pace. All around us the view is identical; flat white surface meets clear blue sky. There are no shadows, no bumps, no growth, no fixed marks, no nothing. We joke that if there were an Antarctic flag, it would be half white, half blue.

The only interruptions in our day now are snowquakes, back with a vengeance, keeping us on our toes. Since I am on the last sled, the others usually encounter, or trigger, them before I arrive, so I miss a lot of the firsthand excitement. But by watching Geoff's and Keizo's sleds ahead of me I can tell when they hit a quake. Keizo has three particularly skittish dogs—Bjorn, Arrow and Ray, whom I'd given to Keizo for additional power—and occasionally I'll see those three dart off to either side, as if they'd seen a ghost. In their panic they generally run in the wrong direction, toward the quake. Sometimes they run to the side, but more often they turn and charge back into the team, tangling the lines and drawing Keizo's rage. Geoff had the same problem early on, but his dogs seem to be getting used to the quakes. My dogs usually freeze in their tracks at the first hint of rumbling, then afterward run very hard for the next quarter-mile, as if they think they can outrun whatever that commotion is.

We are averaging twenty-four miles, or one third of a degree, each day, and the easier pace and lack of storms allows for more socializing than we're accustomed to. Today we had our first lunch break in many weeks during which all six of us could gather comfortably together. We sat beyond the shelter of a sled, in a circle facing each other, a little like kindergartners having their milk and cookies. We've been so isolated these past few months, but now with mild temperatures we can satisfy our hunger for conversation. Today we spent the half hour discussing the fall of the Berlin Wall, which Jean-Louis had heard about during his monitoring of the radio news from France. Victor in particular is stunned by the turn of events in Eastern Europe. From where we sit, it all seems very far away, as if we're hearing the news of another planet.

I'm tenting with Geoff now and carrying the heaviest load on my sled, including Jean-Louis's and Dahe's personal gear. When I come in at night, usually last, the four of us have a chance to talk as we set up camp. After I've staked out my dogs I walk past Keizo and Victor's tent and stop there to chat. Weather permitting I'm able to touch base with everyone during the course of the day, which is a first for me on the expedition. This is such a change; I guess I hadn't realized just how low my moods had taken me in the isolation of the storms during the first half of the traverse. These blue horizons are really waking our spirits.

Essentially our days have very little pain or suffering to them. It is easier to climb out of your sleeping bag in the morning, easier to go outside for the first time each day. For the first four months the wind dictated the coming day's pain level. If it was blowing its usual twenty miles per hour when we got up, we knew we were in for a harsh day of travel. From Siple on the winds blew nonstop, directly into our faces. Since we left the South Pole Victor's morning weather report has been identical day after day: blue skies, temperatures twenty to thirty below, calm winds of ten miles per hour. The dogs are sleeping well at night and no longer feel a need to bury themselves beneath the snow. When we stop during the course of the day they stretch luxuriously in the sun and curl up next to one another to nap.

This travel reminds me of the factory job I had when I was young, assembling water softeners. In the morning Geoff and I pack up the tent, then walk to our respective sleds carrying our thermoses. Once we're off, the cairn building is like watching the clock on the factory wall—every forty minutes we stop to build a cairn, counting them down to lunch. In the factory it was the same: constantly watching the minute hand and waiting for lunch. I spend the days writing letters in my head, designing the environmental meeting center I'm building at the Homestead, plotting future expeditions. I dig deep into my mental filing cabinet for precious natural sensations we've been devoid of these past months: I long for the smell a strong wind carries in a driving spring rain, or what it feels like on an early morning in the middle of October. I hear the sounds of forests, feel humidity, smell the air of a summer's day on the lake. Flowers may be my favorite daydream; I think a lot about roses, gladiola and tulips, both their beauty and their fragrance. Here those memories are like precious jewels. In the evening we are fatigued, as much by the monotony as by the physical effort. The one advantage Antarctica has over the factory is that there are no radios blaring Top 40 music nonstop all day long. Here we are accompanied only by the sound of skis schussing, our own rhythmic breathing and our hearts pounding. In fact, getting a song stuck in your head can make for a maddening day. Geoff has had Roger Miller's "King of the Road" going around and around in his head for some time now, and at the end of each day we laugh, trying to remember more words, more verses.

Each of us spends these hours inside our heads differently. Victor counts the miles that lie between us and Vostok that day, first backward, then forward. He thinks more about the future, he says, than the past. "It is easier for me because I always have a job—leading," he says. "The rest of you are following, so my days are not as monotonous."

Geoff spends his days calculating and recalculating figures in his head, from the miles yet to travel to the amount of white gas we'll have used in our crossing. Dahe says he prefers to think about the past, about his wife and his son and their life in China. "For the first three months I concentrated only on my skiing," he told me. "After the South Pole I re-created my whole life, everything I could imagine: my family, my parents, my colleagues, my childhood friends, the travels I've taken."

Jean-Louis claims to have already re-created his entire life once, on his trip to the North Pole, including walking every step of the small town in southern France where he grew up. He'd done a similar remembering when we crossed Greenland. There, he recalls concentrating for days on the memory of a special vacation he had as a boy, working on a farm. Here, he says, "Sometimes I think I have nothing more to think about, the past is exhausted."

Instead he spends his time contemplating the glimpses of news he picks up on the radio. He received in the mail at Patriot Hills half a dozen back issues of the newspaper *Diplomatic World* and still carries them, though he's read them cover to cover many times. For a while each day he says he takes on a different job, like president of France, King of the World, a ditchdigger, and spends the day thinking about what it would be like.

"Mostly I tried to re-create the warm, and what it was like to feel the sun on your back," he says. "In Greenland I spent three weeks thinking about sailing a big catamaran across the ice." Some days he would look for his girlfriend's (Sylvie's) face in the sky. "At first I could visualize her face, but after a few weeks it became difficult to imagine even what she looked like. Sometimes I felt like a prisoner in jail, looking longingly at the picture of his wife."

Keizo's thoughts take him to Japan and his parents and their home. He daydreams about his girlfriend, Yasue, too, who is living in St. Paul while he is in Antarctica. He longs to sing during the long days, but the high elevation leaves him breathless whenever he tries. Instead he focuses his attention on his dogs. "During the storms there had been no time for boredom; every step demanded utmost concentration," he reminds us. "Now our travel seems like a job—at the end of each day I say, 'Whooo, another day finished, how many more to go?'"

DECEMBER 19, DAY 146

Today we made a smashing 26.2 miles in crusted soft snow, even while building a dozen cairns along the way. These are mileages we did not anticipate making in this stretch, especially because of the high elevation. Our sleds are getting lighter, the dogs don't seem to be bothered by the altitude of ten thousand feet, and the miles just keep clicking by. Each day when we stop we ritually gather around Geoff's sled and check the odometer on the wheel he's been trailing since we left in July. We're starting to get into a numbers game now, and we can't wait at day's end to find out exactly how many miles we covered and how many are left to go.

As a result of our fast pace we are planning for just two

resupplies by air instead of the three we assumed would be necessary. We should have one day of food left around the twenty-seventh, so we'll aim for getting a plane in on the twenty-eighth. That's cutting our margins very tight, but we feel exceedingly confident right now and want to limit outside help as much as possible. If it were solely up to us, we would have preferred attempting to cross the area of inaccessibility without any resupply. But the Soviets, and others who are watching out for us, insisted such an attempt wouldn't have been worth the risk.

The biggest surprise here is the smooth, hard-packed surface. So far we have seen no hint of the deep snows we'd been warned would cover this region. Our second most pleasant surprise is the performance of the dogs. So far the elevation does not seem to have affected them at all. They sprint ahead after we build a cairn, and when they stop they are not breathing hard. But none of us knows for certain the long-range effects this elevation may have on them, especially when we get back into the cold as we near Vostok. In another month we'll be seeing temperatures of −60° to −70°, which in combination with elevations by then of more than eleven thousand feet could cause big problems, for dog and man alike.

Our biggest fear is that we might yet encounter soft snow. We can't afford to be delayed if we expect to reach the coast before winter comes roaring off the seas surrounding Mirnyy, early next March. Soft snow would limit our mileage and endanger our schedule. So far the winds have helped out, simply by continuing to blow, even lightly. We'd been told that the winds would die down from just past the Thiel Mountains until we were halfway across the area of inaccessibility. It now appears we will have winds until right around 86° latitude, because we are still skirting the Transantarctic range and the Ross Ice Shelf. After 86° we start traveling deeper into the interior of the continent, where we will see more high pressure systems. As a result, wind will decrease and snow depth will increase. If deep snow slows us, if our mileage is cut in half, the dogs would have to work much harder, and then the elevation might become more of a factor. Once again we find ourselves, ironically, praying for the winds to continue to blow.

Since we knew we were entering the worst place in the world from which to make radio contact, we had arranged in advance with the Twin Otter at the South Pole to meet us at a specific latitude and longitude on the twenty-eighth. As a result of that prearranged meeting we are putting a lot of faith in the cairns, which I feel comfortable with. If we resupply around 86° or 85° that means 150 of these little cairns (three hundred miles). The plane flies at about 140 miles an hour, so it would see a cairn every fifty seconds, which should be enough of a trail. Victor continues to do an excellent job leading us, so we've been traveling a pretty straight line since we left the South Pole. Once the pilot picks up the shadows of the cairns, he should have no problem sighting us, as long as the sun stays out.

We're not expecting cloudy days and in fact will have twenty-four-hour light all the way until we near Mirnyy. But for all our confidence, we are hardly allowing ourselves to be lulled into thinking it's easy street from here to Mirnyy. There is a lot of adventure to come, which is why we are so thankful for this break in the weather. A regeneration, physically and mentally, was a necessity; without this respite there is little chance we would make it across.

DECEMBER 20, DAY 147

Snowquakes continue to keep us alert, and Geoff had problems today with his dogs freaking out at the rumbling sound of the ground-level phenomenon. After each distraction it takes him five minutes to calm his team, untangle them, and get them back under control. These are definitely the loudest I've ever witnessed, sounding as if a freight train is about to emerge from the ice pack and run you over.

This afternoon Keizo had trouble with Bjorn, who was caught chewing on his harness. Except for fighting, chewing is a dog's worst offense; harnesses are valuable pieces of equipment and hard to replace. If caught, such indulgence requires swift punishment, but punishment works only if you catch them in the act. This time Keizo was able to tiptoe up behind Bjorn while he was chewing, to deliver a disciplinary whack. Just as he brought his hand down on Bjorn's head the surrounding area collapsed in a loud, violent snowquake. Poor Bjorn—his ears flat back, legs quivering—must have thought God himself had spied him chewing. I felt sorry for him at the time, but I'll bet he won't be gnawing on his harness for a while.

The skies across this region are incredibly clear, so we don't see any of the aural phenomena—the sun halos, arcs of blowing crystals, snow dust—that we saw daily as we neared the South Pole. In fact, the skies look the same every day—blue, with high, scattered clouds—even though this is the area over which the hole in the world's ozone shield opens widest during the spring months of October and November. From the ground there is no hint of this environmental catastrophe.

The so-called ozone hole in the stratosphere, fifteen miles above the Earth's surface, has brought world attention to these Antarctic skies. The hole is the result of one of man's biggest chemical experiments; in the mid-1980s it was confirmed, after years of suspicion, that the annual thinning of the ozone shield here is due primarily to man-made chlorofluorocarbons (CFCs), which are found in everyday goods from refrigerators to air conditioners, aerosol sprays to foam cushions.

While scientists had noticed the gap by the early 1970s—at first they blamed it on the exhaust of jet airplanes—it was not confirmed until 1984, by a British Antarctic Survey team. This was no pinprick, they insisted: every spring in Antarctica, from September through November, a hole in the ozone the size of the United States was opening, allowing dangerous levels of ultraviolet rays to come unfiltered down to Earth. (The additional ultraviolet light that reaches the Earth increases the risk of skin cancer, weakens immune systems, kills crops and sea life, and eventually plays a role in warming the Earth's atmosphere.)

Ironically, the chief of the British Antarctic Survey, Joseph Farman, had been trying to draw attention to the thinning ozone shield as far back as 1977. His studies showed that beginning in September the atmosphere over Antarctica would lose more and more ozone, until November, when the stratospheric winds would change and the hole would close. But Farman was told his studies were an aberration, since none of the sophisticated satellite monitors or computer models employed by NASA and other global scientists were transmitting the information that he was seeing. Finally, convinced that he was correct and frustrated by his lone stand, Farman went public with his findings in 1985, writing about them for the British science magazine *Nature*. While his colleagues were initially skeptical of the report they nevertheless rushed south to confirm whether or not he might be right.

His discovery was soon verified, even by NASA scientists who claimed their satellites had, in fact, spotted the depletion in 1984 but that they had dismissed it as a computer malfunction because of the drastic nature of the decrease in ozone levels. While it was clear that Farman's finding was, as one report dubbed it, "the monitoring scoop of the century" and that the ozone shield was thinning, no one was sure exactly what was to blame. CFCs were immediately suspected, but not everyone was immediately convinced they could cause such severe damage. Yet every year, the hole grew bigger.

Eventually two potential culprits emerged: CFCs or the extreme cold and wind characteristic of the skies over Antarctica. In May 1988, two hundred researchers from nine countries who were meeting in Colorado reached a consensus, based on several years of newly gathered data from probes carried aloft by balloons, instruments aboard NASA satellites and even from a supersonic jet flown directly into the heart of the open hole. The ozone layer over Antarctica was thinning, and CFCs were responsible.

Their initial hope was that the thinning of the ozone layer would be confined to the air over Antarctica. But by 1988 studies showed a similar if smaller hole opening annually over the Arctic and Greenland. Worldwide the Earth's ozone shield has thinned by 5 percent since 1978, affecting parts of Europe, North America and the Soviet Union. Each year more of this protective layer disappears, and this season, as we struggled through the storms on the opposite side of the continent, things took a drastic turn: NOAA measurements taken by balloon released from the South Pole station showed that ozone at nine to eleven miles altitude dropped to 15 parts per billion. Normally it is 2,000 parts per billion.

DECEMBER 21, DAY 148

Today is the longest day of the year everywhere in the Southern Hemisphere, and the sun is at its peak. From today on, the sun begins its slow spiral down. Now bathed in twenty-four-hour light, by March 1 we will have six to seven hours of darkness per day.

The only problem I'm wrestling with these days is Zap Junior, one of twenty-six sons of my longtime lead dog Zap (who died six months before we came south, at the age of thirteen). Today Junior started collapsing on me, his back legs giving out for the last hour and a half of travel, forcing him to walk and my team to be slowed. He didn't appear to be breathing too hard when we stopped; I felt his heart and it seemed to be pumping at an even pace, so I attributed his weakness to a cramp or a muscle pull, but couldn't be sure. I just hope I don't have to put him on the sled, because he weighs over a hundred pounds. I finally had to unclip him from the harness before we reached camp, and he limped into camp ten to fifteen minutes later. His illness is a mystery, since his spirit seems to be fine, his appetite is good, and Jean-Louis gave him a once-over and pronounced him fit. Unlike his famous father, whose spirit was always up and who was a seasoned veteran of both Arctic travel and the cocktail circuit, Zap Junior, though built like a horse, can be kind of a sissy. When the going gets tough he has a tendency to get depressed. He was one of two dogs that stayed behind when we left Patriot Hills and was introduced at the South Pole, so perhaps the elevation is affecting him more than the others. If he starts fading drastically I plan to trail him behind the sled rather than carry him. Other than that all the dogs are in good shape, but for the to-be-expected minor cuts on their paws from the sharp ice.

Because of Junior's malaise, I came into camp late and my chores kept me out longer than usual. But in these warm conditions I don't mind staying outside. Geoff and I alternate shifts every other night, in part to enjoy these calm nights. One evening he's inside doing the predinner chores, setting up and lighting the stove, while I am outside cutting snow for water and shoveling snow over the tent flaps. Tonight he made an exceptional curry meat dinner with rice, and we passed the evening talking and joking.

Living with Geoff, as I have since we left the South Pole, is very comfortable. Because it is his tent I feel as if I am his guest, and thus I try to respect his systems and sense of orderliness. We are getting along particularly well, partially because when you tent together you come to depend upon each other more than when you simply travel together. I am learning from his camp style too: every knot is tied perfectly, each box packed exactly the same way each morning, everything is placed inside the tent in the exact same place it was the day before. The biggest change for me is simply living in a pyramid tent, which is a totally different configuration from the North Face domes I'm used to. It took me several days to reorient. Geoff has kept diligent track of exactly how many nights in his entire life he's slept in a pyramid like this one: now it is over six hundred.

Sleep is finally coming easily across this stretch of Antarctica, and most nights my dreams carry me far away from here. As we struggled across the peninsula, I nearly forgot what a good night's rest was like. As a result of this spate of good sleep, I'm getting stronger and stronger each day. The change in our diet helps too. Just prior to reaching the Pole, I'd confined myself to a nearly all-cheese regime, but at the Pole we picked up one hundred pounds of beef per sled, and it's already begun to strengthen our needy muscles.

The biggest unanswered question in camp these days: "Is Thule pregnant?"

DECEMBER 23, DAY 150

Finally a day that wasn't exactly the same as the one before. Low clouds came in early in the morning, and it looked as if warm weather was on the horizon. Later in the day it did warm up, rising to −20°, and for the first time since Mt. Rex the wind was not blowing directly in our faces but out of the southwest and over our shoulders. This means that the wind now will be at our backs all the way to Mirnyy; that knowledge alone made the day seem much warmer.

Despite the pleasure we took in looking at the clouds, we had to focus tightly on ground level, as some medium-size sastrugi stretched ahead. The waves of ice were just big enough that we hoped they would not last, since they would make it impossible to land a plane here.

All day Jean-Louis sang to Keizo's dogs to encourage them, kind of a high-pitched birdcall, like a pigeon cooing with a pebble stuck in its throat. He was actually singing in Italian, but it was garbled by the face mask he wore. My cheer for the dogs when they are fatigued is even more high-pitched, and comes out "gibbie, gibbie, gibbie." Sometimes I alternate "dubba gubba" to goad them on. I'm sure an outsider listening in on this would think we were a bunch of lunatics, but the dogs listen closely to the expression of our words. Intonation is extremely important in getting them to run when they are tired or bored.

On a positive note, we managed to make contact with the Soviet bases at both Vostok and Bellingshausen tonight, which means we'll be able to talk daily to them if necessary. It also means that Victor will replace Jean-Louis as our conduit for passing and receiving information over the radio.

DECEMBER 24, DAY 151

We were able to make shaky radio contact with the South Pole tonight and have bumped our resupply up to the evening of the twenty-sixth, because we're running short on food. We may have cut the timing of the resupply too close; we are dependent upon Adventure Network pilot Brydon Knibbs's ability to follow the shadows of our little snowmen. If we get another front of clouds such as we had yesterday, the flight could be delayed. We can hardly predict when those fronts will come, and it is likely that Brydon will hit one or more such cloud banks as he flies, which will make his job of following the shadows of our cairns more difficult. Because of those risks, we thought it would be wise if he came a day early.

Junior's condition has worsened. I had him trailing on his neck line next to the sled two days ago and he seemed to have no problem. But by ten o'clock this morning he was starting to lag and by lunch he was really dragging. I hoped the half hour rest might revive him, but it did not; by three o'clock I had to throw him on top of the sled. I'm still uncertain what's ailing him; his appetite is good and he's not breathing hard, so I don't think it's either digestive or respiratory. It appears there is something wrong with his back legs, almost as if he pulled a nerve or something in his back, similar to what I did earlier in the trip. I'm afraid I'm going to have to send him out with the resupply plane, and then run my team a dog short.

DECEMBER 25, DAY 152

I spent today alone on the back sled, haunted by the fact that my dogs are sagging, and unable to put my finger on why. It is no longer a minor problem—I am running fifteen minutes behind the second sled, so my team doesn't get a break when the others stop to build snow cairns. I am late for lunch and into camp, which eliminates my spending even a few minutes with the others.

Since I am late into camp in the evening I automatically assume the tasks of the "Outside Man," which includes cutting snow blocks for water. Tonight the blocks come from one of Dahe's five-foot-deep snowpits, which he digs every thirty miles. It is the responsibility of each tent's Outside Man to retrieve blocks from Dahe's "well," filling nylon bags with perfectly cut blocks. That simple chore is often the best time for socializing. You kneel at the edge of the pit, relax for a few minutes, all the while packing away snow and chatting with whoever has joined you at the "well." Dahe is often still there, carefully scraping and bottling samples of snow and ice. Though our exchanges are brief, I always walk away from my visits to the "well" feeling satisfied. The scene reminds me of an African riverbank, with the natives gathering at the river's edge to draw water for cooking and bathing. Except for the cold, our missions are very similar.

Once inside the tent Geoff wishes me a happy holiday, and we agree that the area of inaccessibility may be the best place to spend it, if for no other reason than it is always a White Christmas here.

DECEMBER 26, DAY 153

It is amazing how we have acclimated to this weather. Overnight the temperature rose to −15° and we overheated inside
and had to sleep with our bags fully unzipped. At home in
similar temperatures it would be on the chilly side, even in the
northwoods of Minnesota.

We're all surprised that the winds have maintained their
steady pace and that we are still crossing whitecaps of sastrugi.
The surface is not that difficult for us to travel over; though
Geoff's sled tipped once today, it is an annoyance rather than a
hindrance. It does make it a little harder to ski and you have to
watch the sled carefully so that it doesn't tip, but since the
snow is on the soft side there is little worry of the sled's breaking if it were to fall. The biggest advantage to our days remains the hard-packed surfaces (today we made twenty-five
miles). I don't think it's going to be until 82° or 81° latitude,
another three hundred miles, that we start seeing the wind cut
back a little bit, which is fine with me, because less wind means
deeper snow. The closer we can get to Vostok on hard surfaces
the better off we are.

After comparing notes with everyone else, it seems that it is
our thinking caps that are suffering most these days. The same
thoughts keep recycling through your head, mile after mile,
day after day, and you simply get tired of thinking. You can't
appease yourself by telling yourself it's almost over, because it
isn't. We have become like snow nomads, with no sense of
place; the only continuity to our days is packing up, traveling
and unpacking. Our isolation is compounded by the spiritless,
soulless emptiness of the landscape that engulfs us. If a person
wasn't at peace with himself on a trip like this it would drive
him crazy. If you were a primarily negative person it would be
extremely difficult to survive in Antarctica. I used to think that
space travel would be exciting; now I've had a glimpse of how
exacting a psychological toll it must take.

We are expecting Brydon shortly after midnight, because

that's when the cairns' shadows will be at right angles and easiest for him to follow. We stopped tonight as close to 86° latitude as we could determine, since that was the agreed-upon location for resupply. However, since radio conditions prohibited Brydon from ascertaining where we'd stopped, he left the Pole flying close to the ground, counting on finding our trail of snowmen.

We heard the plane before we saw it, and he flew right to us. He could stay just an hour, given the plane's tightly calculated fuel allowance, so we hurriedly unloaded the Twin Otter and made arrangements with him to resupply us once more, at 82° latitude, on January 9.

DECEMBER 27, DAY 154

We took a scheduled day off and laid out plans to travel twenty-five to twenty-six miles per day for the next ten days, then rest a day before continuing toward Vostok. After today's rest, Zap Junior appears to be back to 100 percent and the team is strong again.

DECEMBER 30, DAY 157

We made twenty-five miles today, and our satellite message was the same as it has been for the past three days: "Sastrugi + + + +."

DECEMBER 31, DAY 158

Messner and Fuchs arrived at the South Pole early this evening, worn and frostbitten but vowing to keep skiing. They had hoped to arrive ten days earlier, but conditions were more difficult than they had expected. For Fuchs, it was a record of sorts, as he became the first man to ski to both poles in the same year. Their plan is to rest at the Pole for three days, then continue toward McMurdo following the same route that Robert Scott's ill-fated return took in 1912.

Our satellite message tonight was simply *"Bonne Année,* Happy New Year."

MILES TRAVELED: 2,369.5

MILES TO MIRNYY: 1,371.5

JANUARY

INACCESSIBLE
NO MORE

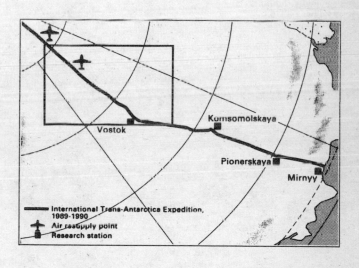

International Trans-Antarctica Expedition,
1989-1990
Air resupply point
Research station

Vostok

Komsomolskaya

Pionerskaya

Mirnyy

JANUARY 1, 1990, DAY 159

We requested by satellite that our Argos readings now be sent from Toulouse to Leningrad rather than to Punta Arenas. From there the Soviet Antarctic Expedition will relay the information via Immarsat (satellite telephone) to Vostok, 357 miles from where we are camped and with which we are now in regular radio contact.

We heard today that the *UAP* is on its way to Mirnyy, hopefully to meet us there March 1. While the ship did not serve its original intent, it has served as a communications base for us in Punta and may still take us off the continent. (When the ship was first conceived its role was to transport us to Antarctica. The plan was to sail it from Paris to Duluth or New York City, where it would pick up dogs, equipment and men. But once the Soviets offered us a ride south on the Ilyushin-76, sailing became unnecessary.) The ship has also proved a valuable base for scientific study; as it sails for Mirnyy, the pair of Saudi Arabian oceanographers onboard are taking seawater samples and making bathythermic soundings to depths of seventy-five hundred feet. They are working at the very limit of ice-free water, and their studies of that region are a first.

The *UAP* is a unique ship, the world's only sail-powered polar vessel, and is rigged with futuristic computer and satellite communications equipment. That it was built must be credited to Jean-Louis, who has long desired a seaworthy polar ship. He hopes to use the ship after the expedition for educational and exploration purposes in both the Arctic and Antarctic seas. The first thing he'd like to do is tag and follow herds of migrating whales. He also hopes within the next three or four years to re-create the famous drift of Norwegian explorer Fridtjof Nansen, whose ship the *Fram* floated him closer to the North Pole than any man had been before, between 1892 and 1895.

The *UAP* was in part modeled after the *Fram*—both feature walnut-shaped hulls that allow them to "pop up" out of the pressure of the ice as it freezes around them, rather than be crushed. The *UAP*'s aluminum-reinforced hull, sixteen millimeters thick, was designed by computer to withstand the pressure of such crushing ice floes. It is thirty feet wide at its maximum, 135 feet long, and sleeps twenty. In addition to the twin turbo diesel 365-horsepower engines it has twin masts and is capable of speeds of fourteen knots under motor and up to twenty under sail. It weighs 120 tons and can carry 30 tons of fuel.

The role of the Saudi scientists in the expedition was the result of another of Jean-Louis's diplomatic efforts. At Christmastime in 1988 he lectured at the shipyard that was building the *UAP* and afterward was approached by a French businessman who wondered why Trans-Antarctica did not include a team member from the Arab world. Jean-Louis answered that we would not have expected a people from the sand-locked Middle East to have experience with Antarctica, or even the cold. But the businessman, who had many contacts in Saudi Arabia, encouraged him to consider including an Arab in some capacity. Jean-Louis liked the idea and within weeks had communicated with Saudi Arabia's HRH Prince Sultan bin Abdul Aziz, who quickly responded that he would be interested in having two Saudi oceanographers join the expedition. Jean-Louis was then invited to Riyadh to meet the pair of scientists the prince had in mind, as well as the minister of education and other high-level Saudis. He returned with a monetary pledge from the prince and an agreement that the scientists would conduct their research in the name of the University of Jidda and Trans-Antarctica.

JANUARY 4, DAY 162

Thule is grossly pregnant, and we hope we can get her out of here before the puppies are born, perhaps carried ahead to Vostok by our next resupply plane. Having puppies on the ice would be a hassle we had not planned on, and at day's end we debated what we should do.

"If Thule has the puppies, I lose a dog and the expedition loses its lead dog," Geoff said. He was none too pleased that Thule was in this condition to begin with, blaming Keizo and me for not watching out for her better when she was in heat. I suggested that if she had a small litter of just two or three puppies she might be able to nurse them en route.

"But she can't run if she's nursing, can she?" Geoff countered. "If she is nursing, she's out of the picture for some weeks. The biggest question is, who is going to take her place? It's a pity that the word got out that she was pregnant to begin with." Apparently the film crew had taken back word that she was pregnant, and the Twin Cities newspapers and Knight-Ridder chain had already run stories about our mother-to-be. Back home, people were anxiously waiting to hear about Thule's pups.

"Personally, I feel if she has the pups we should hit them all on the head. She can have pups anytime," said Geoff.

While I understood his sentiments, I knew we couldn't do that. "We have two or three days to think about it, but it is a big decision, because the press does know," I said. Deep down we all hoped to take home a litter of "Antarctic puppies."

This was a dilemma that separated us from our predecessors who traveled by dog. The only way Amundsen made it to the South Pole was by killing his dogs as he traveled. When he set out the second time it was with fifty-two dogs; when they returned it was with just eleven. The rest had been killed, and cached on top of snow cairns, to serve as food for the surviving dogs on the rugged return trip. That allowed them to carry less weight in dog food than we and was a key reason Amundsen and his men succeeded where others had failed. But they were certainly not alone. Explorers have killed dogs for food, both for the surviving dogs and themselves, for centuries. But the public's acceptance of killing sled dogs for food has changed over the years. Geoff told a story about an English explorer named Andrew Kroft, who in the 1930s made the then longest unsupported trip across Greenland. When he came back home he readily admitted to the press that the only way he had made it was by feeding his weaker dogs to his stronger dogs, a truth he later admitted he wished he'd never shared, given the public's outrage over the truth.

"I don't understand why the press should have such an influence on the way we run our expedition," Geoff said. But the reality of modern-day adventuring is that the media are an integral part of big expeditions. Without media coverage it is hard to get sponsorship; without sponsorship it is impossible to afford this kind of expedition, thus impossible for us to fulfill our goal of educating people about Antarctica and its importance. It is really a simple formula, but occasionally even we find ourselves questioning it.

JANUARY 5, DAY 163

Today was stormy, and when we exited our tents it seemed for a moment that we'd been transported back to the peninsula. Visibility was just five hundred feet, wind was blowing, snow falling, quite unusual conditions for the area of inaccessibility. By the time we harnessed the dogs and began to travel, the weather was breaking into squalls; then it began to clear. For most of the day we traveled beneath spectacular light; the crepuscular lighting from the storm clouds diffused the yellow rays of the sun, resulting in extraordinary, ever changing and fragmented shafts of light streaking to the surface. It was a good day to ponder the role of the "Earth's fiancée" in the planet's ecosystem.

Largely due to the Antarctic Treaty, the continent's guardians have done a good job protecting the continent, but we need to be increasingly cautious about Antarctica's future. Its ecosystem is fragile and should be maintained by a hands-off approach. Despite its isolated place at the bottom of the world, and though populated year-round by fewer than two thousand scientists and support staff, it is one of the best places on Earth to study weather and the growing effect of man-made pollution on the planet.

Many of the planet's environmental problems surface here first, and sometimes most critically, for a variety of reasons. The continent lies at the hub of the planet's weather system, and the turbulent air above it acts as a giant pump that helps circulate air masses around the Earth. The oceans that surround Antarctica absorb more carbon dioxide than do all the world's vanishing rain forests and are home to the nutrients that form the base of the food chain in the Pacific, Atlantic and Indian oceans. As a result, Antarctica serves as a kind of near pristine laboratory. The days when explorers arrived here with simple mapping equipment are long gone. Today balloon-launching rigs, astronomical telescopes, gamma-ray spectrographs, gas analyzers, antennae, tracking stations, seismographs and computer centers are the tools of the new "explorers."

The continent has a major, if not completely understood, influence on the world's weather. As Antarctica's white ice sheet reflects the sun's heat back into space, an overlying mass of air is kept frigid. This air rushes out to sea, where the Earth's rotation turns it into the roaring forties and fifties— old sailors' terms for the fierce winds that dominate the oceans between 40° and 60° south latitudes. If scientists can figure out just how these winds affect the global flow of air, it will be easier to understand and predict the planet's weather.

Adverse effects on global climate are likely to appear here first because of the central role the continent plays in the Earth's weather and because of the pristine nature of its physical environment. The effects of global warming—the green-house effect—are one of the main focuses of study by the scientists who flock here each austral summer. Recent satellite monitoring shows that Antarctica has shed more than 11,000 of its 5 million square miles of ice since the 1970s, and one school of scientists believes that this melting is a direct result of the increased amount of carbon dioxide being put in the air by factories and cars in the "civilized" world. Similar melting is being recorded in the Arctic and Greenland.

This melting has a variety of effects. Antarctica is shaped like a bottle cap; when it warms, ice flows to the sides and falls into the ocean. This not only changes the saltiness and temperature of the teeming, fertile waters but also causes the levels of the seas to rise, which leads to bigger ice shelves breaking off and drifting away. The increase in fresh water being added to the ocean ultimately leads to a raising of the water's temperature, which may affect all sea life, from phytoplankton to krill to blue whales, and spark permanent changes in weather patterns around the world.

We must be careful in coming years if this lively ecosystem is to survive uninterrupted. The environmental profligacies of the civilized world are beginning to take their toll, even on Antarctica. It is sad to think that, given the opportunity, man could irreparably alter this place through carelessness and greed.

For the past week we have had no radio contact, and tonight we futilely attempt to reach Vostok, the South Pole and X-ray Bravo (code name for the Twin Otter standing by at the South Pole). We did manage to raise Martyn Williams at Patriot Hills; at least we could hear him. Our hope is that this stormy weather breaks within a day or so, but we are concerned it may hang on for a while. The temperature is near zero, but the way the fog is hugging the ground it appears to be settling in for a long stay.

Last night I had one of the strangest dreams of the entire

expedition. I dreamed all night that I was pouring concrete; mixing and washing forms, struggling to keep up with the mixer, mucking about in freshly poured pools of wet cement. I have no clue to what the dream might have meant, but at least it was a solid sleep.

JANUARY 6, DAY 164

The whiteouts are back. Today when we made snow cairns we would step fifteen feet away and they would disappear into the noncontrasting whiteness. These surprising conditions caused delays all day, but more important, we prayed the clouds would lift soon, because they obliterate our carefully laid trail of snowmen, our only link with the outside world. Otherwise the flat surfaces were ideal for the dogs and the sleds.

It was a calm day, and we made twenty-three miles in unbelievable warmth. The high was zero, but to us it felt like 40° and the first thaw of spring. In the morning, while we packed up the sleds, the dogs stretched out on the warming snow and "Summertime" played on Jean-Louis's cassette recorder. He said the morning reminded him of a Saturday in Paris and that he almost expected to come upon people out washing the winter's dust off their cars. We dressed lightly in thin stretch pile long underwear and Gore-Tex shells, the lightest we had dressed the whole trip.

As we skied this morning, still stopping to make cairns, I marveled at the fact that no one has ever traveled across this place, that we are truly penetrating a frontier. Fewer and fewer wild places remain on this planet, and I feel fortunate to have seen a few of them before they were spoiled. But the magnitude of this expanse is mind-boggling; there is no wildlife, no culture for thousands of miles. This plateau will likely be untouched for centuries to come. We are surrounded by flat whiteness, a thousand miles in front and behind us, the same distance as separates New York City and Denver, and not a mountain or building, no people or cars, not even a bump in the surface disturbs its flatness. We call it "mono-flat"; there are no landmarks to indicate our progress, just whiteness. The only trace we are leaving are the five-foot-tall markers of snow and ice we erect every hour, which should be knocked down by the winds within two years.

Despite the unseasonable temperatures there was no sun today, so lunch was still cold. In my memory we'd had only two comfortable lunches the entire trip: the first was on October 29, when we found the cache at Fisher Nunatak, when it was so warm we actually lay down shirtless on our sleeping bags and worshiped the sun. The second was three weeks ago. We were convinced today that if the sun had been out it would have set weather records for this part of the planet, since Victor informs us that zero is the record high at Vostok. But by the time we made camp tonight the temperature had dropped to −15°, and we were all chilled.

JANUARY 7, DAY 165

When I heard Victor's footsteps crunching toward the tent this morning, after a particularly good sleep, I had to admit an instant of resentment. There are many mornings lately when I would just as soon stay in the bag awhile longer.

When we quit today, after twenty-five miles, our position was just under 82° latitude, so we continue to make good miles. But the sameness drags on. Even our satellite messages are getting boring: "Clouds. Windy. Sand snow. Dogs, men okay." This is our twelfth straight day of travel and the dogs need a good rest, so we have scheduled a day off two days from now, following our second resupply. We haven't had a good rest, a solid rest, since . . . I can't remember when.

I spent chore time tonight talking with Keizo. We have had the least time together of anyone on the trip—we are each responsible for a dog team, which keeps us separate during the day, and we have not, and will not, tent together. Still, we may be closer than any of the others, in an almost teacher/student relationship. My junior by more than a decade, at thirty-three he has fewer adventures under his belt than the rest of us. Yet his patient, enduring attention to detail sometimes reminds us all that there is a lot we can learn from his Zenlike approach to both this kind of travel and life in general.

I first met Keizo at a Halloween party at the Homestead in 1985. He was working at the nearby Minnesota Outward Bound school, I was preparing for the North Pole. I'm sure his first sight of me that night caused alarm: I was dressed for the holiday in decades-old polar clothes, a World War I gas mask and snorkel, and wrapped in dog chains. Though our meeting was brief and jocular, when it came to finding an experienced dog handler for the team I contacted him immediately.

By then he'd moved on to Snowmass, Colorado, to work with dogs at the Krabloonik Kennels. An escapee of the strict order of his homeland, he is the first to admit he is a very non-Japanese Japanese. Though a model student (his parents brag that he never missed a day of school) and a master's graduate of Kobe University with a degree in economics, he had quit his job in his hometown of Osaka as a sales planner after just three years.

"An ordinary Japanese," Keizo had told me soon after he agreed to join us, "graduates from college, gets a job, marries, has kids, retires and dies. Most people never change jobs once." But Keizo had a very nontraditional and inspirational hero, Japanese adventurer Naomi Uemerura. Uemerura, an acquaintance of mine, was the first man to traverse Greenland north to south and the first Japanese to reach the North Pole, on a solo dogsled trip in 1979. Keizo quit his job for the "outdoor life," intent on modeling his future on Naomi's example. Unfortunately, his role model did not live long enough for his heir apparent to introduce himself: in 1984, on a dangerous solo climb of Mt. McKinley, Uemerura vanished. He had been at the Homestead just two months before, and I worried then that his vision may have been beyond his reach. But he lived his life the way *he* chose, and Keizo was taking the necessary steps to lead his life in a similar fashion.

After quitting his job, Keizo had bicycled across the hottest place on earth (the Sahara Desert) and then come to the U.S. and crossed it by bike, though his English was rudimentary. He learned from that trip, he says, that, unlike the Japanese, Americans live their lives the way it suits *them* best. He decided to stay, and moved to northern Minnesota, to work as a dog handler with Dave Oleson, a veteran Iditarod racer. When I called to offer him a spot on our team, he was visiting back in Japan but accepted my offer and moved to the Homestead to start training dogs in September 1987.

Like the rest of us, his dream of coming to Antarctica had roots in his childhood; as a boy his father had once taken him to see the ship that Japanese explorer Nobu Shirase had sailed to Antarctica in 1911. Shirase had sailed south, with dogs and men, hoping to be the first to the South Pole. Ultimately he was satisfied being the first Japanese to set foot on the seventh continent. Learning of Shirase prompted Keizo to read Amundsen's biography, and he was hooked.

"In Japan, nobody is interested in adventure, or exploring," says Keizo. "Everyone thought Naomi was a crazy guy, but then he became a hero, the government 'admitted' his activities and eventually awarded him honors. Because of Naomi's successes, they don't think I'm so crazy." Keizo's dream after the expedition is to return to Japan and open an Outward Bound-like school.

Generous, kind, soft-spoken—those are traits most often assigned our Japanese teammate. (Geoff says it is those very traits that make Keizo's dog team the most rambunctious. He is too forgiving, too kind.) I have never heard him complain: once he cleared a stream at the Homestead, rock by rock; another time he chopped wood for ten days straight, ten hours a day. He insisted that each day in every experience he learned something new.

JANUARY 9, DAY 167

The Adventure Network plane met us yesterday afternoon at one o'clock, and we decided then to take the rest of that day and today off, only our second rest day since we left the Pole, 550 miles back.

Hooking up with the plane was a challenge. We had agreed to an eight o'clock radio check with the pilot, Brydon Knibbs, to be followed by another at nine and then again at eleven. We made all those contacts yesterday morning, with the belief that he was still on the ground at the South Pole waiting for the skies to clear. But when we got him on the radio at noon he asked if we could turn our beacon on in twenty minutes, because he was just an hour away. To our surprise he had left the Pole two and a half hours before, flying low due to the intermittent clouds and tracing our cairns. What he didn't tell us until he landed was that along the way he had been forced to set down once, get out of his airplane, and turn on his Global Positioning System, a hand-held, battery-operated device that gave him his exact location by latitude and longitude. In other words, he'd been lost. But by one o'clock we could hear him in the clouds, directly overhead.

Since we hadn't expected him until later in the day we weren't prepared to stop, but decided to make camp when he landed, in part to get ourselves set up on a new time zone so that we would be in synch with Vostok. The change required us to set our watches ahead ten hours; it will be confusing at first, because we will depart tonight at 10:00 p.m. (Chilean time), which is 8:00 a.m. tomorrow in Vostok, Mirnyy and Moscow. Other than some minor jet lag, the biggest problem with the switch is that we will now be traveling into the sun most of the day. That will also make our days warmer, since the angle of the sun will be highest in the afternoon, instead of the middle of the night.

When Brydon arrived yesterday we discovered yet another Adventure Network screwup. The original plan was that he would fly from the Pole fully loaded, drop off our food, then continue on to Vostok. He would rest there a few days and then bring us twelve more boxes of dog food on his way back to the Pole. But instead of coming fully loaded from the Pole, he brought only a partial load of human and dog food.

His explanation rang hollow. He claimed he didn't think he'd be able, given the cloudy weather, to find us early so he had brought just eight boxes of food, when we needed twelve. Since we needed additional food now, he was going to have to fly ahead to Vostok and pick up four more boxes of dog food and fly them right back to us. At this point we can't figure out if these Adventure Network guys are just bad businessmen or if they're trying to soak flying hours out of us by these seemingly simple miscalculations.

Brydon's story got more twisted the longer he stayed on the ground. He was very tired, and it turned out he'd flown to us not from the South Pole but all the way from Patriot Hills. Our agreement with Adventure Network stipulated that they maintain a Twin Otter at the Pole for us as we crossed the area of inaccessibility but that if we were given advance notice it would be acceptable for them to use the plane for some of their tourist business between Patriot Hills and the Pole. All we asked was that they alert us and keep track of that time away, so that we could deduct it from the $100,000 a month we were paying for the plane's service (plus $2,000 per hour flying time and $200 per gallon of fuel). Instead, the Twin Otter had spent most of its time at Patriot Hills, not the Pole, and had been flying tourists between the two bases without informing us they were "off duty."

Brydon flew ahead to Vostok an hour after he found us, and he took along Thule, who was going to have her pups any day. He landed there, picked up food for us, and was back within five hours. We heaved a great sigh of relief when he took off, and Jean-Louis and I had a big laugh as we watched the Twin Otter disappear into the overcast sky. So far we'd survived the peninsula, the NSF *and* Adventure Network. From here on things could only get easier.

We had to send Thule out. Even though she was still leading Geoff's team, her pulling power was starting to diminish. Victor sent a note along with her for the doctor at Vostok, who contacted us last night by radio with a long list of questions including date of conception (we of course had the exact time, latitude and longitude, and mate) and whether or not he should house her in the operating room. We assured him anything above 10° would be fine. They were very excited to have her, and hopefully she will give birth soon and within two weeks after we leave Vostok be back at the front of Geoff's sled.

Dahe also sent some of his snow samples from the area of inaccessibility ahead to Vostok. They are the first such samples taken from this region, and potentially a tremendous boon to Dahe's place in the glaciological world. In those samples was a history of the weather patterns in this area going back hundreds of years. His samples of snow and ice are anxiously awaited in Vostok by a French doctor who is studying ice there this winter and will then be transported to laboratories in New Hampshire, France and China for further study. We hope they will be carefully handled on their long trip.

With Brydon I sent a letter to Messner, who we understand through Adventure Network is back on schedule and recently made ninety miles in two days, pulled by an airborne kite. I encouraged him to proceed to McMurdo, reemphasizing that we were 100 percent behind him.

Brydon left behind several copies of the South Pole's daily news summaries from around the world. We were surprised by all the good news: new freedoms in Germany, dictatorships collapsing in Chile and Romania, Noriega behind bars, Mandela nearly freed. The bad news was mostly environmental, involving a handful of dangerous oil spills. Overall it was a decidedly optimistic report from the outside world, which gave us heart.

From Jean-Louis's journal: "Sometimes at lunch people will ask if I have any news from their country, since I try to listen to the radio reports every day. I thought there would be more interest than there is about what is going on outside and I am surprised by the isolation they seem to prefer. I would have preferred carrying one tent for all six of us, to encourage more talk.

"Much has gone on while we've been away. Laurent [Chevalier, the French film director] brought me copies of *Paris-Match* at the South Pole, and I showed Victor pictures of hooligans running in the streets of Leningrad. He felt very badly and was ashamed of his countrymen, but I told him not to worry, that hooligans are everywhere, that it was a good sign. He was amazed, and relieved, to learn that we too in France had hooligans, that in some ways they meant freedom.

"Victor was always very apologetic about the corruption he knew existed in his government. I assured him that all governments had corruption, that men are the same no matter their country or beliefs. Victor was glad to hear that too."

JANUARY 10, DAY 168

We traveled today in a sort of jet-lagged haze, and about noon I started to fade badly. It is extremely difficult concentrating when your body is thrown off-kilter like this, because of the time-zone change. By camp time we were all showing signs of exhaustion. We stumbled into our tents, and our only relief of the day was our first cup of hot tea. After dinner and melting water for the next day's thermoses, we crawled into our bags and within minutes both Geoff and I were fast asleep.

Sleep, whether exhausted or not, is aided by the bluish

color of Geoff's pyramid tent. In the past I have favored sandy-colored, yellowish tents, convinced that that color produced the best indoor light for relaxing. In my experience, reds and oranges make for very disruptive tents; when the light comes through them it is harsh and jangles my nerves, especially on long trips. I'd never used a blue tent before, but here, in this twenty-four-hour sun, it provides a cool relief from the day's march. By comparison, the yellow tents we'd brought were best for that transition period when you wanted every last ray of the setting sun to provide light and a warm-appearing surrounding inside. But we have found when you're in nonstop light like this for any length of time, you develop a craving for darkness. Victor assures us that the sleeping quarters at Vostok are pitch-black. My only hesitancy about getting back into the darker days ahead is that accompanying the loss of light will be drastically colder days and nights.

It's sobering knowing that bitter-cold temperatures are around the corner, and that we have one thousand miles yet to travel. None of us is looking forward to −50° and the return of the winds. That kind of temperature takes a mental and physical toll: we estimate it requires two thousand calories just for regular daily body maintenance, that we burn another two thousand a day skiing, pushing and pulling, and that the cold saps another two thousand.

Contributing to the cold in this area is the altitude. Between here and Vostok, and then for the next three hundred miles, we will be traveling at eleven thousand feet. The effects of the altitude are exaggerated here by the cold high pressure air mass, and as a result, according to Victor, eleven thousand feet in Antarctica is equivalent to fifteen thousand feet elsewhere. We still get breathless periods during the night, and sometimes when you are running or even when you're eating if you skip a breath you find yourself gasping for air.

Victor came to our tent with bad news from Vostok just before we fell asleep. Thule had four puppies, but she did the

unmotherly thing and ate them all. Geoff was both saddened
and relieved, and surprised. She had been eating well and they
had given her plenty of milk to drink at Vostok. Yet her reaction is not uncommon, especially since it's her first litter. She
may have been confused by the new surroundings, by the
warmth and by being separated from her mates. The only
good news is that Geoff will get his lead dog back sooner than
expected; she should be ready to run by the time we reach
Vostok. In a way, I'm disappointed: I'd hoped we'd be able to
bring back some of our own Antarctica-bred puppies.

JANUARY 11, DAY 169

Frost covered the tent walls when we woke, and Victor reported it was −35°; the temperature has dropped fifteen degrees each of the past two mornings. Summer, which seems to
have hardly a chance down here, is already over. On the plus
side, the sky is clear.

It turned out to be our best travel day since the Pole, as we
made 26.5 miles, due primarily to good, smooth surfaces. It
was very cold, though, with the wind cutting across our faces
at a forty-five-degree angle from the northwest at a steady
twenty-five miles per hour. We would never have predicted
these kinds of winds on the plateau.

The loose, crystalline surfaces that allow our eight-hun-
dred-pound sleds to glide along reek of cold weather. You can
see the cold in the ice crystals: simple hexagonal crystals, nothing like the complex flakes we're used to back home, which are
produced under much warmer conditions. Here you pick up a
block of ice and it is rigid and solid, almost hollow. It feels very
foreign, and is actually many layers of thin ice, each a sixteenth
of an inch thick. This is an indication of strong winds and
sunny weather. The striations in it are indicative of annual
accumulation, and here it appears they get between two and
three inches of new snow each year.

Despite the new cold, my dogs are running well and are very excited. They are in perfect shape at this point; I couldn't ask for anything more from them. Their appetites are strong and we have ample food, so I've been giving them one and a half blocks a day. Gordie's appetite is immense now that the cold weather's coming back; he could eat three blocks a day. He is so big—110 pounds—that he borders on inefficiency, because he requires a lot of food. His strength is valuable, but he requires about three times the amount of fuel one of Geoff's dogs needs. If we were running this trip tight on food, Gordie would not have been brought along.

The true stars of the expedition have been Geoff's dogs. Their spirit is constantly high, they pull at a continuously strong pace, and because they are smaller they eat less, all a tribute to Geoff's dog driving and training experience. He has proved to me that a sixty- to seventy-pound dog is the best for these conditions. By comparison, my dogs average between ninety and one hundred pounds.

JANUARY 12, DAY 170

Another cold day, and the winds picked up all morning until stabilizing around eleven o'clock. It was a southwest wind off our left shoulders, which was better than yesterday when it blew into our faces.

The steadily dropping temperature is what we expected as we near Vostok, and throughout February we anticipate it will drop daily, possibly as low as −80°. But it is not the cold that concerns me as we near Mirnyy, it is the lack of visibility. If we can't see the trail we won't be able to travel, due to the crevasse fields that surround the coastal Soviet base. By then we won't have the option of waiting out storms because the weather will only get worse, as we drop from eleven thousand feet to sea level in the last two hundred to three hundred miles. If the conditions stop us before Mirnyy, they may prevent us from moving for many months. If we are stopped short of the coast, for any length of time, the expedition will be over; we're not prepared to spend the winter here.

Jean-Louis was on the radio this morning with Vostok double-checking our position. We estimate we're about five days away, and it is important at this juncture that we have our longitude accurately fixed so that we don't veer right or left of the base. Victor has done a remarkable job keeping us on a beeline course since we left the Pole, in fact since the Thiels. His accuracy helps enormously, especially when we must average twenty-six miles every day; if we were weaving back and forth it would cost us days. One thing that keeps Victor on a straight course is that he is desperate to see his old cronies and to catch up with news from the Soviet Union, where much has changed since he left home last July. For him, Vostok is the ultimate carrot.

Our visit to Vostok will be much different from our stay at the South Pole. People here have been awaiting us anxiously for months. While the crew at the South Pole is used to seeing lots of visitors, few people drop by Vostok. It is an old, very isolated outpost, perhaps the most remote in Antarctica, and our arrival is the biggest event there in decades.

Looking at the map last night we approximated that we are less than a thousand miles from Mirnyy. That alone gives cause for optimism. It also jarred us each into starting to think about our respective futures, since that kind of thought has been on hold for the past three years. It is just dawning on us that we will have a life after Antarctica. That is what preoccupies our individual daydreams now, thoughts not so much of home but of future adventures.

This morning as we traveled my thoughts drifted to Canada and traveling there by dogsled. I've been hungering for a map of Canada to study at night, filled by an intense longing to look at a topography laced with wild country and crisscrossed by rivers, mountains, plains, forests, lakes. In lieu of a map, I've been trying to paste a picture of Canada together in my mind. I succeeded this morning, and it was almost as if I were traveling in Canada, and it was very pleasant. Unlike here, travel in Canada brings new adventure every day; monotony and boredom never surface. The back country of Canada seems like home to me, whereas traveling across this place is truly like crossing another planet and I doubt I'll ever travel here again by dogsled. I think Victor, Geoff and Dahe will all work here again in some capacity; Jean-Louis hopes to sail around the continent; and Keizo and I will most likely return as visitors at some point. But this trip has served as a good reminder to me that my home is in the North.

JANUARY 14, DAY 172

I had more energy this evening than on any day of the trip, which I'm attributing to a new dietary supplement I'm experimenting with at lunch: I'm now dumping an additional eight ounces of cheese into my hot soup mix. God, I'm sick of this food! For the past few weeks I've been tiring dramatically by four-thirty in the afternoon. Getting tired here is related directly to how much fuel you're running on, so skimping on food, as bland as it has become, is dangerous. We're still trying to cram in six thousand calories a day, but we burn that off pretty quickly.

We talked at lunch today about arriving at Vostok and how natural it seems that the six of us, though of different nationalities, have completely forgotten our cultural differences here. Someone at the South Pole asked me what it was like traveling with a Japanese teammate, and I had to stop and think for a second, because it had been a while since I'd considered Keizo "a Japanese." To me he is just another man. That led us to talk about how important it is that Antarctica remain a place where peoples from all countries can work together, where national boundaries are no impediment to cooperation.

It has been more than fifty years since German aviators claimed part of the continent for the Third Reich by dropping hundreds of stakes emblazoned with swastikas. While the post-war Germany did not press the Nazis' claim, seven other nations with histories of Antarctic exploration—Argentina, Chile, France, New Zealand, Britain, Norway and Australia—insisted in the 1940s that portions of the continent belonged to them. The U.S. made no specific claims but refused to recognize those of others. Then in 1946 the U.S. mounted the most massive expedition in Antarctic history. Dubbed Operation Highjump, the naval exercise deployed thirteen ships, fifty helicopters and 4,700 sailors. Its unstated purpose: to ensure the U.S. could one day stake its own claim if it wanted to.

Thankfully, scientific cooperation preceded international conflict, in the form of the precedent-setting International Geophysical Year (actually eighteen months long) in 1957 and 1958. Sixty-seven countries participated in this massive study of the interactions between the sun and Earth, and Argentina, Australia, Belgium, Chile, France, Britain, Japan, New Zealand, Norway, South Africa, the U.S. and the Soviet Union established bases here.

After the project ended, President Dwight Eisenhower invited the eleven other nations that had built bases in Antarctica to join the U.S. in a treaty that would govern the continent. Signed on December 1, 1959, the Antarctic Treaty became effective on June 23, 1961, with the condition that on its thirtieth birthday it could be reviewed and possibly changed.

The treaty is simple and designed to protect and preserve the Antarctic environment and heritage: it says that Antarctica —defined as the area south of 60° south latitude—"shall be used for peaceful purposes only; that there shall be freedom of scientific investigation and a free exchange of scientific information; that there shall be no military measures nor weapons testing, no nuclear explosions, and no nuclear waste disposal; that there shall be free movement and inspection among the various nationals working in the Antarctic; that the countries

shall take measures to further the treaty's objectives, including
the preservation and conservation of living resources; and that
the countries shall discourage activities that are contrary to the
treaty's principles." Any United Nations member capable of
establishing a research station and scientific program may join
the "Antarctic Club." The member nations automatically become "consultative parties," and may vote at the biennial
meetings of the treaty countries. Today there are more than
sixty-five research stations on the continent, financed by
eighteen countries and one independent organization (Greenpeace), with more than three thousand summertime employees. About two thirds of the bases maintain winter-over staffs.

The treaty did not, however, eliminate all territorial jockey-
ing for position. The U.S. and the Soviet Union have strategically placed bases in areas claimed by others; several nations
have built post offices and schools in Antarctica to solidify
their presence. Argentina went so far as to fly a pregnant
woman to its Esperanza base so that she could give birth to the
first native of Antarctica. But since the 1950s no nation has
overtly asserted any specific claim.

Treaty business is conducted during biennial meetings, at
which policy "recommendations" are adopted, by unanimous
vote only. Over the years more than 160 recommendations
have been adopted. At the two most recent meetings, in San-
tiago, Chile, and Bonn, Germany, the sanctity of the treaty
was threatened. The key sticking point is the result of an
eight-year effort by the treaty nations to obtain international
backing for some kind of minerals agreement, which would
delineate the procedures for commercial mining and drilling.
That recommendation first ran into problems in September
1989 at a meeting of member nations in Wellington, New
Zealand, when Australia and France refused to sign it. The
agreement as it was written then would have permitted the
exploration of Antarctica's oil and mineral resources. But the
French and Australian prime ministers, in a joint statement
released in August 1989, claimed, "Mining in Antarctica is not

compatible with protection of the fragile Antarctic environment."

At the same time, a coalition of Third World nations led by Malaysia insisted that any of Antarctica's alleged riches be equally distributed among all nations. The protesters claimed the treaty members were exercising "modern day colonialism" in Antarctica.

As far back as 1938, Douglas Mawson wondered "from an economic aspect, the frozen South may not attract immediate attention, but who can say what a train of entrepreneurs the future may bring?" Today that future has arrived, and profit is the prime motivation behind the push to open Antarctica to mineral exploration. Troves of cobalt, chromium, manganese, uranium, platinum, coal, iron, molybdenum, gold, nickel and diamonds are thought to exist beneath Antarctica's ice. (These theories were developed primarily by looking at a map of the former Gondwanaland, which shows how Antarctica split from what are now Africa, South America and Australia. It is thought by some that the veins of underground riches in those lands most likely continue in Antarctica. A more recent theory suggests that Antarctica was once affixed to the western edge of North America; that 570 million years ago, today's South Pole sat less than a thousand miles from the future site of Las Vegas.) With present techniques, mining in the interior seems unlikely because of the glaciers' constant shifting and extraordinary depth of up to two miles. More important, any guess at just how much mineral wealth lies beneath the ice is still based on assumption; in most cases minerals have proven to be less than 1 percent of the total rock sample analyzed.

But developers continue to prospect for petroleum in the seas surrounding Antarctica: in 1974 the U.S. Geological Survey estimated that the continent and adjacent seas might hold as much as 45 billion barrels of oil and 150 trillion cubic feet of natural gas, quantities roughly comparable to the existing reserves in the United States. In 1987, in an effort to identify such reserves, treaty members decided to allow more extensive exploration and established procedures for drilling and extracting rock form the continent and its seabed, where the Japanese are already searching for oil. But any such long-term exploration would be extremely costly and dangerous, because of the depth of the surrounding seas and the icebergs and fierce winds that patrol Antarctica's coastline.

While Australia, France, New Zealand and others now believe that mineral and oil exploration must be completely banned (and others are for a moratorium on exploration), there are some nations, particularly the United States, that believe exploitation is inevitable. Their stand is that it is better to have regulated exploitation than a legal vacuum in which no restraints of any kind are imposed on even the most environmentally hazardous explorations. In the U.S., Senator Albert Gore of Tennessee is Antarctica's most vocal political supporter and is leading a drive for a one-hundred-year moratorium on mineral exploration and the preservation of Antarctica as a "global ecological commons." "The whole theory of protecting Antarctica with mining that is carefully circumscribed by safety procedures is the approach that failed in Alaska's Prince William Sound. We shouldn't make that mistake again," he says.

Both supporters and opponents of the mineral rights agreement concur on the need to protect the wildlife and habitat of Antarctica's land, coastal waters and atmosphere. The most vocal supporters would like to see Antarctica turned into a world park, a notion first proposed by New Zealand in the mid-1970s and since then enthusiastically supported by Greenpeace and by several million signatories to a world park petition. The concept sounds strikingly similar to the agreement treaty members hammered out for Antarctica back in 1959, but adds the idea of complete protection for the region's wildlife and wilderness, thus eliminating any possibility of mining. Limited scientific activity could take place, with scientists of all nations working in cooperation. And the area would continue to be free of nuclear and other weapons and all military activities.

At the 1991 treaty meetings in Madrid and Bonn, the world park idea was considered but viewed by many members as simplistic and potentially harmful to the scientific work done in Antarctica. The mineral rights agreement was finally rewritten, though there were rumblings among treaty signers that some countries would quietly like to see the treaty sabotaged. Since any recommendation needs unanimous support to be adopted, there are apparently treaty signers who hope the process is disrupted enough to allow exploration without anyone having to vote on the record "for" or "against" such exploitation. Such theorizing holds that some treaty signers might eventually vote for "national interest" over "international accord." In fact, the lone opponent of adopting the fifty-year prohibition on exploration was the United States, angering the twenty-five other voting treaty members who had hammered out the compromise. Environmentalists were also miffed; Greenpeace's Paul Bogert told the *New York Times*, "[This] shows the Bush administration is not interested in protecting the environment. . . . What we're seeing is a foreign policy extension of domestic energy policy: the continued reliance on and addiction to fossil fuels." Ultimately, the United States agreed to a fifty-year ban on oil and mineral exploration, but only after amending the proposal to allow any nation to "walk away" from the agreement at any time. Said Greenpeace's Bogart after the final vote in June 1991, "The U.S. took a delicate agreement concerning the future of a continent and replaced it with an agreement to act unilaterally. There's no doubt that the mineral ban is a positive step—but it's been weakened."

Tourism is another issue the treaty members must wrestle with. Since Chileans first began flying visitors to the peninsula in 1956 and luxury cruises started a decade later, each year brings more tourists down south, threatening to trample wildlife and pollute otherwise pristine habitats. More than five thousand people, mostly American, sail over on cruise ships from South America each year. Demand is such that Chile has opened a hotel near its base to accommodate the growing crowds.

For any flaws, the treaty has fostered international cooperation on a level unknown on any other continent; such an agreement should be cherished, and we will come off the ice convinced that Antarctica deserves to be preserved, not exploited. I've seen too many frontiers destroyed by man's pollution and exploitation—beginning with Alaska in the late sixties and early seventies—and it would be a shame to see the same happen to this wilderness.

JANUARY 15, DAY 173

We haven't received an Argos position in days because communication between Leningrad and Vostok has been sketchy, so we're not certain of our exact longitude. Geoff took a sun shot yesterday with his sextant and we're close to 107°, thus in line with our target. It would be helpful to have an Argos reading now as we close in on Vostok—if we are right or left of longitude at this point we could end up going miles out of our way, or possibly miss the base altogether. Yesterday it was cloudy, with reasonably good visibility, but not good enough if we were trying to spot from a distance the antennae that surround the base.

Somehow the dogs sense a change of pace ahead and are pulling almost in overdrive. I'm not sure if they think the end of the expedition is over the next undulation or if they just sense a rest stop is ahead, but they've been carrying their tails higher the past few days, an indication they're excited about something. They, too, long for outside stimulation—birds to chase, other dogs to bark at, new people to pet them—and somehow sense that some of that is ahead. Surface conditions have aided their excitement: very fast with little sastrugi.

Tonight we saw our first clouds come in from the north, our first weather system to come directly from Mirnyy. Until now all our weather has come from the other side of the continent, from the McMurdo and Ross Ice Shelf side. It is an ominous sight, because we've been warned by Vostok that the weather in Mirnyy this late summer has been particularly stormy. In fact the ice surrounding Mirnyy is so thick it looks as if it will be too dangerous to break a path for the UAP with a Soviet icebreaker. Instead, it will sail on to Australia.

JANUARY 17, DAY 175

Victor is so excited he can hardly contain himself; every day he skis faster and faster. His body language radiates his excitement, and he literally beams at day's end when we check the odometer and he can calculate precisely how many more miles to Vostok. In some ways Vostok is his hometown, and he is acting like a five-year-old kid whose birthday is tomorrow. Unfortunately, we still do not have our definite position. Frustrated, and in an attempt to raise *anybody*, Jean-Louis sends a fictional message over the Argos: "Major geographical discovery." Even that gets no response.

Though Victor is most excited about our arrival, we are all thankful to have this thirty-four-day march over with. We have taken only two days off since we left the Pole and lost a half day due to time-zone change, so we are all a little weary.

JANUARY 18, DAY 176

Today we will cross the last twenty miles' worth of the area of inaccessibility. There is little hurrah over the achievement; it is not like climbing a mountain—you can't look back and see how high you've climbed. Any celebratory mood is related to the fact that we'll soon see other people again. For a geographical first, it is pretty lackluster, and hardly great adventure. Traversing the peninsula was a knock-down, drag-out battle. What we have just crossed was the most boring terrain on the planet; it hardly seems a majestic triumph. What we feel is relief.

We spot Vostok from six miles out, and at first sight it looks like an oil rig you'd find off the north coast of Alaska. But the main preoccupation here is not drilling oil but drilling ice. As we draw near, what appear to be buildings in front of the tall drilling rigs start to distinguish themselves in the fog. As we close in, these buildings begin to move. Toward us. Slowly. Ominously. They aren't buildings after all, but the trax—World War II T-34 tank chassis fitted with Caterpillar treads—that are the Soviets' chief form of transportation in East Antarctica.

Topped by a twenty-foot-tall antenna and a satellite radar dish, they look like hybrids of submarines, airplanes, Winnebagos and Eyewitness News vans. Two stories tall and crammed with sophisticated navigational gear, these forty-ton vehicles are driven, usually in packs of a dozen or more, round-trip twice a winter over the eight-hundred-mile route between Vostok and Mirnyy. They travel at five miles per hour and are the interior's supply liaison, pulling behind them twenty-ton sleds loaded with fuel, construction supplies and everything the base needs for wintering-over except perishable foods, which are flown in during a ten-day window of fair weather in late January and early February. Each tractor is manned by a team of three and in the rear is a living compartment with a small cooking sink and bunks for six. (The Soviets were hardly the first to rely on motorized vehicles in the Antarctic. Both Shackleton and Scott, doubtful that dogs would survive here, brought gas-powered vehicles. Shackleton's, an Arrol-Johnston car he brought down in 1907 to use for towing loads over the Ross Ice Shelf, was quickly rendered useless in the soft snow. Scott brought three specially built tracked motor sledges in 1911, but two fell victim to mechanical problems, the third broke through the sea ice while being unloaded.)

A jumble of men pile out of the tractors as we approach, rushing as one toward us, and mobbing Victor. I am in the back, and it is a remarkable scene silhouetted by the sun—the dogs' heads are bobbing in excitement, men are slapping each other on the backs, everyone is taking pictures.

As we follow the tractors to the base, we can just make out the six flags of our countries flapping in the breeze at its center. We head the dogs in that direction and spy a handmade Welcome sign, in English. As we near, fireworks are set off, and the dogs freak out, turning around 180 degrees and running back from where we'd come. A Twin Otter can land right next to the dogs and they don't budge, but fireworks send them into a panic.

We were shown a place sheltered from the wind where we could leave the dogs. The base was just a handful of simple, low-frill buildings that included a generator shed, a combination dining/living room and a bunkhouse. It reminded me of the Homestead back in Ely, a place where lumberjacks and dogsledders would feel right at home.

Inside they had prepared a big reception for us in a small room, hosted by Victor's best friend and Vostok's station chief, Alexander Sheremetyev. We engaged in a traditional Soviet toast of bread dipped in salt and vodka, then moved on to a table spread with red and black caviar, sturgeon, salami, sweetbreads, kiwis, cherries, apples and oranges. We washed down the rich food with bottled water, champagne and shots of Russian vodka. It was a warm reception, with many verbose toasts of welcome.

Afterward we were invited to the sauna, a small, five-man room inside the generator shed. The sauna was 250°, average for the Soviets, but only Victor and I were able to stand it for long. I scrubbed myself for a couple of hours, relieving my body of five months of dried and dead skin, and then went outside and sat in the −20° weather for ten minutes, under a clear, windy sky. It was quite a treat, and my sore muscles and sallow skin appreciated it.

We had dinner of chicken and potatoes with Alexander. At my urging a map of Canada was produced, and I spent two hours studying its details. Later that night there was a small party in our honor featuring a four-person rock 'n' roll band playing makeshift instruments including a can filled with sand and a plastic bucket made into a drum.

Early in the evening our confirmation of reaching Vostok and having crossed the area of inaccessibility was made when Jean-Louis spoke by Marisat (the marine telephone used at Vostok) to Cité de la Science, the Paris science museum at La Villette. They had been dialing Vostok simply to test the lines and were surprised to find Jean-Louis at the other end. Later he sent a satellite message to Argos that read simply, "Vostok, houra [sic]." When asked about our "major geographical discovery," Jean-Louis explained he'd sent that message out of frustration at not being able to reach anyone as we neared the end of the area of inaccessibility.

As midnight neared, Jean-Louis and I took a break outside. A nearby thermometer read −30°, but it dropped as we stood nearby. The "home stretch" awaited us, and we stood silently for a few minutes then talked about our luck so far.

"The British told us we wouldn't be able to traverse the peninsula in winter," Jean-Louis reminded me, "and it was hard, even doubtful, but we did it. The Americans and the French told us we wouldn't be able to cross the area of inaccessibility, and we too were unsure. But we made it. The Russians are now worried about our ability to reach Mirnyy in time. I say, no problem."

JANUARY 19, DAY 177

It is almost as if we're on vacation here. The men are laid back, though the base lacks the frills the Americans had at the South Pole, luxuries including videos, a game room, bars, library and workout rooms. Instead these men entertain themselves in timeworn fashion: reading, talking, playing pool and cards. In the room where the pool table is, four or five men are always sitting around a kettle peeling potatoes. It doesn't appear things have changed much here in the past thirty years. Most of the men enjoy their long stints here and prefer coming and going from Vostok by the trax rather than plane, and then choose to go home by ship instead of plane. They love their work, living in these stark conditions, and the camaraderie of men. Despite Antarctica's harshness, for some of these men it is an easier life here than it would be at home.

The Soviets have the largest national presence in Antarctica, and Vostok is regarded as a prestigious base because of its remote interior location. Currently they have a significant science project under way that occupies much of the time of the twenty scientists based here. They are attempting to drill down twelve thousand feet, which will provide an analysis of the ice core going back 250,000 years. They have already drilled to the 160,000-year level, but unfortunately the drill broke at about seventy-five hundred feet and they are now trying to extricate it from the hole so they can start all over again. Vostok also sits in the center of the geomagnetic field, and over the years a legion of international scientists has worked here studying it.

There is less wind here than at the South Pole, so the men don't spend as much time plowing snow. They're actually very fortunate to have set their base down here. If they were a hundred miles to the south, toward the South Pole, they would have been subjected to constant winds and their buildings would be constantly drifted over. Without knowing it, the Soviets had built Vostok in an area of soft snow and light winds.

One of the significant things we learned about the area of inaccessibility, which no one had been able to judge or estimate before, was the constant rate of high winds, which died down just outside Vostok. Within twenty miles of this base the snow's consistency, thus the surface, changed remarkably, implying that the Soviets' predictions about deep snow across the area of inaccessibility may have been based on their travels just beyond Vostok.

Including us, there were forty-seven at the base—twenty winter-over—and many of the men (no woman has ever been based at Vostok) had been there more than a year. Of the forty-one Soviets, five were with the trax and twenty were scientists. That is a much higher ratio than the South Pole, where barely 25 percent of the summertime employees are scientists.

We visited the men in their rooms, where they lived in very close quarters. The two main buildings are no bigger than double-wide trailer homes, and many rooms are a combination of science and living quarters; bunk beds are often wedged between stacks of instruments and experiments on tables. Even in the radio room, off to one side, are two bunks.

The only problem for us while at the base was the heat. For the past five months our body temperature has adapted to the cold, actually dropping one and a half degrees. According to Jean-Louis "the body makes its own thermostat," and in the buildings of the station, heated to 60°, our bodies were having a difficult time with the transition.

JANUARY 22, DAY 180

We left Vostok at eight o'clock this morning; the temperature was −45° and dropping. I'm afraid this is the warmest temperature we are going to see for the next three weeks, and already I can tell that some of the dogs aren't wild about the conditions. Gordie whined off and on all last night. But the surfaces are fast—today we made twenty-nine miles, a new record. Time passed slowly, like the first day of school after a long holiday.

We will travel to Mirnyy alongside the trail left by the trax and their heavy sleds. The Soviets are taking our security very seriously, and in order to gain their support we had to promise to keep close to the trail. We are to be resupplied by the tractors every two hundred miles or so, and they had left Vostok before us, headed on a routine trip back to Mirnyy.

Tonight is our first with new tent partners. Victor is with Geoff, I'm with Jean-Louis, and Keizo and Dahe are together. The initial result of the switch is that it took longer to put up camp as everyone sorted out their new duties. I'm back in the dome, which feels more like home than Geoff's pyramid and is much warmer because of its sandy color. But warmth is all dependent upon which side of the tent you sleep on—I was on the sunny side this first night and overheated in my bag, even though the temperature dipped to −48°. The only thing that is saving us now is the sun—if it were −48° and pitch-black on a January night in the Northwest Territories, it would be unbearably cold. But with the twenty-four-hour sun and calm winds, this −48° is not a problem, since the sun prevents moisture from collecting in the tent.

From here on it's figuratively downhill for us (though not literally: we will still climb several hundred feet in elevation before starting our descent toward Mirnyy). We're on schedule and should arrive at Mirnyy on March 1, unless we run into very bad weather as we near the coast. I have a hunch that within a few days the temperatures will drop rapidly. If we're lucky, we'll stay just ahead of winter and avoid the worst of it. We are in good shape: everybody's getting along, the dogs are rested, and Vostok was by far the most relaxing stop we've had in the past five months. I'm amazed that our bodies have endured so well. We've been traveling every day since October 1, with just eight days off, and those were mostly consumed by repairs and meetings. Now past Vostok it feels good to have a strong body, relaxed muscles.

JANUARY 23, DAY 181

We are nearing the end of the Antarctic summer, and it is a balmy −41°. The partially sunny skies heat up the tent and we don't mind going outside in the morning to do the chores. In fact, I find myself looking forward to harnessing dogs and packing sleds. We've probably had only a handful of calm days like this, and they evoke good times.

We are reminded of civilization almost every morning now, and will be for the next ten days, when three Soviet planes fly overhead about nine in the morning, carrying perishable foods to the base as it prepares to hunker down for a long, cold winter. The trio of planes—a boxcarlike Antinov-28, the Soviet counterpart to the Twin Otter, and two Ilyushin-14s—return an hour and a half later. For them we are a novelty, something to look at other than whiteness. They fly low over us and tip their wings, sometimes even circling and buzzing us, anything to break up their day.

Today was another record breaker: we made thirty-one miles in nine hours. We are eight hundred miles from Mirnyy.

JANUARY 25, DAY 183

We capped the highest elevation of the expedition yesterday, 11,400 feet, and as a result I fell into a deep sleep last night. There were flaws in even such sleep, though. At this altitude when you take particularly deep breaths, as I did last night, you wake up gasping. Each time it took me about an hour to gain my normal breathing pace back. It's an awful feeling, like suffocating. You suck in air, as much as you can grab, yet your breath never quite comes back. It's a kind of torture peculiar to this high plateau.

During the day the altitude affects us only when we make quick moves or skip a breath. It is the altitude, in addition to the cold, that is encouraging us to travel fast, long days, to get farther north as hurriedly as we can, if only so that we can sleep better, and sing out loud as we travel.

JANUARY 26, DAY 184

Today the temperature dropped to −50°, with an eight-mile-per-hour wind, making for windchills of −75°. But that −50° was a "daytime" (i.e., sunshine) temperature. In darkness this temperature would be nearly impossible to travel in: flesh would flash-freeze in seconds, the dogs would be too cold to pull. The morning was chilly, with a crosswind, and the sun angled to the side, which helped fog our glasses and freeze our feet. Thankfully, by noon the sun began to peek into our faces, which helped defog our glasses and thaw our nearly frozen digits.

This morning a pair of Ilyushin-14s that were headed for Vostok buzzed overhead and returned two hours later. We understand that one of them is piloted by a sixty-two-year-old who has been in Antarctica off and on since 1958. While such visits give us something to look forward to, an almost-human contact to break the monotony of our skiing, the planes are a reminder of parts of civilization we neither miss nor encourage in Antarctica. Minutes after the planes pass, the air is awash with the thick smell of their exhaust.

Two days ago we had calm, very cold weather that created a wind that in turn caused ice crystals to form in the air. Because it was so bitterly cold and clear you could hear the planes coming for five minutes before they appeared and then smell the kerosene they left on the ice crystals in the air long after they were gone. The sound of their engines echoed off the ice, a wall of sound that made it sound as if we were in the middle of a World War I air battle. At first our dogs were frightened, cowering low to the ground as if they'd seen a ghost. Now I think even they look forward to the comings and goings of the planes.

Our next goal is the Soviet base of Komsomolskaya, known as Kosmos, two hundred miles from here. It was one of the Soviets' first Antarctic bases but was closed shortly after the IGY. For the past twenty-eight years it has been used for only two months in the summer, as a refueling stop for the trax on their way from Vostok to Mirnyy.

JANUARY 27, DAY 185

A very miserable, very cold day. Luckily the wind was at our backs, which made all the difference. If we'd had these temperatures on the peninsula (-50°, with winds between ten and twelve miles per hour) we would have been forced to quit. Today my hands fell victim to the cold; all day they tingled, almost numb. On days like this it is impossible to keep out the cold, no matter how many layers we pile on. To revive my fingers I make a fist one hundred times, then shoot my fingers back into my gloves, which warms first the forearms then pumps warm blood to the fingers. Unfortunately that warmth lasts just ten minutes, and the exercise must be repeated over and over.

At lunch break, I ate alone on the leeward side of my sled. It is on these windy, cold days that we are most isolated from one another. The only thing that makes this life the least bit tolerable is that the end is in sight. Thankfully by now we are all in excellent shape, so when we pull in in the evening, none of us is particularly tired, just frozen.

Jean-Louis and I have already refined a very simple rhythm together at day's end. We work together unpacking the sled and setting the tent up, then he strings out the antenna, which takes about ten minutes, and goes in and sets up camp. His first responsibility is firing the stove, then setting up the radio. In the meantime I stake out and feed the dogs, untangling them from a myriad of crossed, knotted and ice-packed lines. I rearrange the sled and then stake out the tent and shovel snow around it. Usually I'm in the tent just ten minutes after Jean-Louis.

I had specifically saved our pairing until the end of the trip, and our evenings together are very relaxed. I wanted to spend the ending with my partner, and I knew there would be all sorts of winding-down logistics that we would have to sort out together. We talk, have tea before dinner, gear down. We had avoided tenting together earlier, knowing our conversation would be too logistical, too heavy. Now, while not yet reflecting on any success, we talk some about life after Trans-Antarctica. It is comfortable inside: if our sometimes recalcitrant stoves are working properly we can pump the temperature near the top of the tent to 40°, even when it's −50° outside, and the Soviets gave us some meat at Vostok, so dinners are better. The first nights we were together we listened to music, but since we've been listening to the same half dozen tapes for the past six months they're getting pretty familiar. Jean-Louis generally reads himself to sleep, while I work on my drawings.

It is amazing how we have adapted to Antarctica. This is the best I've adapted to cold conditions in my travels. Temperatures of −50° seem like nothing, and −40° with a wind is no big deal. Surviving this experience opens up a whole new frontier for me; in the past I have shunned many parts of the Canadian Arctic and its Barrens because of their severe winter temperatures. Now I feel I can go to those places that used to seem truly out-of-bounds. But nothing except for having spent a half year in this icebox down here could have convinced me it was possible. Cold is a very good teacher about your own limitations.

JANUARY 28, DAY 186

Our fifth consecutive day of −50° temperatures. Weather reports we are getting from Mirnyy imply that Antarctica's winter is coming faster than ever this season, and our satellite message today is "Cold weather. We race with winter."

Our usual morning rhythm is as routine as the evening's. Jean-Louis is up first, woken by a small alarm clock, at six. He lights the Coleman stove and begins to cook and warm the tent. His preferred breakfast is steamed fruit (apricots and raisins, which we'd gotten from the Soviets at Vostok), mixed with semolina, a ground wheat. I'm on the last of the hot cereal, a breakfast that I have to admit is a bit bereft of taste after all these months. Mornings have become my least favorite time of day, and it usually takes me a full ten minutes to crawl out from the warmth and comfort of my bag.

By six-thirty I do my daily writing or tape recording and put on hibiscus tea with lemon grass, then cook up oatmeal. It is a solid rhythm, which helps my body and mind gradually warm to the mood required to step out into a −50° day.

We have a rendezvous planned with the trax for twenty-nine miles from where we camped, to pick up dog food. None of us is looking forward to the meeting, though we appreciate the help the Soviets are lending. We truly don't like breaking our travel/camp/travel/camp rhythm, and meeting the trax is an interruption in that rhythm. To the outsider a chance to have coffee with new people might sound like a welcome break. But the Soviets' insistence on partying and good times does not always square with our daily efforts.

Accordingly we stopped a little after six, and two miles ahead we could see the large trax looming on the horizon like big, hazy buildings. The silhouette of these machines on this otherwise bleak horizon is the most vivid glimpse we have of what it must be like to land a spacecraft on another planet. If it wasn't that a few of the Soviets speak Pidgin English, I could easily be persuaded that we were on Mars or Pluto.

Just before we stopped we passed a mile marker dressed up like a scarecrow, in old Soviet polar gear, topped by an old boot. The dogs spotted it from half a mile away and veered straight for it. As we closed in, you could see it was holding a

sign that read simply 1,000 KILOMETERS, the distance from
Mirnyy. Panda, despite my stern shouting, headed right for
the scarecrow, full of curiosity, followed by Hank. They
sniffed and snarled at its feet, and surprisingly neither lifted his
leg. It was starkly beautiful, stuck here in the middle of ten
thousand square miles of ice and snow.

MILES TRAVELED: 3,036

MILES TO MIRNYY: 705

FEBRUARY

THE RACE IS ON, TO
GET OUT OF THIS COLD

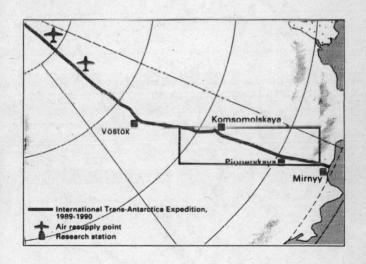

International Trans-Antarctica Expedition,
1989-1990
Air resupply point
Research station

Vostok

Komsomolskaya

Pionerskaya

Mirnyy

FEBRUARY 1, DAY 190

Outside the wind is humming through the guylines, always a
bad sign when it's −47°. But we are preparing to put up with
whatever weather the day holds, because after two more days
of travel (our tenth and eleventh straight since leaving Vostok)
we're taking a day off. Despite the wind we're making record
distances each day, averaging more than twenty-five miles, an
even faster pace than we traveled in Greenland. As we get
farther north the terrain will start a slight descent, and that
should pick up our pace even more.

Morning travel, with the sun to our side, is definitely the
coldest, and our lunch breaks are getting even more unpleasant. Yesterday's was the coldest we'd had in four or five
months, one where I almost wanted to give up even trying to
eat and just take off into the distance running, simply to warm
my frozen bones. Fortunately a small wedge of warmth comes
across our faces now in the afternoon, starting around noon
and lasting until four o'clock, when the sun hits us head-on.
On either side of that wedge, before noon and after four, it's
getting colder and colder each day. The farther north we ski,
the less heat the sun is generating. Yet mechanically men and
dogs are running very well, we're in good shape, and we will
keep up the pace. We must.

Judging by the snow conditions when we shovel and pound
tent stakes into the ice, we are traveling through a generally
very windy area. The surface is crusted and very hard, which
means we can expect wind, thankfully now at our backs, the
rest of the way to Mirnyy. For the next ten days the winds

should increase, the temperature will stay the same (around −50°), and the windchill will drop.

So far the dogs don't seem to mind these conditions, though I'm concerned for them since there is little cover, no blowing snow or soft ice for them to blanket themselves with. At day's end we get a rest from the cold and wind, lying warm in our Quallofil and Gore-Tex and double-thick bags. The dogs get no such reprieve.

It's a good thing we're on schedule, because if we were a week behind I'm sure the cold that's coming would drive us into our tents for the winter. Building a semipermanent camp somewhere along our route and hunkering down for several months, or wintering-over, was never a consideration, due to the toll it would take on both men and dogs. Instead we opted to travel in some of Antarctica's harshest seasons, so that we could get on and off this frozen land within one year. Overnight the cold has become increasingly penetrating, the −70° and −80° windchills swiftly driving any and all heat from your clothing. Your feet and hands get cold first; even the small of your back is iced over. Each day I think about what it would be like to get lost or separated from the team in this cold. You wouldn't last long.

As we head farther north the horizon is filled with blowing, hazy ice crystals, sparkling in the sun. That phenomenon only increases the glare, once again reminding us just how inhumane these conditions are. In order to protect your eyes you have to wear the equivalent of welder's glasses to fend off the ultraviolet that hangs in the bright light, threatening to burn flesh or eyeball. While I've been in weather similar to this before, I've never been so isolated and in such hostile surroundings. In the morning the instant the stove is turned off the cold penetrates the tent, brutally. An hour into our day and we might as well be on Mars, trudging like bulky spacemen across a desolate, unidentifiable surface, into a horizon with no landmarks, seemingly no tomorrow.

For us, the race is on to get north, to get out of this cold.

We're making superb mileage, and tomorrow we should reach Kosmos, where a cache awaits us.

During the course of the expedition Jean-Louis has been reading and rereading a story about a visit to Antarctica written by noted wilderness writer Barry Lopez. Jean-Louis's intention in reading the story out loud is to practice his English, but the story—especially Lopez's romantic, vivid descriptions of Antarctica—is getting on my nerves. It is frustrating that he, who visited the continent for just ten days, can describe the place with such accuracy and poignancy while, after six months here, I am in some ways dulled to Antarctica's beauties.

My concern is that I am not capturing Antarctica and its romance properly. Lopez's view seems fresh, flowery and evocative by comparison to my own descriptions. For him everything was new; his advantage in such a short stay was that his mind and descriptive powers were not bludgeoned by the monotony and remoteness that is the real Antarctica. I understand; it is easy to step off a tourist's plane for a few days and conjure up images that paint Antarctica as a kind of cold paradise. Many days now I see it as quite the opposite.

FEBRUARY 2, DAY 191

Tonight I am sitting in an eighteen-by-twenty-four-foot shack, buried under several tons of snow and ice. From outside all you see of this place is the bare hint of a metal roof. Otherwise it is impregnably and forever buried. A trapdoor opens on a snow-and-ice stairway that leads down ten feet into the main room, a meat locker–size space split into two. In one snore five men, asleep on stacked bunks. We traveled seventeen miles today to reach Kosmos; we have covered 344 miles in the last eleven and a half days, a remarkable pace that has left us all exhausted.

In the background I hear the sound of a film projector. It is always dark in these rooms, and the Soviets who are based here for two months have turned one into a cinema, where they show Soviet-made World War II dramas and the like. The accommodations are typically Soviet: submarinelike living, with people stuffed into every corner, yet somehow still very comfortable. Everything is worn, from the furniture to the doorknobs, the blankets to the floors, and the place looks as if it could have served as one of Admiral Byrd's shacks from the 1930s. But we're not complaining, since it is dry, comfortable and very warm.

We left at the usual time this morning, and about ten o'clock I saw on the horizon what looked like two barrels far ahead in the distance. At the time I assumed they were mile markers; given the lack of depth perception in a place where there are no landmarks, I guessed they were a few miles ahead. But we traveled on and on and the barrels did not get any closer. By eleven o'clock it looked as if there were three barrels; by noon the barrels had grown to tractor size and we began to assume what we saw must be the base. But we had heard that the base was covered by snow and did not expect to be able to sight it from any distance.

We stopped for lunch, and then by two o'clock we could distinguish men near what we'd thought were barrels; they were walking toward us. The dogs picked up their pace when they saw the movement, and then smoke flares shot into the air. Obviously this was Kosmos, and the "barrels" we thought we saw were trax awaiting our arrival.

Pulling into the long-abandoned base was like entering some kind of polar spook house. From a mile away we could just make out the tail and rear fuselage of an airplane, an Ilyushin-14, jutting awkwardly out of the snow. As we neared we saw another crashed plane, obviously down for several years. On either side of the trail two large props, bent and broken, served as the gateway to Kosmos. Scattered amongst this graveyard were half a dozen monstrous, spent fuel sleds. As we neared the center of the base its entire staff of a radioman and two diesel mechanics emerged from the ice-buried shacks. Victor searched for a place for us to set up camp and skied to the far side of the base, near a yellow sign that read RADIATION. Apparently when the base was in operation they had used a nuclear battery to keep weather instruments going in the winter. None of us was too eager to set up camp on top of anything remotely radioactive, so we skied two hundred feet to the opposite side of the camp and stopped for the day. The temperature was −58° when we arrived, and the winds were picking up, which we've learned in the past weeks indicates temperatures should drop again in the next few days. Winter is definitely on its way.

Kosmos is the eeriest scene we've come across these past six months, resembling a Gypsy caravan dropped here in the desolate, frozen outback of Antarctica. A diesel generator housed in a sagging shack sits next to the main building, and its constant roar is a discomforting break in the otherwise noiseless surroundings. On the snowy stairway leading down into the main building, twenty canisters sit in the snow, the films the crew will watch during their stay.

The main hangout is the eleven-by-fourteen-foot kitchen, its dominant feature a long, scarred wooden table surrounded by benches. Shelves begin just above seated head level and rise to the top of the ceiling, every nook and cranny crammed with boxes of food and canned goods. Prominently positioned on the wall is an official portrait of Mikhail Gorbachev, surrounded by dozens of labels steamed off emptied vodka and whiskey bottles. While Gorbachev has admitted that alcohol is one of the potential ruinations of the Soviet Union, the mixing of his photo with all these labels was not done out of disrespect. It does give an indication, though, of the two most important elements of a Soviet polar man's life: the leadership that sent him here and the spirits that keep him going once arrived.

To the left of the kitchen is a radio room with three bunks; to the right a ten-by-ten-foot mess hall. As we sat and talked in these quarters, the steady *click-clack* of Morse code emanated from the radio room. Because reception in this area is very chancy, the residents still rely on the otherwise antiquated Morse code for their main communication with Mirnyy, five hundred miles away.

In our travels both before the expedition and once on the ice here in Antarctica, the Soviets, bureaucrats and polar men alike, have proven some of our best allies. The Russians we've met in Antarctica remind me of rural Americans; they are wholesome, friendly, social, very warmhearted. Stuck in our tents in the far reaches of this continent, it is impossible to think of them as an enemy.

The Americans and Soviets are said to be plotting the first truly shared Antarctic base not far from Kosmos, yet another step forward in the international scientific efforts already well established here. The proposed new station would be built about 82° south latitude and 45° east longitude, equidistant from the South Pole and Vostok. It would sit at the highest altitude in Antarctica, thus ideal for astronomical research with as little atmospheric obstruction as possible. Despite the brutal cold at the site there would be virtually no precipitation and only mild winds all year long. Eight hundred miles from the South Pole and reachable only by ski plane or tractor-train from Vostok, the new outpost's realization is far off and due to staffing problems and long-standing "claims" of original Antarctica claimants, perhaps just talk. But the fact that the two nations would even consider such an expensive, cooperative undertaking is a good sign.

FEBRUARY 4, DAY 193

As we pulled out of Kosmos the dogs went into a group howl, a sign that they are rested and ready to run, and we had a good morning of travel, over very fast conditions. Just before noon we spotted a trax ahead of us, then a pair of them. At first we assumed they were gas trailers that had been left behind on the Mirnyy-Vostok run earlier in the year, but when we shouted the dogs to a halt we could hear a distinct, loud rumbling in the distance ahead.

As we traveled on, the pair of trax became three, then four. We quickly surmised this was the convoy we knew we would run across at some point on our way to Mirnyy. Fourteen trax in all, each pulling sleds heavily loaded with supplies for the crew at Vostok, the convoy was on its annual run. I turned my team over to Jean-Louis and skied ahead to photograph our meeting: it was an amazing scene, our three sleds of ash-and-lashings compared to this rumbling chain of forty-ton diesel-spewing tractors, set against a backdrop of the flat, white horizon. The contrast was bizarre; we were so fragile by comparison. Despite their ominous appearance, such convoys are the most economic form of resupply and travel in Antarctica. Flying, as the Americans do, is many times more expensive. (Ironically, due to budget cuts, the NSF is considering establishing its own trax runs between McMurdo and the South Pole.)

As soon as they spotted us the trax came to a stop and the ground ceased rumbling. Men popped out dressed in the standard Soviet polar uniforms of black and blue, appearing from where we stood as stark silhouettes against the sunlit ice. Compared to us—in our dirty-but-still-vibrant orange, teal and purple suits—their drab dress made them look as if they had just climbed out of the coal mines of West Virginia.

There were twenty men altogether, and they gathered around the sleds and the dogs, excited to greet us. We chatted a bit, peeked inside their mammoth vehicles, and took more group pictures. They toasted our accomplishment-to-date with a shot of cognac chased by hunks of salami, all done hurriedly. Forty minutes later we were on our respective ways. It was an odd encounter, but one that I had been anticipating for years. We knew that somewhere on the stretch between

Vostok and Mirnyy we'd run across this otherworldly convoy, and it signified yet another milestone passed.

FEBRUARY 6, DAY 195

Today we quit a half hour early, yet still covered nearly twenty-eight miles. It was a good day, dipping to −54°, another spent passing time in our minds. Jean-Louis's satellite message was *"Ciel bleu, sol blanc, plat."* ("Blue sky, white ground, flat.")

FEBRUARY 7, DAY 196

While we're still living day by day here, it helps to have something over the next horizon to aim for to help the days pass more quickly. Our next goal is another abandoned and buried Soviet base, Pionerskaya, eight or nine days' travel from here and hopefully just twelve days outside Mirnyy. We had heard a portable ice-core drilling station and team of men might be stopped there, but we wouldn't know for sure until we arrived. From Pionerskaya on, the weather will worsen and we fear the cold storms that will blow in our faces off the Indian Ocean.

Already the weather is worsening. Today a wind of twenty-five miles per hour blew from the southeast and the temperature was −40°, meaning the windchill was −104°. Visibility dropped to three hundred feet and we slogged through drifting snow, the trail of the sled ahead vanishing before we could reach it. Unfortunately, the continent's most brutal winds are yet to come.

It is the windchills that make us worry for the dogs. They are sleeping on hard-packed surfaces, unable to burrow in. The only consolation is that in just three weeks the expedition will be over, and we take some small comfort knowing of their months to come lounging in the dog yard at the Homestead. I'm not sure they understand the end is near, but I hope so.

My biggest physical problem during the day is a dripping nose. Each day I have to take my hands out of my gloves, literally forty times a day, to swipe at my nose. As a result, my right hand is cold all day long. It would help if I could cover my nose, but then my sunglasses fog. For a few days I tried jamming Kleenex into my nostrils to eliminate the constant drip, drip, drip, but it works for only an hour or two and causes my nose to chafe, crack and bleed. The only option is to drip and wipe, drip and wipe, drip and wipe.

My second biggest complaint these days is dietary. For 196 days now we have eaten oatmeal for breakfast; dried fruits, chocolate and nuts for lunch; and a combination of pemmican, noodles, potatoes or pasta, and cheese for dinner. The only spice comes from the dried soup that I liberally dump into every dinner. I'd kill for a fruit salad.

FEBRUARY 8, DAY 197

We had some delays today, mostly because Geoff had to repair a lashing on his sled. While he was repairing I lay down next to the dogs and fell asleep, curled in the snow. Despite the slowdown we made twenty-six miles.

In the mornings now Jean-Louis and I together take down the camp and pack the sled and lash it. He then walks down the dog line and unclips each dog, then rolls up the stakeout chain. While he's doing that I'm clipping the dogs one at a time into the gang line. I like the whole process of rigging the sled for travel, and it gives me a few moments with each of the dogs as I hitch them up to the sled. I talk to them and give them a good rub and do the same at lunch. Due to the length of this trip this may be the best rapport I've ever had with a team, and surprisingly little discipline is needed to keep them in line.

Jean-Louis and I have had some heart-to-heart talks during the evenings, which is what I'd hoped for. Many of our conversations focus on the future. My immediate plans are concentrated on building an educational meeting center at the Homestead and plotting at least one more major expedition in the Arctic. Jean-Louis's focus is going to be on the UAP, once he squares the $1 million personal note he shouldered to get it finished.

The world is full of dreamers, but few people ever manage to pull off their dreams. Despite some differences in style, what Jean-Louis and I share is our ability to achieve ours. This expedition, for all its challenges and occasional missteps, should make our achieving the dreams we still harbor a little easier for both of us. Our involvement with various governments, both logistically and diplomatically, will ensure that we'll be able to work with them again. Though any expedition planning demands many hours, if not years, of hard work, completing this trip assures us that putting together the next one will be that much simpler.

I think that is what has changed most for me in the past five years: my opportunities now appear limitless. Five years ago I was still struggling to define my dreams to those necessary to pull an expedition off—sponsors, the media, government agencies. If we make it out of here safely, still a big question as far as I'm concerned, my future plans will hopefully require less struggle. It was difficult to reach this point, physically, mentally and spiritually. Nothing was gained without a price. But looking all the way back to my first adventures—kayaking the Yukon, working on a fire-fighting crew in Alaska, dogsledding by myself deep into Arctic winters—I'm satisfied each step was worth its price. I wouldn't necessarily want to go back and live the first half of my life over again, though it had many highlights. But memories of each struggle are, and will always be, firmly etched in memory.

FEBRUARY 9, DAY 198

Today was the first time we saw billowy cirrostratus clouds, which reminded us all of summertime. It was a great day, with a high of −30°, and we covered twenty-eight miles.

For the first time in months, since before the South Pole, we made a descent. All of a sudden the terrain started rolling, then headed sharply back uphill before dropping down nearly two miles over hard-packed surfaces. It was as good a travel day as you could expect anywhere on the frozen parts of the planet. We also had a brief snow squall, and while the accumulation was next to nothing it is an indication we've begun the descent off the plateau toward the Indian Ocean.

Today is the sixth since we left Kosmos, and we're planning to take Day 10 off.

FEBRUARY 11, DAY 200

Another typical twenty-six-mile day. The only thing that's changing is the topography, which is gradually becoming rougher, the ice more solidly packed and wavy each day, a result of the increasing winds.

Today was different in one respect: we have now established regular daily radio contact with Mirnyy. Until this point we've had to transmit back to Vostok, which then relayed our messages to Mirnyy. In part the awkward communication is because Mirnyy's transmitter is old and works irregularly. In fact, on a few occasions the trax drivers have asked to borrow our radio, because theirs were out of order. From Mirnyy we got word that we "better hurry" if we can, in order to avoid what they predict will be an early winter of storms and severe cold. They also report that ice conditions in the ocean around Mirnyy require departure as soon as possible after March 1.

FEBRUARY 12, DAY 201

After a journey of ninety-two days, over 1,550 miles, Messner and Fuchs arrived today at New Zealand's Scott base on McMurdo Sound. They had an arduous trip that boasted bad weather, poor radio communication and difficult times skiing across the sastrugi pulling their 150-pound sleds behind them. Aided by windsails, they made fast time once past the South Pole. Though disappointed that they had not been able to make a true coastline-to-coastline traverse, they told the press it had been "a worthwhile adventure."

FEBRUARY 14, DAY 203

This evening we witnessed a first: a sunset, the first we'd seen in one hundred days. Due to the lack of moisture (and pollution) it was virtually colorless, just a wan hint of yellow. But with the blowing drifts and perfectly flat horizon in front of it, it was still stunning. At the same time, low on the other side of the sky, rose a three-quarter moon with a very dark earth shadow, the darkest I'd ever seen, and then stars began to tumble into the dusky sky. It was a wondrous scene not witnessed anywhere on the planet, except for where we stood.

The sun will now be setting between twelve and thirteen minutes earlier every day, another sure sign that winter is coming. These first "sunsets" are actually just the sun skimming the Earth, as it is out of sight for only fifteen to thirty minutes. By the time we reach Mirnyy we will have approximately six hours of darkness per day.

There is absolutely no pleasure in eating anymore. I force down oatmeal in the morning just to have enough strength to travel. I eat lunch only to ensure that I have the strength to make it to camp. Dinner is dreary. The only true taste pleasure I look forward to is a cup of tea when I first come into the tent in the evening. Our pleasure scale these days resembles the horizon we've been staring at since we left the South Pole—no highs or lows, real flat. My mind and my body feel completely flushed, drained. My powers of smell have dissipated. Today's sunset was the closest thing to beauty we've seen on this plateau; since the Thiel Mountains the colors we have seen range from white to blue.

FEBRUARY 15, DAY 204

It wasn't until you took your gloves off for two seconds to undo a tangle in the dogs' lines that you realized just how cold it was today. Your fingers ached instantly, and within five or six seconds they would lose sensation. The winds blew steadily at thirty miles per hour, visibility was less than 150 feet, and the temperature dropped to −53°, resulting in our coldest windchill of the trip, −113°. Despite that, we managed to travel thirty miles in a short day, quitting at five. The surfaces were good and hard, and if we'd stayed on our skis until six we could have made thirty-four miles. Our satellite message was a simple "Cold."

Time passed reasonably quickly, as it does often in these stormy days, but it was a very miserable, quick lunch break. There was some debate about whether we should just skip lunch, but as tired as I am of the food I voted to stop. It is important to get a little bit of fuel in the machine; otherwise it can be an even longer day. When we camped we were seven miles from Pionerskaya.

I'm considering proposing that we take an extra rest day at Pionerskaya, and I know from past experience that such spontaneous changes require careful advance warning with Geoff. I have sensed recently that he is growing irritated, anxious to reach the end, and rightfully concerned that we need to get to Mirnyy as quickly as possible, if only to protect the dogs from this worsening cold. His conservative ways continue to be a valuable check and balance, so I will talk with him before making any plan.

As soon as I fell asleep tonight my dreams took me very far from here, to scenes of lakes and sunny beaches, hot sand and friendly people. After such dreams I hate waking up to the reality of Jean-Louis's morning clamor—the alarm clock, the stove rattling to fire, ice being dropped into the teapot, the radio turned on—reminding me, painfully, that I'm not really on some sunswept beach.

FEBRUARY 16, DAY 205

We arrived at Pionerskaya about noon, hungry, tired and cold. For the past two weeks we have been traveling downhill and downwind, so though the weather has been bad we haven't been traveling into its teeth. Today, lost and searching for Pionerskaya, we traveled for six miles directly into the wind, and by the time we found the base my face was badly frostbitten. When we finally arrived we found the small buildings surrounded by four trax, which transport a small, portable drilling rig and a small "house" that the drill team lives in as they work their way across the stretch from Mirnyy to Vostok. The job of this eleven-man scientific team is to do six-hundred-foot test drills of the ice core every forty to sixty miles, as well as conduct geophysical examinations of the region.

FEBRUARY 17, DAY 206

The weather continues to worsen. Each day is more brutal, more inhospitable than the one before, and it is as if this place wants us out of here and wants us out of here fast and so is throwing in our face some horrible teasers of what's to come. Yesterday it was zero visibility. Today it is −100° windchills.

Both the extreme weather and the length of our outing are

starting to wear on us. Rumor had gotten around that I was going to suggest staying at Pionerskaya for two days and, after hearing that, Geoff blew up at me. His tirade was born of his legitimate concern that we not take risks, or slow down for any reason, in these cold conditions. His concern was for the dogs, which was fair, but during his outburst he unloaded a variety of complaints about me he'd obviously been storing up all these months. He was cutting ice blocks to build a wall to protect his dogs when he confronted me, and we stood in the cold as he aired his pent-up complaints. First he blamed me for Tim's death, then for allowing us to get caught in the cold storms on the peninsula, and he questioned my leadership skills. He was also angry because we were planning to meet up with the French film crew before Mirnyy, which would inevitably slow us down. My response was to say nothing, just nod my head and allow him to get his anger out. The man is like a rubber band: he stretches and stretches and stretches, then snaps. He closed his rebuke by saying that if we lost a dog to the weather between here and Mirnyy he would hold me personally responsible "for the rest of my life."

I kept to myself afterward, numbed by Geoff's anger and accusations. I felt bad that he had directed all his anger at me. I wondered what I could have done differently to appease him these past months. Maybe I could have participated more; sometimes Geoff goes out of his way to help others, perhaps it appeared that I wasn't always pulling my weight. But my "weight"—the ultimate responsibility for my teammates—was carried in my head always, a burden less visible than navigating or helping someone put up a tent.

After we parted I returned to my tent and drew for about five hours until I got so tired of the drawing and design I couldn't look at it anymore. Then I watched the minute hand on my watch go around for another three hours, and then ate a little bit. Needless to say, Geoff's final taunt had put a lot of pressure on me and in part due to his anger it was evident that we could not stay at Pionerskaya an extra day. Finally I bounced what Geoff had said off Jean-Louis, to get a reading from a third party. "He obviously was pouring all this stored-up anger out on you this morning," said Jean-Louis as we sat over tea in our tent. "I understand what he is saying about Tim; maybe you could have carried him on your sled more. But at the time you thought, and I agreed, that running him alongside to keep his circulation going was a good idea.

"I think the main problem between you and Geoff is that you are a leader, and Geoff is a follower. But you are not the strict military leader that he is used to following, and he is confused by that."

Until now Geoff and I had gotten along remarkably well. Jean-Louis is right: Geoff likes a military kind of precision to his traveling and his leadership. Besides Robert Scott, one of his heroes is the British mountain climber Chris Bonington, who runs his expeditions with extreme discipline. You step out of line, you get disciplined. That's the way Geoff had been raised since he was a small boy. He has told me many stories about getting his wrists slapped with a ruler as a seven-year-old for spelling words wrong. As a result he harbors a general dislike of authority figures, and I guess here on the ice I am his authority figure.

Despite our differences, Geoff is an invaluable member of the team. It was his conservatism that in fact encouraged me to invite him when we first met. His caution makes him seem overly pessimistic; Jean-Louis accuses him of being a "backseat driver." But Geoff's conservative way has been an important piece of our decision making down here; he always forces you to look at the worst-case scenario, which perhaps has made us move more cautiously when I might have encouraged us to go ahead more quickly, and, perhaps, more dangerously. On these trips, it is good to have a "Geoff" as an anchor.

From Geoff's journal: "I felt that Tim's death could have been avoided, by carrying him on the sled, wrapping him up, and his death upset me a lot. But my complaint was really sparked because we were having to delay due to the film crew. I would have preferred just getting to Mirnyy. I always considered the film crew an imposition—I didn't trust them, nor fancy ruining the expedition or chancing my life for their gain.

"We cut short our days, even taking a couple off, and consequently were caught in the weather we so wished to avoid. High wind, drifting snow, cold temperatures swept across us for nearly ten days. The dogs became dispirited and some badly iced. . . . Thule, my lead dog, suffers the most. We knew the temperatures were getting worse and there we were just hanging around, stalling. The dogs were getting run down and iced up again. So, rightly or wrongly, I challenged Will.

"Will and I get on very well usually—we accept each other. But there is a big difference between us, like the difference between chalk and cheese. What we do respect is each other's differences. I've been on many expeditions, and the climbing companions that I take all my holidays with, we have vicious arguments, we fight all the time. But we still get on. It's totally different with Will—we don't argue really. I get mad at him, and he probably gets mad at me, but rarely do we let our anger out. Sometimes I can't understand why myself.

"Still, we are friends. After Greenland, for example, we all wanted to zoom off, as if school had just let out. But we parted with the knowledge that we wanted to get back together, soon. We have become like family—you love to get together, and you love to get away from each other."

FEBRUARY 18, DAY 207

Though the weather remained very bad overnight and into the morning, we must travel today. Visibility is down to seventy-five feet, yet because they are well rested the dogs are anxious to run, which makes traveling even more difficult when you can't see the sled ahead of you. Several times, traveling in the number two position, I couldn't stop my dogs before they ran into and over Geoff's dogs, which resulted in the pair of us stopping and untangling our teams several times during the day. More than once I lost my temper with my dogs as I bent to untangle them, which was the wrong thing to do since I overheated and my sunglasses fogged, reducing my visibility to near zero.

On one occasion when I finally got my dogs untangled they charged off the trail, veering twenty degrees to the right. I assumed they were following the scent of Geoff's sled, which had gone before, but I couldn't make out any tracks in the hard-packed snow. I hollered my dogs to a stop and walked back to Jean-Louis and Keizo, a sled length behind. They agreed we weren't on, or near, the trail. None of us knew where Geoff and Victor had gone. Jean-Louis skied back for five minutes, hoping to run into them, but had no luck. We pushed on another twenty minutes and saw no sign at all—no paw prints, sled marks or dog excrement on the trail—so we debated what to do. Jean-Louis thought we should go back and check again, which meant skiing into the raging wind for over half an hour. My hunch was that they were ahead of us, so I hesitated to retrace our steps. Just when we were about to turn around, Victor came into view in front of us, skiing back in our direction. Geoff, he indicated with his ski pole, was eight hundred feet away the whole time. If we'd traveled ahead just two minutes, we'd have run him over.

The day continued like that. Geoff in front, me catching up to him about every ten minutes, him catching up to Victor, and then all of us stopping and waiting for Jean-Louis and Keizo. Despite the stop-and-go traveling, we made twenty-five miles. The dogs, full of energy, remained difficult to control all day long, and it took many sharp commands to get them to stop.

When we were separated from Geoff and Victor we were all reminded of just how easy it is to get lost in these kinds of conditions. Whenever Victor or Dahe related their experiences of being lost in similar storms, their usual joviality disappeared. Those were the most sobering experiences of their lives, and they'd each learned a good lesson: never take anything for granted in Antarctica.

FEBRUARY 19, DAY 208

We spent the day in our tents, due to strong fifty-mile-per-hour winds. But I woke to the oddest sound: songbirds chirping. I looked up and Jean-Louis was in his sleeping bag, cuddled with a tape recording of bird songs he'd saved until now.

I tried to sleep during the afternoon, then did some drawing and undertook our by-now-standard pass-the-time routine. We had a one-o'clock radio check with Mirnyy, and another at nine o'clock. The big news is that one of the Ilyushin-14s that had buzzed us earlier, near Vostok, had engine failure yesterday and was forced to crash-land somewhere between Kosmos and Vostok, three hundred miles from Mirnyy. The pilot was the sixty-two-year-old twenty-five-year-veteran of their Antarctic air fleet, Victor Golovanov, and although the five-man crew is apparently okay, the plane was "finished." A search-and-rescue mission was being planned from Mirnyy; due to poor visibility and outdated Soviet communications equipment, the rescue was to be conducted using our radio as a patch between the downed airplane and Mirnyy.

We are low on dog food so we need to travel tomorrow to the next cache laid by the trax. The only change in our schedule resulting from this day off is that we'd planned originally on finding that cache today, and celebrating Geoff's fortieth birthday. Both have been postponed.

These storms are a result of the warmer weather near the coast, so they are a mixture of blessing and curse. As we close in on Mirnyy, temperatures should rise, while the severity of the storms will increase, creating conditions we haven't seen since October. At the same time visibility is dropping each day.

I haven't seen Keizo and Dahe since we stopped thirty-six

hours ago. Victor has been over a number of times for radio checks, and Jean-Louis and I chat a little bit. Since the winds were too strong for us to properly celebrate Geoff's birthday today I went over to his tent early this morning with a gift of a Cadbury chocolate bar. We talked briefly, and it seemed that his anger of the day before was already behind him. I know him well enough to know that he apologizes for any tirade by being nice the following day. Today we chatted, pleasantly, for ten minutes.

I didn't feed the dogs tonight, a trick I learned from the Eskimos, who never feed their dogs during storms; it is better for them to keep sleeping, safely buried, than to shake out of their snowy shelter for food only to have to burrow in and warm up all over again. While I'm always concerned for the dogs, Geoff's threat of holding me responsible for any dog's death puts even more pressure on our situation. Finding a frozen dog now would be the ultimate tragedy.

We heard from Mirnyy that the *Professor Zubov*, the scientific research ship that will take us (and the Soviets heading home before winter sets in) from Antarctica to Australia, is stuck fifty miles from Mirnyy, blocked by icebergs the size of city blocks. For the past several days an icebreaker has been moving ahead of the *Zubov* to clear a path, but its progress has been stopped. Onboard the ship are a handful of journalists; Bob Picard and John Pierce from the Homestead, who will help us get the dogs back home; as well as the new crew of scientists bound for Mirnyy and Vostok.

FEBRUARY 20, DAY 209

In the morning we stopped and started a lot, in a storm similar to the worst we experienced on the peninsula: fifty-mile-per-hour winds, temperature of –25°, zero visibility. Victor and I were on foot because it was far too difficult to ski and the better traction made it easier to control the dogs. Deep sas-

trugi had returned, and Dahe fell at least fifteen times during
the course of the day. As a result of the combined conditions,
you were forced to keep one eye constantly on your feet, yet if
you concentrated too much on the surface, when you looked
up again the sled in front of you had disappeared. It was a
dangerous situation, and we couldn't afford to stop and make
camp since we ran out of dog food last night and must make
the cache today. The concentration, and the cold, gave me an
Antarctic-sized headache; at lunch it was so miserable we set
up the emergency tent to eat in.

Throughout the afternoon conditions slowly improved.
Victor put on skis around three o'clock, and by five visibility
improved to almost five hundred feet and we found the cache
without a problem. Just before we made camp Yeager collapsed, and I carried him on top of the sled for the last hour.
He'd been having trouble with his paws—they were cut badly
by the icy crystalline surfaces—and his fur was matted with
snow and ice. It wasn't anything too serious, but I decided he
should sleep in the tent tonight, which proved very comfortable for him, though at first he was confused, acting as if he
thought he was being punished. He lay quietly in an empty
cardboard dog food box until after radio check and then slowly
inched his way over to lie on the foot of Jean-Louis's sleeping
bag.

It is getting noticeably darker every night, and by nine
o'clock it is difficult to read in the tent without a headlamp.
Starting our rapid descent to the sea, we are already down to
about seventy-eight hundred feet, which promises warmer,
wetter weather.

Tonight we had a long radio check with Mirnyy, where they
are still overseeing the search-and-rescue operation looking
for the crew of the downed Ilyushin-14. Hopefully, aided by
better weather, they'll find them tomorrow. Our tent was loud
and crowded as Victor read telexes back and forth. We also
talked by radio with several of the journalists who had arrived
in Mirnyy late today aboard the *Zubov*. Jean-Louis spoke with

film crew director Laurent Chevalier, Keizo with a reporter from a Japanese newspaper, and then I got on with Jacqui Banaszynski, a reporter from the St. Paul *Pioneer Press.*

She asked a dozen questions and closed by asking whether or not I was thinking about home. I told her not too much, that I was still into the trip and the demands of our daily travel. I was not, I assured her, allowing my thoughts to wander too far from the steps in front of me, especially given the stormy conditions. We're not home yet, I cautioned her. We can't let our guard down.

FEBRUARY 21, DAY 210

This morning Jean-Louis got out the two little guidebooks to Northern Hemisphere birds he'd carried across the continent, and for an hour we studied the pictures. As we looked, we found ourselves studying not just the birds but the whole photograph, including the flowers, the blades of grass in the background, the trees, the clouds. He would study one page for three or four minutes, hand it to me, and I would do the same. It was as if we were slowly preparing ourselves for the world beyond Antarctica, by reminding ourselves of some of the outside world's colors, beauty and intricacies.

FEBRUARY 22, DAY 211

With strong katabatic gusts at our backs we covered record distances in the morning, averaging almost five miles an hour despite visibility down to 150 feet. At times we were going almost too fast; the sled was slipping to the side, and I was afraid one of the runners would collapse and break.

We made camp at seven o'clock, and by then it had calmed and warmed to −25°. We could see the full 360-degree horizon, and visibility was probably thirty miles. If these conditions lasted overnight, my prediction was that we would have a good stretch of clear weather ahead. We have a full nine days' travel left.

The search for the Ilyushin continued until late tonight, employing the second Ilyushin-14, the Antonov-28 and a Soviet helicopter. Finally, about nine-thirty, the wreck was located half buried in a snowdrift and the five-man crew picked up. They had waited for five days inside the plane, without sleeping bags or food.

FEBRUARY 23, DAY 212

The terrain is starting to roll as it drops down gradually, and once again it resembles the rolling plains of Saskatchewan. From the top of the crests of deep sastrugi we could see seven or eight miles ahead; when we dropped into the trough of the wave we could see only snow and ice a few feet from our faces. All day long it was like surfing big, frozen waves of ice; up and down, up and down, up and down. Otherwise travel was uneventful, through a fine mist of blowing drift but nothing too severe.

We had arranged to meet the trax, which were now traveling twenty miles ahead of us, because the Antonov was to deliver the film crew to where they were stopped. As we approached the trax at day's end, the dogs spotted them first and raced toward the spot where one of the film crew members had set up a tripod. Geoff was in the lead, but as we neared the camp, out of excitement, my dogs raced past him. When we pulled to a stop, we could see several friendly faces, including Arkady Sosnikov, a friend of Victor's who was chief of the Mirnyy station the year before and is now head of the Soviet Arctic and Antarctic Research Institute; Laurent and his film crew; Galena Dobrotina, who was in charge of finance for the Soviet Antarctic Expedition; and several reporters. It was the first real charge of energy we'd received from the outside world since Patriot Hills, and the scene reminded us that we hadn't been forgotten these past seven months.

Unfortunately, Geoff went into another tantrum when Laurent ran to film his arrival at camp. Geoff angrily shoved the camera back into Laurent's face, shouting, "You don't show the truth. You don't show the truth." He pulled his sled to a halt and stomped away in a huff. At first we thought he was joking, but he staked out his dogs, set up his tent, and disappeared inside without acknowledging anyone. The last we saw of him was his hand zipping up the tent from inside. While we all knew of his dislike for the intrusion of the film crew, his reaction also implied a disdain for the others, who had flown in from Mirnyy. Given our oft-stated goal of cooperation, his example was a poor one for our friends.

One of Geoff's irritations with the film crew went back to August, when we were on the Weyerhaeuser Glacier. All three sleds were mired in deep snow, and I had gone ahead of my team to help Keizo. Victor was shouting and yelling to encourage Keizo's dogs; all the while Laurent was standing in the distance filming. His pictures would show what appeared to be a struggle, maybe a hard day, when in fact except for this one moment, our travel that day had been relatively easy. Geoff thought it showed that we couldn't control our dogs, and he was offended by Laurent's filming. I didn't think anything of the situation, but to Geoff it was very offensive and he's been upset with Laurent ever since.

That night we had a small celebration dinner, with everyone but Geoff in attendance. Unfortunately, he is a man who can't control his anger. After he explodes he is most upset with himself for getting angry. When he blew up at me at Pionerskaya, he admitted he did not know how to argue without getting angry. I am just hoping his rationality returns by the trip's end. Basically he is a kind, thoughtful person, not the irrational, angry man he's exposed recently. Fortunately, I haven't gotten angry back at him. I've just stuck my hands in my pockets and let him deliver his verbal blows. That is the only way to handle his anger.

FEBRUARY 24, DAY 213

Due to a pair of growling dogs I lost sleep last night, the first time that has happened in some weeks. I couldn't discern exactly who it was, so finally I went out in my fleece socks and administered some discipline to my team with an empty cardboard box, thinking that would squelch their growling. I came back in and tried to thaw out my hands and feet by rubbing them for half an hour, when there was a muffled bark, followed by another. Within an hour the whole pack was growling and barking. I would have given anything to have known who started it.

I unzipped the tent door and, armed with my cardboard box, headed for the stakeout chain. Then I saw one of Keizo's Eskimo dogs loose near his tent. I knew that had to be the culprit, so I pulled him to his chain and delivered a stern warning. I was so cold when I came back I got only about a half an hour of sleep before sunrise, which I knew would make for a very tiring day of travel.

I began the day by going to Geoff's tent to talk with him about his rude behavior in front of our friends yesterday. But instead of agreeing with me he blew up at me once again, saying I was "inconsiderate" and that I had "barged" in front of him with my dogs when we came in. "It was your fault," he said over and over.

Jean-Louis came to try to calm him down, but instead got riled himself, and they exchanged unpleasantries for a while. Jean-Louis's approach was to try to convince Geoff to drop his anger, not to let it cloud his vision. Unfortunately, that kind of rationale doesn't work with Geoff. He is unable to see his anger, or how he carries it and allows it to build, or how it is perceived by others. It was a very sad way to start the day.

After that ruckus calmed down, we were off and had a fast travel day and made twenty-seven miles. After lunch Jean-Louis approached Geoff with his hand outstretched and they shook, agreeing on the "need to cooperate" these last few days. If only it had been Geoff who'd first stretched out his palm for forgiveness. We are all like brothers sometimes—it is natural that we should disagree, as long as the lines of communication stay open. It is especially important as the trip nears its conclusion that the cooperation that has gotten us this far not dissolve.

FEBRUARY 25, DAY 214

Perfect weather today helped mellow everyone, and good cheer, relief, even a sense of accomplishment, swept the team. We're each starting to look at a future beyond tomorrow. For instance, Victor traveled with me for a while today and I asked him what was on his mind. "Mirnyy, our arrival in Mirnyy," he blurted as we ran alongside the sled. And then? "Natasha!" Victor's wife had been flown down by the Soviets to meet us at Mirnyy, and Victor was ecstatic.

Laurent had brought Jean-Louis a photo magazine from France with pictures of the revolution in Romania. While we'd heard bits and pieces of news from Jean-Louis these were the first visual images from the evolving world theater that we'd seen. I was struck by the story they told.

When we completed our trek to the North Pole we returned home to the tragedies of the space shuttle, Chernobyl, a crisis in Libya. When we step off the Soviet ship onto either New Zealand or Australia in a few weeks, the news of the past that greets us will I think be much more optimistic. It seems in these past seven months the world has changed more than in any previous such time period in any of our lives.

Today was a historic one of sorts for us too: we saw our first bird since leaving Seals Nunatak last July. A skua, an aggressive Antarctic sea gull, dive-bombed the dogs and landed nearby. On one of its approaches, heading right toward my team, Panda made a futile, running leap in an attempt to snatch it out of the air. He made three identical lunges and each time was snapped back hard into his harness. The bird flew alongside us for an hour, taunting the dogs, and we talked about its visit long after the sun had gone down.

We also had our first above-zero day since October, with the temperature climbing to 1°. I joked with Victor that it felt, finally, as if we really *had* been transported to Miami Beach.

FEBRUARY 26, DAY 215

Another first: we saw open water for the first time since we flew from King George Island to the mainland last July. We had camped on a high overlook, about thirty-five hundred feet above sea level, and starting midmorning as we traveled over the gently rolling terrain the bright blue of the Indian Ocean came and went from our sight.

There wasn't a sense of "Hurrah, we're here" when the ocean came into full view. We simply crested a hill, and there it was stretched out in front of us. (Actually it was still thirty miles away.) The lighting was soft, not glaring as it had been the past months; thus it was a comforting, friendly scene. Billowy white clouds on the horizon served as backdrop to the indelible dark blue ocean, which was studded with icebergs. We couldn't have asked for a more beautiful sight. None of us spoke as we gathered our sleds together, filling our eyes with the finest scenery we could have imagined.

Our minds had been flattened by the past four months of

visual starkness. Our eyes did not feast on the scene in front of us but rather they rested, all of our senses absorbed completely. The blue of the ocean said one thing to us: completion. We did not talk about the scene, but it was one of the most vivid pictures the six of us would take away from this place. Our goal had been to go coast to coast; in one beautiful glance this sighting made sense of the past 214 days.

We traveled nineteen miles today, as the weather so far continues to cooperate on this "home stretch." The dogs are running extremely well; in fact, the hardest part of our recent days has been calming them down as we make camp, trying to convince them the day is done. Every day now my sled overtakes Victor, and I have to do a lot of shouting and yelling to slow my dogs. It's actually a pleasant problem.

We are winding this trip down in good moods, the miserableness and tensions of the past few months already forgotten. Geoff seems to have put his recent irritations behind him. After blowing out the candles tonight, Jean-Louis and I lay in our bags minutes from sleep, and I asked if he'd be interested in meeting on June 1, 1994, at the North Pole. He said sure, why not. I seriously think that's where we'll meet again, at the top of the world, he in his ship, me with my dogs. . . .

FEBRUARY 28, DAY 217

Today we saw the ocean from three or four different vantages, and the icebergs just keep getting bigger and bigger as we draw nearer.

Even as we close in on Mirnyy sometimes I have a hard time fathoming exactly where I am on this planet. I still don't have a sense of what we've accomplished, or where we are. I look at these icebergs in the ocean and realize we're on the edge of a continent, and the continent's edge then has a reality to me. While I can draw a mental picture of Antarctica at the bottom of the Earth, I'm having a hard time putting this cold place into words. But the little glimpses of a bay full of icebergs make sense. If we'd sometimes felt as if we were on another planet, now we were sure we were in fact on Earth.

It is a good thing we're almost home, because we're down to the last inch and a half of our last candle. Inside the tent the Coleman is sputtering. Somehow I think even our equipment senses it's time for a break.

MILES TRAVELED: 3,725

MILES TO MIRNYY: 16

MARCH

KEIZO MUST BE LOST

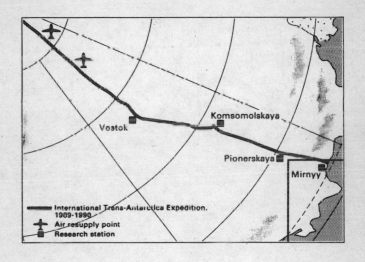

International Trans-Antarctica Expedition.
1989-1990
Air resupply point
Research station

MARCH 1, DAY 218

Eleven p.m.—sixteen miles from Mirnyy

Strong winds, gusting up to fifty miles per hour, blew up while we slept last night. I didn't think much of this new storm —it seemed that we'd experienced everything Antarctica had to throw at us at least twice by now—though it did force us to sit today. Jean-Louis was up early to hear the radio news, and I stayed in my sleeping bag until late in the morning. Victor came in around noon and informed us the weather was worsening and to be careful if we went outside the tents. Still, I didn't think much about his report. We'd been away from heavy, freshly falling snow for nearly four months now, and it seemed like a novelty rather than a danger.

I ventured out about one o'clock and it was blowing so hard I could barely distinguish the outline of Keizo's tent, just fifty feet away. I locked my eyes on his dogs, followed them to his tent, and was then able to see ski poles stuck in the snow every five yards, which led me to Geoff's dogs, then his sled, then his tent. During the whole walk I was groping, almost blindly, grabbing on to each pole I came across to keep my balance.

The afternoon was spent talking with the others, and the weather outside was just one topic of conversation. But by four-thirty the winds violently shaking the tent became our main concern. At six Victor poked his head in and asked Jean-Louis and me if we had seen Keizo recently. He had checked his tent, and only Dahe was inside. We quickly counted heads and shouted outside for Keizo, with no response. It didn't take long for us to begin fearing the worst. Keizo must be lost, somewhere out there in this blowing storm. We agreed quickly to meet near the trax, which were parked a hundred yards upwind, to organize a rational search. We dressed warmly; though the temperature was a relatively mild 10°, the wind was cutting. Victor strung more skis between the trax and tents, and we used them to steady ourselves in the vicious wind as we struggled to the meeting point.

On my way I stopped at Keizo and Dahe's tent, to make sure Keizo hadn't returned. There was only a very worried Dahe inside.

We quickly discovered that mounting a rescue with an international group would be a challenge. The four of us (Dahe stayed in the tent, hoping for Keizo's return), the four-man film crew and half a dozen Soviet trax drivers were stymied at first in our organizing efforts, in part because of the language barriers but also due to the near-hurricane-force winds. Before we could coordinate a systematic approach, people were scattered, shouting worriedly for Keizo as they uncoiled ropes and climbing gear, risking getting lost themselves.

We combined the rope that Geoff and I carried on our sleds, about 300 feet, then tacked on a 40-foot stringer, which gave us a radius of almost 350 feet. The plan was to anchor one end of the rope to a sled and then proceed in a circle the entire radius, with a man placed every 20 feet along the outstretched rope. The first decision was whether to begin looking upwind or downwind. My vote was for upwind, but Victor, who had been lost in these conditions, argued vehemently that when you're lost you always head downwind.

After a few false starts we got the rope stretched to its full length and began to circle, everyone shouting, "Keizo . . . Keizo . . . Keizo" at the top of his lungs. In this wind our shouts carried just a few feet into the darkness. I ran up and down the length of the rope, trying to keep the men separated and encouraging the Soviets to keep shouting.

It took about forty-five minutes to make one complete circle; once we completed a 360-degree swing we unhitched the rope from the sled and attached it to the next one. We concentrated on downwind sweeps, though we did make one upwind. By nine o'clock it was pitch-black, we couldn't see three feet in front of our faces, and we were stumbling in the deep snow, clumsily trying to stay on our feet. We reorganized and reswept the areas we'd already searched. "Keizo . . . Keizo . . . Keizo." At ten o'clock the decision was made to call off the search until daylight, and we agreed to meet six hours later, at the first hint of dawn.

Before we split up, we met in one of the trax and outlined a plan for the new day. We wrote down the names of each searcher and assigned a position on the rope. My concern was that we needed to get men positioned so they could see the next man up the line; I was concerned about leaving "blind spots" on the rope—i.e., one man looking upwind, while the man next to him was looking downwind. If that happened we could easily miss the area in between. Considering the worst, I assumed Keizo might be frozen, unable to move or respond even if he could hear us. We couldn't count on his yelling back; we had to see him. We would continue to overlap our 360s until we found him.

Before crawling into our sleeping bags at eleven-thirty, we sent four flares into the sky, hoping if Keizo was awake—or alive—they might give him an idea of where we were camped.

None of us slept. I prayed Dahe would come running in the night to report that Keizo had shown up. At best we hoped he'd somehow dug himself into the snow, the standard procedure if lost in these conditions. Mimic the dogs, bury yourself to protect yourself from the night. All of us were scared. I couldn't stop thinking about Keizo and heard him singing his song about the wind, but I tried not to allow myself to get too sentimental. I tried to block out the worst-case scenario, hoping we would find him come daylight.

As I tried desperately to grab a few hours of sleep, ringing in my ears was a conversation Keizo had had with a reporter, standing on the tarmac at the Minneapolis airport last July as we readied for departure. "While I am afraid of dying, my biggest fear is dying without having done anything, without having fulfilled my goals . . . dying without really living," he had said. "But I—none of us—can dwell on death; it would be impossible to do anything. Certainly just because I'm going on an expedition to Antarctica doesn't mean I'm necessarily going to die."

MARCH 2, DAY 219

Four a.m.

I jumped out of my sleeping bag and into my clothes like a fireman rung awake by a four-alarm blaze. But at four o'clock it was still too dark—I wanted to have at least 80 percent light so that if we went over an area we would be sure we hadn't missed Keizo. By six o'clock the first circle was begun. Geoff was on the far end of the line, Jean-Louis closest to the sled. I acted as runner, making sure people stayed separated, and continued to shout. Even the dogs had taken up the chorus, and were howling, caught up in the troubled excitement. "Keizooo . . . Keizooo . . . Keizooo . . ." we shouted. I did not have a good feeling; I was convinced he was beyond the limits of our farthest perimeter.

The wind was still so strong that you could barely hear the man twenty feet from you shouting into the bleakness. Running into the wind a horrific image filled my mind: carrying Keizo's frozen body to the finish at Mirnyy tomorrow, on his sled in a sleeping bag, draped with the flag of Japan. I shouted more desperately—"Keizoooo . . . Keizoooo . . . Keizoooo." I thought if I shouted louder it might save his life. If we did not find him soon, and alive, the expedition would be a total loss.

Just before completing our second sweep, the rope started to droop, as if the men at the far point were giving up and coming back, quitting the search. I started to run toward the back of the line to encourage them not to give up, when I made out a commotion at the front of the line. As I ran forward I could see Geoff shouting and waving his arms. It seemed as if he'd made contact, but I couldn't discern exactly what was happening. Then I saw a figure in the storm, about a hundred feet from Geoff. I knew it was Keizo. All I saw were his arms in the air, waving frantically. I shot for those arms, risking being separated from the rescue line myself, caught him above the waist, and lifted him off the ground. He was shouting, "I'm alive. I'm alive." He'd been missing in the storm for thirteen hours, just three hundred feet from his tent. Despite Victor's exhortations to the contrary, we'd found him upwind. As we helped him back to the warmth of the Soviet trax, he said over and over, "I am, God. I am, God." Later when I asked him what he'd meant, he admitted: "Thank God. Thank God."

Inside one of the trax we helped Keizo into a warm parka and ladled hot tea into a cup. He was dressed only in a light Gore-Tex windsuit and booties. Through quivering lips, he at first apologized repeatedly—typical Keizo—for being such a bother, causing such distress. The winds outside rocked the forty-ton truck. We had found him about six-thirty, and the windchill was −40°.

"I'm sorry, I'm sorry," he said over and over. "I'm so glad you found me. I'm sorry for big trouble." I told him we were literally at the end of our rope, about to give up searching in that area when we spotted him. We would never have come back to look there again.

"When I heard your voices, I thought it might be God . . ." he said.

"Well," said Jean-Louis, "we did speak with him this morning, and he gave us a quick reply."

Keizo said he had seen the fireworks of the night before but was afraid to make a dash for where he thought they originated, for fear of getting further lost. Geoff came into the trax and hugged his Japanese mate. "Why did you run away?" he laughed.

"I went outside, about four-thirty, to feed the dogs. Then I could not find my tent.

"When I went out, the blizzard was not so bad—only about minus twenty-five degrees. I didn't wear mukluks, only Gore-Tex boots, my wind parka and wind pants, long underwear and wool socks. Very fast the visibility became very bad. When I tried to go back to the tent I found the first ski, no problem. But I could not find the second ski.

"I stayed between the skis for a while, maybe ten minutes, waiting for the visibility to break. But it didn't. Then I tried to move back toward the first ski, but it was very difficult to walk straight ahead, into the wind. I went left, I went right, I tried to go straight, but I could not find the first ski. I could not find anything.

"I stopped many times, and shouted, 'I am here. I am here. Come on.' The most frustrating thing was I knew I wasn't far from camp, that's why I kept walking. Most, I was upset with myself. I did not want to make trouble and cause people to look for me. I thought about that a lot.

"At that time I was not cold; the adrenaline, the excitement was keeping me warm. But I was very worried about my toes; they were getting very cold. Fortunately I found some dog shit and the faint trail of a sled, which I tried to follow, but it disappeared. But that meant I was close to camp, behind it actually, which was a good sign, so I decided to stop.

"I always carry pliers in my pocket, to help unfreeze dog collars and fix broken ones, and now I used them to dig into the icy surface, which was very hard. I scooped out a shallow ditch, about two and a half feet deep, and a hole to put my feet into, because it was my toes that were the coldest.

"Once I was in my snow ditch, blowing snow covered me in five seconds. I was completely covered, like the dogs. I could breathe through a cavity close to my body, but the snow was blowing inside my clothes and I was getting wet. I thought under the snow I would be warm, but I was cold because I didn't wear much. The snow was heavy and packed down on my wind jacket, so my clothes were touching my skin and there was no layer for warm air to gather. I knew my teammates would be looking for me, I believed I would be found, it was just a matter of time. I had to believe that. But I knew I would have to stay one night, because I knew you could not find me in the dark.

"When I was digging it was warm, but once inside it was cold. I worried about losing energy. I didn't know which was better: to move around to keep my body warm, or lie still to conserve my energy. In the hole I curled up and kicked my feet to keep them warm. Every twenty or thirty minutes I would jump out of my snow ditch and jump up and down, rub my arms and shout, to warm up. After a while I stopped the shouting. It was too windy to be heard, very noisy.

"When I jumped up, the wind would push me away from my snow ditch, sometimes so far I would have to crawl on my stomach looking for it. That happened many times. But I always found it, helped by the fact that I'd spread everything in my pockets around it as guides—my pliers, my headband, lip cream, compass, pocket knife.

"When I was in my snow ditch I tried to enjoy the opportunity. . . . I thought to myself, 'Very few people have this kind of experience, lost in the blizzard; settle down, try and enjoy this.' When I did I truly felt Antarctica. With the snow and quiet covering me I felt as if I was in my mother's womb. I could hear my heart beat—boom . . . boom . . . boom—like a small baby. My life seemed very small in comparison to nature, to Antarctica.

"I thought many, many things while I was lost, especially that I could not die at that place, only sixteen miles from Mirnyy. I had big responsibility. If I died there, everybody would have big trouble—I simply could not die. If I died here, it would be a real shame for me, big shame, deep shame.

"About five o'clock it started to get light and I tried to find the sled trail again, but I could not. I thought maybe I would have to stay lost one more night, and I thought I could survive that. But I was worried about my feet. They weren't really cold, but they felt very strange, like they were swelling, like my socks were broken [torn], because I'd kicked my feet all night. It was a sign of frostbite, but I could not take off my socks to rub my feet, because then they would get wet. Now at least they were dry.

"I was in the ditch when I thought I heard somebody yelling. The storm hadn't let up at all and I thought I heard, faintly, 'Keizo! Keizo!' But I thought it was wind noise. I'd been hearing things all night long; the wind can sound very much like the human voice. But I jumped out of the ditch to look and heard the voice again. 'Keizo. Keizo. Keizo.' Two or three times more I went out to look, to see if I could see anyone. I yelled, 'I am here. I am here.'

"Finally I heard a voice just outside the ditch and I knew you were close to me. But I could not see anything. I shouted again, 'I am here.' Finally I saw Will and I just ran toward him, because I knew I might not see him again, it was so whiteout. I left everything behind. If it had been my imagination, a mirage, I'd have been lost again and in big trouble. I was very happy to see the people looking for me in the blizzard. I felt the human love—everybody had watering eyes, crying and wet. I cried, yes, I cried too."

He was in surprisingly good shape, more rested than most of us. When I saw him and he started screaming I thought he was either hysterical or half frozen. But when I reached him it was obvious he was in good shape, healthy. He had remarkable strength left in him, a testament to the months we'd spent in these severe conditions. Thankfully it wasn't one of the cold storms such as we'd seen back in September and October; the temperature when we found him was 20°. Keizo's will is very, very strong; that, too, helped him survive.

We had worried about coming into Mirnyy and seeming

unenthusiastic, dulled by the long trip, but this last adventure assured we would arrive in Mirnyy in grand spirits, fully appreciating the test Antarctica had given us. Ironically, just a few days ago Keizo and I were talking about his future, and we agreed that all he needed if he was going to start his Outward Bound–like school in Japan was some more experience. But while I would never have encouraged him to get lost simply for the "experience," he now knew what it was like to fight for survival.

One of our goals from the beginning was to emerge from Antarctica as a team, as friends. As we sat this morning in the trax and relived Keizo's lost night, I looked around at my five teammates and realized we'd been successful.

Tomorrow we reenter a world that seems very, very far away. It is with great relief and a calm satisfaction that we radio Mirnyy tonight, tell them about Keizo's experience, and assure them we will see them tomorrow. While the storm continues around us, we hope for a clear morning. We plan on rising early and heading for the coast.

MARCH 3, DAY 220

In fact we did travel the final sixteen miles under perfect, clear skies and temperatures hovering just below zero.

We could see the deep blue of the Indian Ocean the entire day. Sunlight danced and glared off the icebergs that had lined up to greet us, and we crested the hill overlooking the Soviet base just before seven o'clock. As we headed down one last icy slope—men shouting encouragement to their dogs, the dogs howling out of pleasure at the scene that spread before them—an aura of peace swept over me as the responsibilities of the past three years and these last 3,741 miles lifted from my shoulders.

As I skied the last half mile I could not erase from my mind a picture of another time, another cold place. It was April

1986, the middle of the frozen Arctic Ocean, when Jean-Louis and I first met. He stepped to the top of a ridge of jumbled sea ice, seemingly out of nowhere, and we embraced, like brothers, though we'd never even been introduced. Everything that we'd done these past years evolved from that fated moment, from that embrace. We had turned our dreams—about adventure and cooperation, about preservation and the environment —into realities. We had the confidence to take risks, and the scene splayed in front of us was our reward, our affirmation.

The Soviets had marked our entryway with red flags and made a FINISH line. A gathering of one hundred, speaking a dozen different languages, swarmed around us as we came down the flag-bedecked chute. As I called my dogs to a stop one last time and stepped out of my skis, Jean-Louis walked toward me. I lifted Sam onto my shoulder, and Jean-Louis— completing the circle begun those years ago in the middle of the Arctic Ocean—wrapped us both in a bear hug.

EPILOGUE

THE CHALLENGE
HAS JUST BEGUN

When we pulled into Mirnyy we were ecstatic, overwhelmed by a feeling of accomplishment and a relief that knew few words. As we sat around a table inside the base's main building, I watched my teammates as the Soviets toasted us with more bread dipped in salt, chased by goblets of champagne. It was remarkable to me then, as it is now some months later, that we made it across Antarctica. Though it sounds clichéd, it was a true and genuine love that propelled us across that frozen land.

We received numerous telegrams of congratulations that day, from Messner and Fuchs, the National Geographic Society, President Bush and the respective political leaders of our homelands. We also engaged in yet another first: live television interviews broadcast from Antarctica, the result of a unique and complex diplomatic and logistical cooperation between the Soviets and the French. I stood to one side while Jean-Louis told a worldwide audience of tens of millions his hopes for this continent we had crossed. "Antarctica is a dangerous land, without mercy," he reflected, obviously harking back to the days we spent struggling along the peninsula. "But it's still virgin and white. All countries should forget their partisan interests and offer it to the world. . . . This continent belongs to everyone."

Our luck stayed with us the days we were in Mirnyy. The storm that Keizo had been lost in had blown monstrous, obstructive icebergs out of the harbor, making possible our departure aboard the *Professor Zubov*. We were fortunate the storm had cleared the way, since there was no icebreaker on hand to break a path for us. As we loaded waiting dinghies that would carry men, dogs and equipment to the *Zubov*, vicious storms set in; as we pulled away from Antarctica, they raged on, whipping the ice-strewn sea and obliterating the mainland from sight within minutes. If we had not left when we did, March 7, we might very well have been stuck in Mirnyy for several months. Symbolically, as we loaded the dinghies and motored to the waiting ship, a dozen of Mirnyy's penguins peered over the ice cliff at us and walked up and down the stairsteps we'd hacked down to the sea, as if to make sure we got away from the continent safely.

It wasn't until nine days later when we stepped off the Soviet ship at Perth, Australia, that what we had accomplished began to sink in. We stepped off into a new world; during the seven months we were on the ice the world had undergone many changes: the Berlin Wall had tumbled to democracy, San Francisco had been rocked by an earthquake, Eastern Europe was reemerging, Nelson Mandela was free. We began to sense how Trans-Antarctica fit into this changing world, as a blueprint for international cooperation.

From the day we set foot in Australia, then as we traveled over the next few months to the capitals of each of our homelands, we were greeted by thousands of people who turned out at rallies and press conferences. The swell of public opinion that greeted us at each stop was affirmation that our goal of drawing attention to and educating people about Antarctica had been successful. They all had the same question: What could they do to help preserve Antarctica? When we began Trans-Antarctica, this is the question we wanted to have asked at its end. In many ways the crossing was just the launching of our goal of preserving Antarctica. The challenge didn't end in Mirnyy; it has just begun.

One of the telegrams I received in Mirnyy was from the College of St. Thomas, my college alma mater in St. Paul, offering me as their tribute to our success the school's "Alumnus of the Year" award. This is what I telexed to them on March 3: "The 1990s will be a decade of global change, demanding a new way of thinking and a renewed commitment to action. For the first time in history, there is hope for world peace. And yet the planet is threatened by an imminent environmental disaster. Your generation must reverse the tide of destruction and strive to preserve the future. As I learned anew in crossing Antarctica, the only limit to achievement is the limit you place on your own dreams. As you seek your own way in the world look beyond personal gain to your responsibility as God's stewards of the Earth. Let your vision be guided by hope, your path be adventurous, and the power of your thoughts be directed toward the betterment of tomorrow. Thank you for your faith in me. From Antarctica, best regards."

The message holds.

ACKNOWLEDGMENTS

.

Reflecting on the hundreds of people who helped nurture and make Trans-Antarctica a success is a pleasure the six of us have indulged in often since we returned from Antarctica. While we were crossing the continent it was the hopes and prayers of volunteers from St. Paul to Paris—diplomats and schoolchildren in nations around the world who we knew were watching our progress—that encouraged us when we faced hard times.

Often, both before and after the expedition, at gatherings small and large, with potential sponsors or interested teachers, Jean-Louis and I were introduced as the partners who had organized Trans-Antarctica. In fact, we both knew that wasn't quite accurate, that our third partner was, thankfully, probably back in the office making sure this grand undertaking actually came off. Cathy deMoll was that third principal, the seventh team member.

In many ways when Jean-Louis and I left for Antarctica, we left the worrying and the headaches with Cathy, and her tasks —like struggling long distance from Tokyo with bureaucrats in Moscow and Washington, D.C., to arrange for a Soviet fuel drop in the middle of Antarctica—were often harder than ours. At least on the ice Jean-Louis and I had each other to commiserate with; often Cathy was alone in her decision making. It is an understatement to say that without her the expedition would not have been a success.

Foremost among the thousands who helped us I would like to thank all the volunteers for their countless hours. Most important, the teachers around the world—and the 15 million students they inspired—deserve credit for our success. In the months since we returned I have heard from hundreds of teachers, thanking us for giving them an avenue to teach in a new, inspired fashion. Those thanks must be returned: on many days, when the temperature dropped to −50° and winds blew over thirty miles per hour, the knowledge that kids in classrooms around the world were monitoring our progress by computer and workbook encouraged us to continue. I will always feel indebted to those students for their attentions; hopefully they gained from the expedition knowledge that will help preserve Antarctica for generations to come.

In the United States I would like to thank the International Polar Expeditions, Inc. office in St. Paul, especially Jennifer Kimball Gasperini, Cynthia Mueller, Ruth Ellickson and Yasue Akimoto. For keeping the Homestead up and running both before and during the expedition, John Stetson, Dave Sheild, Indre Antanaitis, Gaile Antanaitis, Daina Antanaitis, Tweeta Antanaitis, Judy Spanberger, Christine Ruark, Kevin Smith, Jim Schnurr, Kristine Mosher, Jim Musielewitz, Paul Ormseth, Tom Beery, Mick and Marilee Fleming, John Pierce, Bob and Carol Picard, Paula Bergland deserve my sincerest gratitude. In the French office of Hauteurs et Latitudes, in Paris, I thank Michel Franco, Bernard Buigues, Christian de Marlieve, Christine Declère, Jean Collet, Emanuelle Bizien and Anne Soland.

Specifically, I'd like to acknowledge the government agencies that helped smooth our path to and across Antarctica: in the U.S.S.R., the State Committee of Hydrometeorology in Moscow and the Arctic and Antarctic Research Institute in Leningrad; in the People's Republic of China, the National Committee for Antarctic Research in Beijing and the Lanzhou

Institute for Glaciology and Geocryology, in Lanzhou Province; and in Japan, the International Trans-Antarctica office in Tokyo.

Though mentioned in our press releases and boasted on the various patches on our gear, expedition sponsors can sometimes get lost in the shuffle. I hope that was not the case with Trans-Antarctica. Our two lead sponsors were W.L. Gore & Associates, Inc., and UAP, without whom, literally, we would never have taken the first step.

Our major sponsors were DuPont Fiberfill, Hill's Pet Products, SAFT, Target Stores and The North Face. Corporate supporters were Blandin Corporation, Elf, Honeywell Building Control Division, IDS Corporation, Minnesota Power, Nikon, Inc., Northwest Airlines, Norwest Banks, ProColor and Potlatch. Licensors were Marian Anderson, B.A.D. Bags, Dayton Hudson Stores, Grandoe Gloves, Little Bear Trading Company, Bryan Moon Studios, McGilvray Ltd., National Screenprint, Slumberjack and YEMA. Also, the Eastman Kodak Corporation; we used exclusively its Professional 200 Kodachrome, with outstanding results.

Special thanks for always being there when we needed them are due Mrs. Vieve Gore, Senator Dave Durenberger, Gil Grosvenor, Jack Dougherty, HRH Prince Sultan bin Abdul Aziz, Mark Erickson, Jonathan Segal, Patti Steger, Mr. and Mrs. Bill Steger, Grover Washington, Jr., Steve Drogin, Dr. Gretchen Gerber, Chris Somers, John Unland and John Pellegrene. Sadly, I must thank Giles Kershaw in memoriam. He was killed in Antarctica in a gyrocopter accident two weeks after we left Mirnyy.

Once it was assured we'd be able to take the first steps, the next most important element for our crossing were the supplies that kept us warm and fed. For that and more I thank White Bear Travel, Back Packer, Centor Freed, Crazy Creek Products, Midwest Mountaineering, The Coleman Company, Mirro/Foley Company, Adventure Foods, Alpine Aire, Steger Designs, Fox River Knitting Mills, H&R Robbins, The

Omega Source, MAC Tools, Maxit Designs, Laboratoire Fabre, Lumen Food Company, Penn Cycle, French Meadow Bakery, Pac Lite, Pillsbury Research and Development, Nalgene, Ultra Poly Tacoma, Regal Ware Inc., The Great Outdoors, Johnson Camping, Salomon, Exel, Snowsled Workshop, Nortur, Leatherwood Designs, MSR, Classic Discoveries, Biotherm Cosmetics, Stash Tea Company, Twinings, Thor-Lo, EWC, Velcro USA, Nature Made Vitamins, North Star Containers, Land O Lakes, Hershey's Chocolate and Pasta Groups, General Foods, California Vegetable Concentrates, Canada Roy, Bear Creek, Algood Food Company, Orville Redenbacher, King Oscar Sardines, Spice Trade Associates, DANCE, Hunt-Wesson, DuPont Thermax Division, Scott Paper, St. Mary's Medical Center, Shaklee Foods, Carnation, Rockwell Machinery, Berger Transfer & Storage, Global Transportation Services Inc., Trade Press, South Street Seaport Museum, and the Meredith Corporation.

—W.R.S., February 1991

I would like to thank the other five team members for their reflections and insights, many collected in a whirlwind battery of sessions soon after they stepped off the Antarctic ice cap, in hotel rooms and restaurants, on balconies and front stoops from Osaka to Ely. While this is Will's telling of the team's experience in Antarctica, in many ways it is just as much their story.

I should also add a thank-you to the Trans-Antarctica staffs in St. Paul and Paris, especially Cathy, Jennifer, Cynthia and Stef, for allowing me to gyrate from "outsider" to "insider" and occasionally back to "outsider" again, with relative ease.

Others deserve credit: Mark Bryant, the editor of *Outside* (for sending me to Greenland with these guys in the first place); Jeff Blumenfeld and DuPont (for keeping me warm in a variety of frigid settings); the Homestead staff (for consumables and putting up with my sly smile); Deanna Peterson (for screening nearly two hundred hours of audiotape recordings);

Barbara Horlbeck (for reading and consultation in the waning days); Cathy Saypol (for always spreading the good word); Jonathan Segal (for making sure my words were in the right order); Stuart Krichevsky (for keeping the faith); and last but never least, Debra Goldman, for sticking close by, always.

—J.S.B., February 1991

APPENDIX A

EIGHTEEN MONTHS LATER

Since we sailed out of the port at Mirnyy each of the six of us has traveled widely throughout our respective countries, sharing our experiences and impressing upon audiences of government officials and schoolchildren alike our belief that Antarctica must be preserved, not exploited.

For all the congratulatory messages and pats on the back we received, our biggest satisfaction came from the feedback we received from schoolchildren. Fifteen million in classrooms around the world followed the traverse. Our office in St. Paul provided maps, audiotapes, phone hotlines, study guides, teacher's manuals and weekly updates for students from Maryland to Tokyo. In France, Australia, Japan and Great Britain students followed our progress by computer; in the United States the *Weekly Reader* carried a story a week to its 10 million subscribers; in Japan the country's largest daily, *Asahi Shimbun*, covered the expedition weekly and put news stories on-line for home computer distribution to ten thousand Japanese homes and high schools.

In recent months I have spoken to the National Press Club, the Humphrey Institute at the University of Minnesota, the National Geographic Society and the National Science Teachers Association, trying to reinforce the need to protect Antarctica; in September 1990, at the invitation of Congressman Bruce Vento, I testified before Congress and supported the establishment of a world park in Antarctica. Two months later I joined a group of congressmen and environmentalists to encourage the U.S. State Department to join with Australia, France and New Zealand in discouraging mining in Antarctica. (Late in 1990 Congress passed legislation calling for an international agreement to ban mining in Antarctica and to protect the region as a global ecological commons. The sponsor of one of the bills, the late Congressman Silvio Conte, said upon its introduction, "Saving a continent is a once-in-a-lifetime opportunity. Let's not miss it.")

Victor, after completing his reports on ozone levels and the weather for the Arctic and Antarctic Research Institute in Leningrad, resigned his position there to help me organize a future expedition. In December he flew to Paris and picked up the car Jean-Louis had promised him for his help in conducting the urine study for the European Space Agency. Though still not possessing a driver's license, and uncertain of how he would talk his way back into the Soviet Union, Victor loaded the car with food and headed back to Leningrad.

Upon his return to Lanzhou, Dahe was made a full professor at the Lanzhou Institute, with the understanding that he will be allowed to devote himself to his fieldwork. His analysis of the ice samples he took across Antarctica is much anticipated by glaciologists around the world, and since we returned he has traveled in France, the U.S. and Germany detailing his studies for his peers. (Though we had enthusiastic receptions in each of the capitals we visited after leaving Antarctica—including Paris, London, Washington, Tokyo and Moscow—our reception in Beijing was perhaps the most overwhelming. When we stepped off the plane there in May 1990, to an estimated television audience of 500 million, crowds ran toward us as if we were a visiting rock band. We received extensive daily press coverage while we were in China, and Dahe was regarded as a national hero; when he arrived home a biography of his life had already been written. Everywhere we went in his country he was swarmed by throngs of young people, wanting to shake his hand and get his autograph. At one stop he had to be carried away—horizontally—by soldiers, as the crowd pressed around him dangerously. His arms were scarred by the stabbings of pen-wielding autograph seekers.)

Geoff is currently splitting his time between Great Britain and the U.S., delivering talks in both countries. In November 1990 he gave a report on the expedition to the prestigious Royal Geographic Society in London, and Britain's vaunted polar men and members of the royal family were in attendance. His attentions have also been focused on the sled-building business he and a partner began just before we left for Antarctica. Finally, last September, Thule, whom Geoff has taken back home to Keswick, had a litter of seven healthy puppies.

Keizo has toured and lectured in schools and businesses all over Japan. Last January he returned to Minnesota and raced in the annual Beargrease Dogsled Race in Duluth. He also took home dogs from the expedition: Kinta and Monty are now living in Osaka and will be the start of Keizo's dog team for the outdoor school he hopes to open. Last summer he and longtime girlfriend Yasue were married.

Immediately upon his return to France, Jean-Louis sat down and wrote a book about his Trans-Antarctic experience, and when published in September 1990 it quickly sold sixty-five thousand copies across France. He continues to speak throughout Europe, about Antarctica and his future plans. He has lined up the sponsorship of the European oil company Elf and with a major grant from them will use the UAP—now called the *Antarctica*—for educational trips. His first will be to sail back to Antarctica.

Though for the time being we have each gone our separate ways, another expedition will soon bring us together again. Early in 1991 I announced my plan for The Arctic Project

1994, an expedition similar in intent and scope to Trans-Antarctica. The vast Arctic region, much like Antarctica, is one of the most pristine environments left on the face of the earth. But today it is at risk, its cultures sundered by modern times and its environment threatened. There exists no environmental protection for this area, and unlike Antarctica there is no treaty to protect it. As such, it provides the perfect setting for another international environmental/education/expedition effort.

The first goal of The Arctic Project is to garner the necessary international cooperation to build a scientific ice station, which, once frozen into the Arctic Ocean, will drift with the polar currents from September 1993 to March 1995. From this facility an international team of scientists will conduct research to measure man's ecological impact on the Arctic. A major educational component will be coordinated, focusing on the development of curriculum for classrooms worldwide.

The expedition part of the project will be a major traverse. Four people and two dogsled teams will set off in March 1994 from the ice station off the coast of central Siberia, and head for the North Pole. After reaching the Pole we will head south for Alaska. By June 1 we will fly the dogs and sleds out and finish the trip by canoe by August 1. Like Trans-Antarctica, the expedition is designed to draw attention to this relatively unexplored part of the world and will be supported by a consortium of government agencies, scientific groups and private sources. My partner on the expedition will be Victor. Dahe will conduct scientific experiments from the ice station; Geoff will build the sleds for the expedition . . . and I hope to meet Jean-Louis and the *Antarctica* near the North Pole sometime during the late spring of 1994. (For interested teachers, we are continuing our annual educational programs at Hamline University in St. Paul; information is available by writing the Arctic and Antarctic Education Fund, P.O. Box 4097, St. Paul, MN 55104.)

APPENDIX B

THE DOGS

Team 1
Driver: Will Steger
Sled Name: Amundsen

Sam (*Lead Dog*)
Tim (*Lead Dog—deceased 10-22-89, Siple, Antarctica*)
Ray (*Lead Dog*)
Buffy
Panda
Zap Junior
Hank
Yeager
Tommy
Chuchi
Bly
Gordie

Team 2
Driver: Keizo Funatsu
Sled Name: Naomi Uemura

Bjorn (*Lead Dog*)
Kutaan (*Lead Dog*)
Odin
Caspa
Monty
Herbie
Rodan
Kuka
Arrow
Aukluk
Chinook
Kinta

Team 3
Driver: Geoff Somers
Sled Name: Robert Falcon Scott

Thule (*Lead Dog*)
Soda Pop
Spinner
Sawyer
Huck
Chewbakie
Kaviaq
Floppy
Jimmy
Jocky
Jewbak
Pup

Reserves:

Fuzz
Rex

Garret
Brownie
Apak (*deceased 7-17-89, Havana, Cuba*)
Godzilla (*deceased 7-18-89, Havana*)

The dogs that pulled the entire 3,741 miles:

From Steger's team: Sam,* Panda, Hank, Bly
From Funatsu's team: Bjorn, Monty, Herbie, Rodan
From Somers's team: Huck, Chewbakie, Floppy, Jocky

Borrowed from and returned to Krabloonik Kennels in Snowmass, Colorado: Rodan, Kaviaq, Kuka, Kuraan, Soda Pop, Spinner, Chewbakie, Aukluk

Dogs' diet: 5,700 calories/day

2 pounds/day of Science Diet Endurance produced by Hill's Pet Products of Topeka, KS, made of a high-energy-density, high-fat-content and a high-nutrient balance.

* Sam is the only one of the dogs to have pulled to both the North and South poles.

APPENDIX C

TYPICAL DAILY RATIONS

Breakfast:

    Quaker Oats or Little Bear Cereal (4 oz.)
    French Meadow Bakery Granola
    Land O Lakes Butter (4 oz.)
    Twinings Tea
    Stash Tea
    Maxwell House Dehydrated Coffee

Lunch: (6 oz. total)

    Dried nuts and fruits
    Hershey's chocolate bar
    Shaklee Energy Bar or
        Intermountain Bar or
        Pilot Biscuits or
        French Meadow Bakery Granola Bars

Dinner:

Bassett's Meat Pemmican (4 oz.) (a 60/40 mix of finely
ground dried beef or pork and lard)
Adam's Peanut Butter (4 oz.)
Shaklee Spice Soup (2 oz.)
Land O Lakes Cheese (6 oz.)
6 oz. of: Hershey's Egg Noodles or
Uncle Ben's Rice or
Gibb's Wild Rice or
Pillsbury Dried Potatoes

Optional Supplements:

Swiss Miss Hot Chocolate
Canada Boy Powdered Milk
Shaklee Vita-Lea Vitamin and Mineral Supplements
French Meadow Bakery Dried Bread
King Oscar Sardines
Canned salmon
Canned tunafish
Orville Redenbacher's Popcorn

APPENDIX D

EQUIPMENT

The North Face "Himalayan Hotel" dome tent (slightly modified)
Slumberjack Quallofil-insulated sleeping bags (custom-made)
Lestra sleeping bag
B.A.D. Bags duffel bags
Fisher waxless cross-country skis
Exel nordic ski poles
Berwyn bindings
MSR "Whisperlite" and XGK white gas stoves
Coleman two-burner camp stoves
Vuarnet sunglasses
Kodak alkaline batteries
SAFT lithium batteries
Silva compasses
Yema watch
Nikon FM2 cameras
Kodak film
Camp Rest sleeping pads
Nalgene plastic bottles
Crazy Creek camp chairs

Argos satellite data and tracking system
CEIS, Espace—message panel for Argos

Clothing (all manufactured by The North Face):

Fleece pullover, pant, hat, headband, neck band
Gore-Tex wind parka and pants
Gore-Tex one-piece jump suit
Insulated jacket filled with "Thermolite" and
  "Thermoloft" insulation

Accessories:

Duofold "Thermax" thermal underwear
Duofold "Thermax" liner socks
Damart "Thermax" thermal underwear
Steger Designs Mukluks
Steger Designs Over Mitts
Grandoe Gore-Tex gloves
The Masque neoprene face masks
Fox River "Hollofil" socks
Surefoot Insulator insole
Head Lite "Scotchlite" patches

LAUREL EXPEDITION

■ **EIGER DREAMS** .... 20990-0/$5.99
Ventures Among Men and Mountains
by John Krakauer

■ **RIDING THE
DRAGON'S BACK** .... 21000-3/$5.99
The Race to Raft the Upper Yangtze
by Richard Bangs and Christian Kallen

■ **HIMALAYAN ODYSSEY** .. 21125-5/$5.99
The Perilous Trek to Western Nepal
by Parker Antin with Phyllis Wachob Weiss

■ **INTO THE GREAT
SOLITUDE** .... 21244-8/$5.99
An Arctic Journey
by Robert Perkins

At your local bookstore or use this handy page for ordering:

**DELL READERS SERVICE, DEPT. DLE
2451 South Wolf Road, Des Plaines, IL. 60018**

Please send me the above title(s). I am enclosing $ _____.
(Please add $2.50 per order to cover shipping and handling.) Send
check or money order—no cash or C.O.D.s please.

Ms./Mrs./Mr_____

Address_____

City/State _____ Zip_____

DLE-2/93

Prices and availability subject to change without notice. Please allow four to six
weeks for delivery.